Dina Matar is Director and Senior Lecturer at the Centre for Media and Film at SOAS. A former foreign correspondent and editor covering the Middle East, Europe and Africa, she is the author of *What It Means to be Palestinian: Stories of Palestinian Peoplehood* (I.B.Tauris, 2011). She works and writes on Islamist politics, culture, politics and communication in the Arab world and diaspora cultures. She is co-editor of *The Middle East Journal of Culture and Communication.*

Zahera Harb is Senior Lecturer in International Journalism at the Department of Journalism, City University London. A former broadcast journalist in Lebanon working for Lebanese and international media organizations, she is the author of *Channels of Resistance in Lebanon: Liberation Propaganda, Hezbollah and the Media* (I.B.Tauris, 2011).

NARRATING CONFLICT IN THE MIDDLE EAST

DISCOURSE, IMAGE AND COMMUNICATIONS PRACTICES IN LEBANON AND PALESTINE

EDITED BY DINA MATAR AND ZAHERA HARB

To my darling Sam —
Thank you for everything
you have done — for your wit,
intelligence, passion & humor &
support — we'll get there in the end!
Much love always
Kirkland

I.B. TAURIS
LONDON · NEW YORK

Published in 2013 by I.B.Tauris & Co Ltd
6 Salem Road, London W2 4BU
175 Fifth Avenue, New York NY 10010
www.ibtauris.com

Distributed in the United States and Canada
Exclusively by Palgrave Macmillan
175 Fifth Avenue, New York NY 10010

Library of Modern Middle East Studies: 121

ISBN: 978 1 78076 102 2 (HB)
          978 1 78076 103 9 (PB)

A full CIP record for this book is available from the British Library
A full CIP record is available from the Library of Congress

Library of Congress Catalog Card Number: available

Printed and bound in Great Britain by T.J. International, Padstow, Cornwall

Contents

II.   Discourses

III.   Memories and Narration

LIST OF CONTRIBUTORS

Refqa Abu-Remaileh completed her PhD at Oxford University in 2010. Her research examined the creative works of Emile Habibi and the films of Elia Suleiman. After completing her PhD, Refqa worked with the Oxford Research Group's Middle East Programme, a conflict-resolution organization focusing on the Palestinian-Israeli conflict. She created a new strategic thinking group involving Palestinian citizens of Israel. In October 2012, Refqa took up a postdoctoral fellowship at the Wissenschaftskolleg zu Berlin for one year.

Atef Alshaer is a postdoctoral fellow in Political Communication at the Centre for Media and Film Studies and Senior Teaching Fellow in the Faculty of Languages and Cultures at the School of Oriental and African Studies (SOAS), University of London. He has published numerous articles and reviews concerned with culture, literature and politics of the Middle East.

Rounwah Adly Riyadh Bseiso is a PhD candidate at the Centre for Media and Film Studies at SOAS, London. She has worked as an intern for the International Organization for Migration and for the UNDP and UNHCR. She has also worked with the United Nations Human Settlements Programme (UN_HABITAT) and the Palestine Land Society. She is currently the International Programme Coordinator in the Gulf University for Science and Technology in Kuwait.

Zahera Harb is Senior Lecturer in International Journalism at the Department of Journalism, City University London. A former broadcast journalist in Lebanon working for Lebanese and international media organizations, she is the author of *Channels of Resistance in Lebanon: Liberation Propaganda, Hezbollah and the Media* (I.B.Tauris, 2011).

Carole Helou is a news editor with special interest in political advertising in the Middle East. She has a Masters degree in Global Media and Post-National Communication. She has seven years of working experience in radio and out-of-home media in Lebanon.

Dina Matar is Director and Senior Lecturer at the Centre for Media and Film at SOAS. A former foreign correspondent and editor covering the Middle East, Europe and Africa, she is author of *What It Means to be Palestinian: Stories of Palestinian Peoplehood* (I.B.Tauris, 2011). She works and writes on Islamist politics, culture, politics and communication in the Arab world and diaspora cultures. She is co-editor of *The Middle East Journal of Culture and Communication*.

Helena Nassif was born in São Paulo and raised in Beirut. She studied public health, media and journalism in Beirut, Aarhus, Amsterdam, Swansea and London. In 2009 she was awarded the Erasmus Mundus Masters in Media and Journalism within Globalization. She has 12 years of work experience in community development and adult training. She also worked in TV and documentary film journalism where she contributed to documentary films/series aired on Al Jazeera and Al Arabiya news networks. Helena is currently a PhD researcher at the University of Westminster. Her research considers the politics of mass culture in the Levant, focusing on Beirut and Damascus. Her research interests include the politics of fiction and stardom, mediated history, memory and conflict, public everyday culture and visual culture.

Matt Sienkiewicz is Assistant Professor of Communication and International Studies at Boston College. His research focuses on Western interaction with Middle Eastern media, as well as representation in American screen comedy. His publications include articles in *Popular Communication, Middle East Journal of Culture and Communication,*

The International Journal of Cultural Studies and *Columbia Journalism Review*.

Kirkland Newman Smulders is a researcher, writer and documentary filmmaker, specializing in the Middle East, notably the Israel-Palestine conflict, and in mental health. She has a degree in Modern Languages from Oxford University, an MSc in European Studies from the London School of Economics and Political Science and an MA in Near and Middle Eastern Studies from the School of Oriental and African Studies. She has worked for Rockefeller Brothers Fund and Ogilvy & Mather in New York, and for the Prince's Trust in London.

Teodora Todorova is a doctoral candidate in Critical Theory and Postgraduate Teaching Assistant in the Department of Culture, Film and Media at the University of Nottingham. Her work examines emergent solidarities between Israeli civil society and the Palestinian struggle for self-determination articulated in post-2000 attempts to address the call for a Just Peace in Israel-Palestine. She is the 2009 winner of the Feminist and Women's Studies Association (FWSA) essay competition. The winning essay 'Giving Memory a Future: Confronting the Legacy of Mass Rape in Post-conflict Bosnia-Herzegovina' was published in the *Journal of International Women's Studies*, Vol. 12, No. 2, March 2011. Teodora's research interests include narratives of conflict and reconciliation, civil society and grassroots activism, women's and migrant rights, and public mobilization. She teaches Political Communication, Public Relations and Propaganda, and has previously taught modules on Intercultural Communication and Researching Communication.

Hanan Toukan is a postdoctoral research fellow at the Wissenschaftskolleg zu Berlin's Forum for Transregional Studies. Before that she was a Teaching Fellow at SOAS, University of London, where she taught on the politics and government of the Middle East in the Politics Department as well as the mediated cultures of the Middle East at the Centre for Media and Film Studies. Toukan has researched and written on cultural politics, visual cultures, travelling theory, globalism/localism and cultural diplomacy. She received her PhD from SOAS in 2011.

Nadia Yaqub is Associate Professor at the University of North Carolina at Chapel Hill. She is the author of *Pens, Swords, and the Springs of Art: The Oral Poetry Dueling of Palestinian Weddings in the Galilee* (2006) as well as of numerous articles on Arab and Palestinian literature, art, and film.

1

APPROACHES TO NARRATING CONFLICT IN PALESTINE AND LEBANON: PRACTICES, DISCOURSES AND MEMORIES

DINA MATAR AND ZAHERA HARB

At the beginning of the twenty-first century, fewer countries are at war with each other than before, but the world remains beset by endemic and diverse conflicts. Many states are locked in bloody internal conflicts and internecine struggles, while the USA leads a highly public conflict in its self-defined "war against terror" post-September 11, 2001, plunging Iraq into bloody chaos and requiring a long-term presence of foreign troops in Afghanistan. At the same time, diverse conflicts against economic deprivation, dispossession and marginalization of particular groups whether on ethnic, gendered, sexual or religious grounds, as well as struggles over presence and power continue in several regions in the world, including the Middle East. Here, these struggles translated into popular uprisings in Egypt and Tunisia that ended with the overthrow of authoritarian regimes at the beginning of 2011 and spurred other similar protests in much of the Arab world over political representation and basic human needs, including the right to free thought and speech.

As clearly witnessed worldwide, these contests over power and presence were played out, and continue to be played out, on the street, and mediated via diverse systems of communication, including an increasingly overcrowded satellite broadcasting market in the Arab world and popular social networking sites. Within these highly mediated contexts, the potential for new and diverse struggles over identities, visibility and public presence becomes even more likely in various spaces and at different levels, rendering attempts to adequately theorize contemporary conflicts more problematic and demanding new research agendas and approaches on how conflicts are narrated, where and by whom, and how they are lived in everyday life.

Conflict and Media: Problems of Definition and Approach

The literature on conflict is extensive and impossible to detail here. However, to date there is no single theoretical approach that can adequately map, much less explain, all the conflicts in the world today (Cottle, 2006). In fact, to consider conflict as a singular or uniform concept that can be applied to all contexts and different geographical areas irrespective of history disables an analysis of the constituent factors and subjectivities defining and surrounding any particular conflict in a particular region, nation or space. At the same time, to consider each conflict as entirely distinct and/or unique undermines attempts to examine common and largely structural factors causing conflicts, such as economic disparities, marginalization and exclusion of certain groups by others (Maltby and Keeble, 2007). Generally speaking, the term conflict has been loosely used to refer to struggles between opposing interests, groups and outlooks, ranging from cultural and geo-political contests over discourse and power, to street protests, to civil or armed conflict within nation-states, and to the outbreak of armed hostilities between nations.

Briefly, the literature classifies conflicts in the post-Cold War era under three broad categories: those conflicts in which genuine geo-strategic and economic interests are involved; those caused by ethnic or nationalistic politics as witnessed in the war in the former Yugoslavia and those "invisible" conflicts such as the wars in Sudan and other parts of the world which rarely register on international media radar (see Thussu and Freedman, 2003). However, these categories are too general and vague, and cannot adequately or analytically describe complex, multiple or long-term conflicts, such as those in Palestine and Lebanon, which are a mixture of some or all of these categories put together, as well as some other categories not mentioned in these classifications. Furthermore, in the burgeoning literature on communication and conflict, or the scholarship on media and war (which includes studies related to Palestine and Lebanon), much emphasis has been placed on the representation and the reporting of contemporary conflict. In this area, analysis has mostly followed the methods and concepts of Western-centric mass communication theories and approaches which tend to focus on the mainstream media and other conventional forms of communication while ignoring other areas and spaces of expression.

In their edited book *War and the Media* (2003), Daya Thussu and Des Freedman suggest that the mainstream media's role in communicating conflict can be identified as that of critical observer and publicist, and as battleground on which war and conflict are imagined and executed or framed. Other scholars working on the relationship between media and conflict, or media and war, particularly post-September 11, have focused on issues around the reporting of conflict in the news media; the communication of conflict between various parties and to outsiders; journalistic ethics and norms; objectivity, bias and propaganda; as well as representations of contemporary conflict. Most of these studies tend to address the traditional media—such as broadcasting, the press, the internet and other new technologies—often at the expense of alternative diverse spaces in which conflicts are imagined and narrated. In addition, little attention has been paid to what conflicts mean for those involved in them, whether as agents or as subjects, particularly in today's globalizing and "post-traditional" times (Giddens, 1994) when solidarities once taken for granted—based on class, ethnic, gendered, religious or other forms of identifications—are constantly challenged and re-imagined in various cultural and media spaces.

Given the multiplicity of available and expanding discursive and mediated spaces in which contemporary conflicts are played out in different ways, this book uses the phrase "narrating conflict" rather than the more ubiquitous "mediating conflict" which tends to suggest a view of media and other forms of communication as neutral conveyors of information or even as arbitrators between contestants, or that media themselves can become implicated in conflict. Narration allows us to examine the diverse discursive spaces and forms within which conflict is mediated, communicated, experienced, imagined and lived, while not losing sight of the fact that the term narration itself implies subjectivity and agency, if not a provisional and partial reconstruction of lives and histories. In this edited collection, we use the term narration to also include actors and spaces that have been sidelined or neglected in the public and academic discussions of conflict. We hope our contribution can open the field of inquiry and help us better comprehend the meaning of long-term conflict for ordinary people and for political and cultural lives. Ultimately, the concern is to shift attention in the study of communication and conflict from top-down analyses concerned with formal politics and the elites to discussions of the everyday and the non-elites.

Narrating Conflict: Palestine and Lebanon

Nowhere is the competition over the imagination, construction and narration of conflict, as well as its meanings and its centrality to people's everyday lives, more compelling for academic attention, if not more divisive, than in discussing Palestine and Lebanon, which have experienced, and continue to experience, long-term and different conflicts over space, identity, discourse, image and narrative. Their populations have been subjected to persistent processes of terror, counter-terror, violence, counter-violence, similar to what Frantz Fanon (1963) has talked about in his work on post-colonial societies, but particularly Algeria.

History and politics reveal much about why these conflicts—namely the Israel-Palestinian conflict and the Lebanese long-term internal and external conflicts—started, why they continue, how they could be resolved, and how they have influenced or might influence local, regional and international relations. However, many of these studies, as Ted Swedenburg and Rebecca Stein (2005) have argued, are rooted in the national and the political economy analytical paradigms: The first puts the nation or nation-state as the inherent logic guiding critical analysis of these conflicts, and the second Marxist paradigm complicates the narrative of national conflict by paying attention to the struggle over control of the state and the means of production. Both these paradigms tend to underplay the complex multi-vocalities and the diverse experiences and memories that reside within each individual and within the collective, and which have shaped and continue to shape contemporary and lived experiences of state and nationhood.

In recent years, a tentative paradigmatic shift has occurred in analytical articulations of the ongoing conflict between Palestine and Israel, in particular, as scholars began to rethink questions of power and knowledge at different levels of societal interaction, placing an increased emphasis on popular culture as providing significant alternative "political" and "cultural" narratives. A new generation of scholars from diverse disciplines has also started to take up questions that move beyond narrow definitions of the political to explore the social, economic and cultural histories of these conflicts, as well as the diverse cultural trends that can yield "a fuller chronicle of politics and power than political economy or diplomatic models can alone provide" (Swedenburg and Stein, 2005: 11). Central to these approaches is a rethinking of culture as a crucial terrain for the struggle between hegemonic powers and subaltern counter-hegemonic forces and one that takes place across a vast array of spaces and modern institutions, including media institutions and other cultural forms and practices. Revisionist histories, including some studies by Israeli historians such as Tom Segev and Ilan Pappé, and the expanding field of oral history (see Sayigh, 1978, Matar, 2011), too, are providing personal counter-narratives that stand against established authoritative master narratives while also serving to argue against and seriously disturb hegemonic discourses that have informed and shaped public accounts of this conflict.

A full history of the Palestinians' conflict with Israel is not possible to provide here, but as the chapters in this edited collection suggest, for most Palestinians, "narrating in the present" the ongoing and as-of-yet unresolved conflict with Israel, in its diverse forms, remains inextricably linked to the past, and specifically to the year 1948. This is the date of the *Nakba* (the term Palestinians use to describe the events that led to the loss of their land) which marked the end of a lengthy chapter in the fight over the possession of Palestine, the roots of which lay in the emergence in the late nineteenth century of the European-based Zionist movement dedicated to establishing a Jewish national homeland on the land of historic Palestine (Sayigh, 1997). Before 1948, the Arabs of Palestine constituted an absolute majority of its inhabitants and owned nearly 90 percent of the privately owned land. Within a few months of the 1948 Arab-Israeli war, between 850,000 and 1 million Palestinian Arabs, according to most estimates, were expelled or forced to flee from the area, most of which became the state of Israel. About 150,000 Palestinians remained within Israel, which by then controlled 78 percent of the territory of former mandatory Palestine (Matar, 2011). More than 531 Palestinian villages were destroyed and 11 urban areas were emptied of their inhabitants in the resulting war of 1948, "a clear-cut case of an ethnic cleansing operation, regarded under international law today as a crime against humanity" (Pappé, 2006: xiii).

The *Nakba*, the formative event par excellence of the thousands of Palestinians who lived it or even the thousands who imagined living it by proxy (through storytelling and other forms of popular memory) has over the years spurred a folk culture conveyed by songs, ballads, poetry and narratives formed around three motif—the praise and memory of the lost paradise from which Palestinians were expelled, lamentation about the present and the depiction of the imagined return. This folk culture formed the foundational stones for some of the most durable collective memories that have shaped Palestinian popular discourse and collective memory for more than six decades. Indeed, stories and imagery associated with the events of 1948 have galvanized and sustained political energy, even among the Palestinian refugee population and the overall diaspora, despite the overarching presence and dominance of the "other" counter-narrative, that of Israel. Other critical events in the conflict, including the 1967 war with Israel, the 1982 Israeli invasion of Lebanon, the two Palestinian *intifadas* (uprisings) of 1987 and 2000, internal Palestinian divisions and internecine struggles, as well as the lack of progress on the fate of more than 5 million Palestinians in exile have, too, without doubt helped structure the memories and everyday lives of Palestinians, as much as have Israeli occupation practices which continuously squeeze Palestinians into or out of changing and diminishing spaces, while crippling economic and other advancements.

Lebanon, too, has experienced long-term internal and external conflicts, some of them involving Israel. Often described as a country of paradoxes, Lebanon is characterized by a complex political structure and tenuous relations between its diverse confessional groups which have moved between peaceful coexistence and open warfare. Despite Lebanon being one of the smallest nation-states in the Arab world, the legacy of colonial rule, Lebanon's delicate demographic balance, fragile political system, military invasions and successive incursions by Israel, Syrian political claims over the country, as well as its protracted 1975–1990 civil war have all combined to contribute to a deep identity crisis over what it means to be Lebanese. The civil war between 1975 and 1990, the Israeli invasions of 1978 and 1982, ongoing conflicts between various political and sectarian groups that pervade everyday life, the emergence of the Shi'i party, Hezbollah, as a resistance militia to Israeli occupation in 1982 then as the main political party in Lebanon in the first decade of the twenty-first century, the assassination of Prime Minister Rafic Hariri in 2005 and the 2006 war between Hezbollah and Israel have all brought about a dramatic rupture in the national narrative of progression and development forged under the National Pact born with independence from colonial rule in 1943.

The causes and interpretations of the long-term internal and external conflicts are myriad and too complex to detail in this brief introduction, but as the burgeoning work on cultural memory reveals, the proliferation of cultural practices and events to do with the 15-year civil war suggests a rather complex and continuous mediation of personal, often-emotive recollections of events. As Sune Haugbolle (2010) writes, memory studies, especially those produced during the 1990s and before the assassination of Hariri in 2005, show that the debate about the war oscillated between probing discourses and nationalist nostalgia in which contested memories of fraternity and/or sectarian separation competed with and were manipulated by social and political actors. As Haugbolle notes, the civil war was complex with different players and agendas that changed over time depending on the historical context, but it was a period of Lebanese history when the very existence of the nation-state was jeopardized by various degrees of internal and external conflict. At times, the civil war was a "war of others," mainly Israeli, Palestinian and Syrian troops fighting each other and Lebanese groups in turn. At other times, it was a "war for others", in which Lebanese factions fought agendas put forward by others, including outsiders. Between 1972 and 1982, the Palestine Liberation Organization was involved in the Lebanese war to defend the Palestinian refugees in Lebanon. In 1978, Israel invaded southern Lebanon, and then launched a full-scale invasion of Lebanon in 1982, ostensibly to drive the PLO out (see Harb, 2011, for a detailed analysis of the origins and key moments of the conflict between Lebanon and Israel). However, inasmuch as Lebanon became a battleground for external interests, the war was also undoubtedly spurred by contests over what it means to be Lebanese as well as a complex and unfair political system that marginalized some of the country's constituent communities. The civil war ended with the signing of the Ta'if Accord in 1990 and several other treaties that legitimized Syria's involvement in Lebanon's internal affairs until its forces were compelled to leave following the killing of Hariri.

Not surprisingly, the multiple forms and layers of violence created, sustained and perpetuated during the Lebanese civil war as well as continuous tension between the country's various political groups and sects have constituted a recurring theme in numerous novels and other forms of cultural production presented by Lebanese writers and artists living in Lebanon and abroad, not only during the war itself but also in the post-war era. The experience of living through a civil war predominantly controlled and manipulated by militia fighting, the military intervention of foreign forces, the killing and kidnapping of thousands of people, and the destruction of cities and villages has resulted in a collective trauma for both younger and older generations of Lebanese descent. But also crucially, Israeli actions in Lebanon, including the occupation of south Lebanon for over 22 years between 1978 and 2000, and the 2006 war, provide fertile ground for subversive popular politics that finds outlets in diverse forms of cultural expression and media.

Plan of the Book

This book sets out to explore some of the various forms and practices in which the conflicts in Palestine and Lebanon are constructed and narrated. It is divided into three themes: the first explores the cultural practices in which conflict is imagined and narrated, beginning with an analysis by Matt Sienkiewicz of the political and economic environment in which independent Palestinian media makers operate. In this chapter, Sienkiewicz argues that this environment, overshadowed by the conflict with Israel, results in a unique coalescing of internal and external forces, creating what he calls a transnational "censorscape" in which all production must take place and under which transnational production and funding can have the opposite effect. By weaving together the idiosyncratic and occasionally contradictory political concerns of international funders, regional buyers and local authorities, the global collaboration that much contemporary Palestinian production requires creates a set of obstacles that exacerbate an already difficult media environment operating under continuous conflict conditions.

Zahera Harb's chapter discusses the contemporary Lebanese media scene as polarized and as characterized by an *interwoven* relationship between the media and various Lebanese politicians, engendering a model of "media confrontation" between two main opposing camps in Lebanon's contemporary domestic political scene: the March 14 camp and March 8 camp which were led by the two main parties, the Future Movement and Hezbollah. The political confrontation between the two groups also takes place on television broadcasting stations affiliated with the two parties: Future TV and Al Manar, while other Lebanese television stations are divided in support of one over the other. In this atmosphere, journalists become open about their religious and political affiliations, and news programs that set to serve directly this camp or the other are produced. In examining the continuous media battles between the various groups, Harb questions the ethical boundaries that Lebanese journalists retain when reporting internal conflict.

Hanan Toukan turns to post-civil war contemporary art from and in Beirut to unveil local and international perceptions of representations circulating in such art works. She argues that these visual narrations can be seen as counter-hegemonic artistic productions aimed at troubling dominant representations of the Lebanese civil war. Specifically, the chapter analyzes the dynamics by which a group of artists and artist-supporting organizations tried to re-present the "un-representability" of the civil war after it ended. Most of the contemporary art practices that emerged out of Lebanon during the period under study were consumed with the civil war and post-war reconstruction, national identity dilemmas and the violence of regional politics. The documentation and archiving of the war, its memory and its associated trauma were always included within these practices. Combined with the new media that symbolized a break with the past, the contemporary art scene offered an exciting new terrain for international curators interested in the region; however the political content of the work continued to signify a counter-hegemonic location even when it was incorporated into the global arts circuit on terms that, one might argue, conflicted with such a standing.

Refqa Abu-Remaileh examines the literary and cinematic practices of narrating the Israeli-Palestinian conflict in the novels of Palestinian writer Emile Habibi (1922–1996) and the films of Elia Suleiman (1960–). Experiencing the conflict, she argues, was more pronounced for these two Palestinian cultural producers because they grew up as Palestinians inside Israel, which provided them with a different existential experience than for Palestinians who live in the Occupied Territories or the diaspora. Indeed, it was in light of a state of imposed historical, political, cultural and geographical absence that they found themselves in (despite their physical presence on the land) that they began taking active roles as writers and artists in documenting and recording their existence, as well as those of many others, in order to assert their presence. In analyzing the documenting techniques used primarily by Habibi to assert presence in the face of imposed absence, and the sense of de-territorialization and fragmentation is characteristic of Suleiman's *Divine Intervention*, Abu-Remaileh draws attention to the ways in which counter-narrative practices are constructed to question, ultimately, where truth lies amidst conflictual layers of narrative.

The second theme critically interrogates the various discourses (and images) of the long-term conflicts in Palestine and Lebanon. As Atef Alshaer argues in his chapter on the ways in which Islam was incorporated into the ideologies of the Palestinian groups Fatah and Hamas, discourse is a source of representation that sets in motion a state of delineation as it marks out different paradigms of knowledge and authority. Alshaer analytically explores the continuous political contest between Fatah and Hamas for representation of the Palestinian people as well as the ways each faction deploys "Islam" as a discourse to fortify its arguments against the backdrop of the ongoing conflict with Israel, while drawing on Foucault's concept of discourse as a stream of discursive formations. In doing so, the author highlights the shifts over time in the discourses of the two groups in relation to Islam and as their own conflict over power develops, and questions the role Islam may have in the Palestinian public sphere and the official and/or everyday politics and discourses of both movements.

Rounwah Bseiso moves to explore some of the seemingly banal images and discourses of the nation narrated and produced by the Lebanese Al Manar television channel affiliated with the Lebanese party Hezbollah. Drawing on an original empirical study of the promotional videos produced and broadcast daily by the station, she argues that these videos produce and reproduce a historically-specific "cultural discourse" or cultural narrative that underlines everyday practices and lives in the present, and their relations to the past. These videos usually depict Lebanese families and neighbors in ordinary settings and show Lebanon as a unique landscape, serving to produce a cultural discourse that is embedded within the larger grand narrative of resistance that Hezbollah uses to legitimize its existence and its *raison d'être* as a party concerned with the protection of Lebanon's sovereignty. This chapter suggests that in communicating social realities, Al Manar engages in what we might call "a meta-cultural commentary" on Hezbollah's identity, and what it stands for.

Kirkland Newman Smulders offers an insightful analysis of the contested discourses of "victimhood" that Israelis and Palestinians construct, mediate and narrate to support their respective claims to nationhood and to historic Palestine. She argues that the long-running conflict is, during its quieter moments, more of a struggle over public opinion fought on the battlefields of national and international media, than one fought on the ground. Using case studies, she recounts how both sides in the conflict have used and continue to use narratives of victimhood to convince outsiders of the legitimacy of their claims to the contested territory of historic Palestine. She concludes that understanding how these narratives of victimhood are constructed and communicated by politicians and laypeople, the role they play in the conflict, their effects on identity formation and action, and their implications for peace can help open new avenues for containing and resolving the conflict.

In the chapter on the use of visual images in the domestic political battle over Lebanon, Carole Helou underlines the ways in which visual and public discursive contests have become an integral, but almost banal, part of intense mediated political narratives in the political and public life in Lebanon. Helou examines the political battle over posters and visual campaigns used by diverse political and confessional parties in the country, paying particular attention to the ubiquitous billboard "I love life" campaign. In doing so, she examines the meanings and repercussions of these visual campaigns for the control of discourse in the contested public space, arguing that these visual discourses and images provide a new dimension to the continuous battle over narrative, truth and power in the divided country.

The final theme turns to narrated memories of conflict and the ways in which these are structured by diverse contexts and agents. Helena Nassif provides a rare study of experiences of Lebanese adolescents born during the peaceful years between 1993 and 1995 who therefore do not have direct experienced personal memories of the 1996 Israeli offensive against Lebanon or other wars. However, these youngsters, she notes, most probably began to follow the news after Hariri's assassination in 2005, the war with Israel during July 2006 and domestic clashes between Hezbollah and its opponents in May 2008. While images of war, including some of atrocities, are normal fare on Lebanese television, as people are used to images of violence from the region, including neighboring Palestine and post-2003 Iraq, the author provides a moving insight into how adolescents in Lebanon make sense of war news in their region.

Nadia Yaqub explores the ways in which the *Nakba* has continued to structure Palestinian writing and filmmaking though these writers and filmmakers, like the Lebanese adolescents mentioned in the previous chapter, have no direct experience of either pre-1948 Palestine or the war that divided it. Furthermore, their access to those who have had such experience is rapidly disappearing. The despair of political impasse has been the subject of a number of Palestinian films, particularly in the years immediately following the outbreak of the second Palestinian uprising in 2000. Such despair, she writes, is particularly evident in films from 2005 such as Rashid Masharawi's *Waiting* (*Intizar*) and Hany Abu Assad's *Paradise Now* (*Al Jannah al-An*), both of which reflect the utter loss of hope that followed the *intifada*. What is, however, surprising is that in the second half of the 2000s there began to appear Palestinian films that look beyond the current political impasse for narratives of agency and a peoplehood less dependent on political possibilities for the future than on an ethical way of being in the present, however unacceptable present conditions may be. Through a close reading of some of these films, Yaqub demonstrates how these filmmakers refuse to be defined by the defeat of 1948 while insisting on their right to remember it.

In the last chapter, Teodora Todorova examines the proliferation in the past decade of Israeli and Palestinian collective, individual and historical narratives concerned with the events which took place in post-Mandate Palestine and the newly established State of Israel between 1947 and 1949. It begins with the story of the public resurgence of the suppressed narrative of the Palestinian *Nakba* after decades of silence marked by a pronounced lack of officially-sanctioned narratives. The chapter focuses on the ways in which Palestinians have collectively held onto the memory of their dispossession and how that memory has more recently been utilized politically in order to articulate the Palestinian refugees' right of return. This account is fused with a theoretical analysis of the work of the Israeli NGO *Zochrot* (Remembering) which seeks to reintegrate the narrative of the *Nakba* in the Jewish Israeli collective consciousness by making pre-1948 Palestine and its people visible in the Israeli socio-cultural and political landscape. The chapter concludes that the work of critical historians such as Ilan Pappé, alongside progressive civil society institutions such as *Zochrot,* is creating a much needed "safe space" within Israeli society where acknowledgement and witnessing can begin to take place without fear of persecution or retribution.

References

Cottle, Simon (2006). *Mediatized Conflict: Developments in Media and Conflict Studies* (Maidenhead, UK: Open University Press).

Fanon, Frantz (1963). *The Wretched of the Earth*, trans. Constance Farrington (New York: Grove Press).

Giddens, Anthony (1994). *The Consequences of Modernity* (Cambridge: Polity Press).

Harb, Zahera (2011). *Channels of Resistance in Lebanon: Liberation Propaganda, Hezbollah and the Media* (London: I.B.Tauris).

Haugbolle, Sune (2010). *War and Memory in Lebanon* (Cambridge: Cambridge University Press).

Maltby, Sarah and Richard Keeble (2007). *Communicating War: Memory, Military and Media* (Bury St Edmunds: Arima Publishing).

Matar, Dina (2011). *What it Means to be Palestinian: Stories of Palestinian Peoplehood* (London: I.B.Tauris).

Pappé, Ilan (2006). *The Ethnic Cleansing of Palestine* (Oxford: Oneworld Publications).

Sayigh, Yezid (1997). *Armed Struggle and the Search for State* (Oxford: Oxford University Press).

Swedenberg, Ted and Rebecca Stein (2005). *Palestine, Israel and the Politics of Popular Culture* (Durham and London: Duke University Press).

Thussu, Daya and Des Freedman (eds) (2003). *War and the Media: Reporting Conflict 24/7* (London: Sage Publications).

I

PRACTICES

2

JUST A FEW SMALL CHANGES: THE LIMITS OF TELEVISUAL PALESTINIAN REPRESENTATION OF CONFLICTS WITHIN THE TRANSNATIONAL "CENSORSCAPE"

MATT SIENKIEWICZ

For critics and activists alike, the preferred metaphor used to describe the Palestinian West Bank is that of a prison. As Rashid Khalidi notes in his provocatively titled history of Palestinian statelessness, *The Iron Cage* (2006), in the years following the second *intifada* (uprising) that started at the end of 2000, Israel has progressively limited the mobility of West Bank residents. Whereas once a Palestinian could travel into and within Israel with relative freedom, a new matrix of checkpoints, concrete walls and road closures have turned the West Bank into a series of discrete, poorly interconnected cells. Not only is travel into Israel impossible without a permit, but movement between towns and cities under the control of the Palestinian Authority is controlled by the Israeli Defense Forces. Checkpoints dot the West Bank, ensuring an Israeli presence between every Palestinian city and making the complete isolation of each residential zone only a single military decision away at any given moment. For example, the city of Qalqilya, located just miles from Tel Aviv and identified by Israel as the launch-point for major suicide bombings, is encased almost entirely by a 30-foot concrete wall, save for a single entry and exit road manned by the Israeli military.

The isolated, disconnected nature of West Bank life goes beyond the physical level, infiltrating into the realm of culture as well. In particular, the region's media system is cited as playing a role in further fracturing Palestinian society. As Helga Tawil-Souri has argued, private Palestinian television has historically tended to be "hyper-local" (Tawil-Souri, 2007: 4–27) creating the impression that little connection exists between individual cities in the West Bank or Gaza Strip. Station managers, forced to compete with regional satellite superchannels, have become increasingly focused on carving out small, highly concentrated viewership so as to provide value to local advertisers. The result, according to Tawil-Souri, is a system that works against the fostering of a sense of Palestinian national identity that might give momentum to solidarity against Israeli and elite Palestinian interests. Although projects such as the Ma'an Network have worked to overcome this element by linking local stations together throughout the West Bank (Sienkiewicz, 2010: 3–14),[1] there still exists a sense in which Palestinian media contributes to both the physical and cultural imprisonment of its viewers.

Nevertheless, for producers of independent film and television, the fractured, prison-like nature of Palestinian space and culture is just the beginning of the story. Yes, unpredictable road conditions make assembling a crew and scheduling a shoot even harder than these challenging tasks are under normal conditions. And, yes, the inability to find national broadcast outlets beyond the realm of government television serves to work against the creation of a consistent, independent media industry. However, beyond these logistical problems lies another daunting obstacle for media makers interested in producing material that requires a significant budget. For producers with professional ambitions, the West Bank is not merely a concrete prison: it is also a panopticon – a space in which myriad and sometimes anonymous observers watch every frame, waiting for an opportunity to exercise their corrective authority. Western funders, potential Arab program buyers, Israeli media watchdogs and Palestinian government censors all bring restrictions to the content of independent Palestinian film and television. Such limitations only grow when these productions engage in the sorts of politically controversial material that is central to so much of contemporary Palestinian storytelling.

This chapter argues that the political and economic environment in which independent Palestinian media makers operate results in a unique coalescing of internal and external forces, creating a transnational "censorscape" in which all production must take place. I use the term "censorscape" in parallel with Appadurai's (2006)[2] "mediascape" to emphasize the global, fluid nature of the often-unwritten rules and regulations in which Palestinian content creation takes place. Furthermore, I wish to suggest the smallness of the individual producer against the backdrop of a vast interconnected political world that ultimately has a significant impact on what she can and cannot present in her work. Whereas scholars such as Mattelart (1996) and Downing (2001) argue that transnational television distribution plays the role of bypassing local censorship in places with low levels of media freedom, this article illustrates the fashion in which transnational production and funding can have the opposite effect. By weaving together the idiosyncratic and occasionally contradictory political concerns of international funders, regional buyers and local authorities, the international collaboration that much contemporary Palestinian production requires creates a set of obstacles that serve to exacerbate an already difficult media environment.

When asked about his work, Nasser Laham, chief editor of the Bethlehem based Ma'an News Agency and one of Palestine's most renowned journalists, inevitably returns to the same core principle. "To be a Palestinian," he says, "is to be a slave with one thousand masters."[3] He goes on to detail a roster of international powers, each member of which not only places its own demands on the Palestinian people, but also acts as though their generosity has been betrayed if their ostensibly friendly advice goes unheeded. The Americans, the Israelis, the Gulf States, the European Union, the Russians, the Jordanians, the Iranians and the Egyptians all contribute economically to Palestine's fragile economy and each, according to Laham, feels entitled to preferential treatment. In a nation without an established professional media industry beyond the government-run Palestinian Broadcasting Corporation, this situation is particularly restrictive. Whereas in many nations the media is funded either via commercial investment or government subsidy, the independent producer in Palestine lacks either of these options. Thus media makers must choose to work either with a self-financed micro-budget or turn to alternative sources such as foreign governments and NGOs in order to have funding. In the years following the second *intifada* this latter option has proven increasingly viable, as digital technologies have reduced production budgets and "edutainment" projects have grown in popularity amongst donors.

In this chapter, I consider two projects that were financed in this manner. The first, *Spiderwebs*, is an independent feature film produced by a Palestinian women's organization (TAM Media) in conjunction with NETHAM, a branch of the United States Agency for International Development. The second, *The Team*, is a forty-part television serial produced by the Ma'an Network through a grant from Search for Common Ground, a conflict resolution NGO that also receives most of its funding via American government grants. By considering the project proposals, donor notes and final texts of these projects, I sketch out the contradictory demands imposed on Palestinian media makers, underlining the levels of direct and indirect censorship that help structure the stories they are allowed to tell.

A History of Censorship

Academic assessments of censorship in the Middle East have often come in the form of taxonomic breakdowns of national media systems, occasionally combined with broad and dire generalizations about the region's press freedom. This tendency appears in many of the foundational texts on Middle Eastern media, perhaps most influentially in the Rugh's *The Arab Press* (1979), which rates each nation's media as being in the "loyalist," "mobilization," "transitional," or "diverse" modes. In his book-length treatment of the subject nearly 30 years later, Al-Obaidi describes the dominant patterns of media control within the region using a similar nationalist framework to consider whether given countries fit into the conservative paradigm, the democratic paradigm or someplace in between, based on the level of government cooptation of the press. He notes that while all areas of the globe are subject to certain levels of censorship, in the Middle East the extent of top-down control of mediated expression has "exceeded all limits and norms" (Al-Obaidi, 2007: 5). While his account identifies a slow movement away from totalitarian control of the media in nations such as Jordan and Yemen, he argues that it is the presence of transnational technologies such as satellite television and mobile devices that provide the best hope for a more democratic mediasphere.

This focus on new media and international distribution as a means of overcoming localized censorship has become a general trend in the contemporary understanding of media censorship in the region. Indeed, critic Marc Lynch makes a similar claim for the prospects of a new, transnational Arab public sphere. Arguing that Al Jazeera, the internet and other forms of telecommunication operating outside the scope of government intervention promote "dialogue and reason" in discussions of contentious issues, Lynch holds that the era of globalization has provided alternative avenues for forms of expression traditionally curtailed at the national level (Lynch, 2005: 87). The work of Lynch, Sakr (2007a), Amin (2003) and others have all made the point that these apparent international freedoms are likely to have a positive impact in reducing national forms of censorship as viewers become accustomed to more open forms of global media.

However, due to the ongoing struggle for national autonomy within the Palestinian territories, discussions of censorship in the West Bank and Gaza Strip have rarely moved beyond the national level. Jamal, Nossek and Rinnawi, respectively, argue that from the beginning of Israel's occupation of the territories in 1967 through the Oslo Accords of 1993, Palestinian media was directly censored by dueling nationalist regimes intent on taming the flow of information. Most prevalently, the Israeli military apparatus invoked a series of British Mandate-era press laws in order to exercise strict media censorship under an ostensibly legalistic framework. In practice, this meant that "the military authorities limited and revoked distribution permits, banned distribution, confiscated published materials and prosecuted Palestinians found in possession of banned publications." All materials for publication were subject to the review of Israeli censors who were not required to apply a consistent standard when refusing the publication (Nossek and Rinnawi, 2003: 194). In addition to this line-item control of print media, Israel also imposed a complete ban of electronic media in the Palestinian territories, a circumstance that would not change until 1993.

The Palestinian response to these external efforts at absolute control resulted in further curtailment of the press, as the media became an important site in which to establish political power both within the Palestinian community and *vis-à-vis* Israel. Jamal states that by 1972, the Palestinian Liberation Organization came to own the vast majority of print outlets being produced in the West Bank both legally and illegally, using them as a means of declaring resistance to Israel as well as refuting claims of Jordanian ownership of the West Bank in the wake of the Black September violence of 1970 and 1971 (Jamal, 2000). The PLO exercised direct forms of censorship, as statements in support of opposition parties and otherwise controversial opinions were eliminated for fear of providing "either tactical or emotional benefits to enemies"(Jamal, 2000: 47). Nossek and Rinnawi identify the period from 1972 to 1993 as one in which Palestinian media was forced to look outward to avoid internal critiques, following the "developmental" model of media in which the media system's primary purpose is to foster a sense of national unity and purpose (Nossek and Rinnawi, 2003: 187).

Direct Israeli control of Palestinian media ceased in 1993 with the Oslo Accords, but indirect forms of censorship persisted. Perhaps most notably, while Israel at this point began to allow the dissemination of radio and television from the West Bank and Gaza Strip, it dismantled the areas' broadcasting infrastructure and made no effort to facilitate the establishment of a functional Palestinian electronic media system.[4] While the newly formed Palestinian Authority (PA) struggled to form and maintain the Palestinian Broadcasting Authority, small, for-profit stations emerged across the region, broadcasting to sub-sections of citizens and providing an often extremely localized brand of news and entertainment. As a result, Palestinian television has remained a fractured and inconsistent product, leading Tawil-Souri to argue that Palestinian media mirrors the disjointed physical nature of the West Bank and Gaza Strip that results from Israeli road closures and military checkpoints.

From a legal standpoint, the birth of the Palestinian Authority marked the end of sanctioned media censorship, as Israel could no longer enforce arcane laws dating from the colonial period. In 1995 the Palestinian Press Law came to replace former media regulations, providing an ostensibly liberal framework in which freedom of expression was to be granted widely and government censorship would disappear. However, despite the late Palestinian leader Yasser Arafat's claim that the PA would foster a media system in which no criticism was out of bounds, there nonetheless emerged a combination of official and unofficial methods by which media freedom was significantly curtailed. Amal Jamal argues that during this period, media censorship transitioned from being an official "mechanism" to a more fluid "behavior," as the vagaries of the Palestinian Press Law were used in order to control messages from both print and broadcast outlets (Jamal, 2000: 54). The law, while avoiding partisan language, required that all media must be "objective and balanced" and avoid doing "harm to national unity" (ibid.: 51). And although these requirements are perhaps within the bounds of reasonable expectations for a populace struggling for national recognition and self-determination, the implementation of the law was uneven and, according to critics, often implemented for the purpose of intimidation. While censorious actions against media outlets became far less frequent than during the previous Israeli-controlled era, Hillel Nossek and Khalil Rinnawi suggest that "fear of repercussions from the PA" resulted in "the creation of significant self-censorship among Palestinian journalists" during the period (Nossek and Rinnawi, 2003: 199).

Censorship also came in the form of direct shutdowns, particularly of television stations during times of crisis. Jamal reports that in 1998 eight private television stations were forcibly shut down for providing coverage of pro-Iraqi demonstrations, for fear that the publicizing of such events would harm the world's image of Palestine and particularly offend American policy makers whose budgets contributed heavily to the Palestinian Authority's coffers (Jamal, 2000: 52). Such policies appear to have continued well into the 2000s. Members of the Ma'an Network report that in the years following their launch in 2003 they would consistently receive orders from the President's office to cease the broadcast of a specific story or idea. According to producers at Ma'an, this occurred most frequently when a program would criticize a specific individual, directly contradicting Arafat's earlier claim that media would serve as a means of keeping high-level politicians honest.[5]

Such shutdowns appear to have become a thing of the past in the West Bank of today and stations like the Ma'an Network, which represent many of the most visible non-governmental outlets, no longer report the varieties of governmental strong-arming which appeared as a limiting factor in early scholarship. However, the claims of Jamal, Nossek and Rinnawi and others focus largely on the institutionalization of self-censorship, a claim that remains relevant in the contemporary context. While the Ma'an Network and a handful of other independent stations are able to exist without direct support from the PA, the government-run Palestinian Broadcasting Corporation remains not only the West Bank's only nation-wide television outlet, but also a prime purchaser of programming produced independently in the territories. Even Ma'an, an organization that has gained its reputation both locally and internationally by promoting its independence from the political parties of Fatah and Hamas, has turned to selling to the PBC's Palestine Satellite Channel as a means of gaining both income and exposure. In such cases, however, the PBC reserves the right to turn down programming based on political content, providing an incentive to produce programming that will be approved (Sienkiewicz, 2010: 6). The PBC has notably loosened its control over its content, however, particularly in the time after 2007's civil war with Hamas which resulted in the station moving its headquarters from Gaza to the West Bank city of Ramallah and brought with it a wholesale change at the executive level of the organization. Most notably, in 2009 the Palestine Satellite Channel aired the independently produced satire program *Country on a String*. The program included parodic impressions of both local and international leaders and took direct aim at government inefficiencies and failures (Garcia-Navarro, 2010).[6]

Yet, despite the ample attention that both academic and popular writers have showered upon the national elements of media restrictions on Palestinian media, little effort has been made to conceptualize the impact of international pressures and organizations on local content production. Naomi Sakr argues that

NGO-driven media efforts have a fundamentally positive impact on Palestinian self-expression, creating new voices that can expose government corruption. While such efforts inevitably run into problems at the domestic level, she contends that internationally-funded media efforts nonetheless make available a variety of information pipelines that will, one way or another, allow ideas to move past efforts at censorship and enter the public consciousness (Sakr, 2007b). With the booming growth of internationally-funded, non-profit media over the past ten years, Sakr's insight remains both relevant and conceptually important.

For example, over the past eight years, four significant Palestinian soap operas have been produced in the West Bank: the Ma'an Network's *Ma Zi Fi Jad* (*Joking Seriously*), *Shu Fi Ma Fi* (*What's Up*) and *Al Fariq* (*The Team*) and the Goethe's Institute's *Mattab* (*Speedbump*). Each of these products was funded with foreign money filtered through international NGOs and was broadcast on the PBC, as well as local outlets. Having reached this level of production both in terms of quantity and quality, internationally-supported media in the West Bank can no longer be viewed simply as an oppositional element creating new outlets for expression. Instead it must be understood as a core element in Palestine's media industry and one that brings with it both opportunities and restrictions. In the following section I make explicit the means by which the newly internationalized elements of Palestinian television impact content via an analysis of the restrictions on the production, distribution and exhibition of programming produced in the West Bank under the influence of foreign partners.

Producing within the Censorscape: The Case of *Spiderwebs*

Spiderwebs is an 87-minute film produced by Saleem Dabbour, who, in addition to being one of Palestine's most highly regarded cultural figures and writers, is also the chairman for the Association of Women's Committees for Social Work (AWCSW), a multi-million dollar NGO based in Ramallah that serves the whole of the West Bank. Dabbour's biography is a diverse and transnational one that has positioned him to challenge the traditional restrictions imposed on Palestinian media makers. Cigarette burns up and down his legs attest to his role as a student leader during the first *intifada* and provide credibility for his claims to a true understanding of the struggle of Palestinian life. His post-university experiences in Holland, where he was awarded a variety of prizes for poetry and writing, endear him to the European arts community that has so strongly supported the efforts of Palestinian filmmakers such as Michel Khleifi. His work with the AWCSW—which receives large financial grants from governments across the world including the United States—establishes him as a figure who can be trusted to take seriously the regulations and unwritten rules that come along with accepting international funding for cultural projects. Dabbour is also a vocal member of Fatah, the ruling political party in the Palestinian Authority, allowing him access to certain public resources without officially turning his project over to the government.

Armed with these unique credentials, Dabbour has taken it upon himself to produce Palestinian films that are appreciated by large portions of the Palestinian people. Although he respects the efforts of internationally celebrated Palestinian filmmakers such as Khleifi and Elia Sulieman, he admits that he has seen very few of their films. And though no conclusive data on the subject exists, it would appear that Dabbour is not alone in feeling that much of the canon associated with Palestinian national cinema is unfamiliar to most Palestinian viewers. For example, in the city of Bethlehem, the only film produced in the Palestinian territories regularly available at local video stores is *Paradise Now,* a movie made in conjunction with Hollywood producers and aimed at an international audience. With *Spiderwebs,* Dabbour wanted to tell a story that takes on issues such as gang-intimidation and domestic violence in the West Bank, important concerns for the Palestinian people but not the kind of themes likely to resonate with global viewers.

In order to produce the film, Dabbour and his director Rifat Adi turned to international donors, the only sector of Palestinian society capable of covering *Spiderwebs'* modest $75,000 budget. Using connections established in his work at the AWCSW, Dabbour contacted NETHAM, a private organization currently employed by USAID to oversee its efforts in Israel and the Palestinian territories.[7] NETHAM pointed Dabbour to their current "Rule of Law" project. Rule of Law has become a fashionable topic in the world of international development, although, according to Challand, it is rarely approached in a systematic fashion that clearly defines what the concept stands (Calland, 2006: 24). The official NETHAM Rule of Law report calls for projects that increase "accountability among justice sector officials" and improve "public trust in, and access to the justice sector."[8] To do so, the organization funded law courses at Palestinian universities, created awards for law enforcement officials and established a Public Services Office at the Ministry of Justice.

Dabbour's film pushed the Rule of Law project in a slightly different direction, introducing the notion that cultural productions and creative storytelling could play a role in increasing social awareness of the legal system. The application for NETHAM funding describes *Spiderwebs* as an "entertainment-education project" in the tradition of Miguel Sabido's telenovelas that would not only contribute to public awareness of the law but also cause "audiences to adopt new behaviors."[9] This latter, rather bold claim was likely inspired by the need for applicants to establish "verifiable outputs" for any USAID-supported project. The film's narrative is a dramatic, often violent, story in which a local gang terrorizes the city of Bethlehem, a husband mercilessly beats his wife and a corrupt police officer takes bribes in order to keep his eyes averted from the anarchy that is consuming the city. Ultimately, an honest police officer saves the day, arresting the criminals and bringing the crooked cop to justice. While initially critical of the PA's security forces, the story ultimately redeems the system, showing that, if citizens properly report wrongdoing, the good guys will show up and save the day.

When asked about the freedom afforded by NETHAM in producing the project, Dabbour makes the very important point that, without USAID's money, a $75,000 film would be nearly impossible to produce in the West Bank. From this perspective, the American funding of *Spiderwebs* perhaps ought to be viewed as a liberating force, for without it there would not have been a film at all. However, despite the relative autonomy that NETHAM provided the filmmakers, there were nonetheless significant restrictions placed on the script's content. Dabbour points to three words that had to be removed, the first of which was redacted by the United States, with the latter two being changed in deference to local authorities.

Spiderwebs is conspicuous for the total absence of a discussion of Israel and the occupation. Dabbour notes that this was a general, if unwritten, condition of being involved with the Rule of Law project, the expressed goal of which is to concentrate on the internal Palestinian justice system. However, to discuss life in the West Bank without a mention of Israel is inevitably misleading and could very plausibly result in a loss of audience trust in the film. Dabbour chose to address this problem by simply including a mention of a sympathetic character's father being "martyred by Israel." The Arabic word used for martyr, *shahid*, has become a lightning rod for Palestinian producers supported by foreign funding though some organizations claim its association with suicide bombers glorifies death and violence.[10] Although it is a phrase far more often used to describe innocent victims than terrorists, hearings in the United States senate have been held questioning whether or not the term ought to be allowed in media produced with foreign funds.[11] Ultimately, Dabbour was told that the phrase "martyred by Israel" was a provocation and distraction from the purposes for which *Spiderwebs* was being funded. He relented, removing the word Israel and simply describing the character as a martyr who must be respected. Israel is thus completely absent from the film. And although this decision certainly involved Israeli supervision that perhaps resonates with that exercised during earlier periods of the occupation, it is crucial to understand this limiting of Palestinian vocabulary within a global context. For example, the Israeli organization Palestinian Media Watch has direct relationships with a variety of foreign governmental bodies. The organization, along with others of its kind—such as the Middle East Media Research Institute (MEMRI) and NGO-Monitor—has employed the internet in order to make local Palestinian media decisions a global issue. Each day, emails featuring transcripts and video clips from the Palestinian territories are sent to thousands of listserv subscribers around the globe, ensuring that the world's eyes remain focused on even individual word choices made in the West Bank and Gaza Strip.

However, it was not simply Israeli or Western sensibilities that were offended by the first cut of *Spiderwebs*. Two other changes demanded to the script came from local authorities. Again, it is important to consider the positive role that the censoring body played in the film's production. *Spiderwebs* focuses on corruption within Palestinian society and does so with the help of a variety of governmental resources. Yet, the film's budget did not include nearly enough money for the purchase of realistic-looking police equipment or the rental of spaces that could convincingly represent courts and prisons. Dabbour used his positive relationship with the PA to acquire these resources, but this cooperation came at a price. During a description of the problems in Palestinian society, Dabbour had originally written a line of dialogue claiming that the corruption went "all the way to president." Local PA authorities asked the line be removed, likely because it undermines the film's ultimate message that the legal system, given enough time, will succeed in bringing justice. Also, in the original script, the boy screamed at the corrupt officer "you are not an authority (*sulta* in local Arabic); you are a salad (*salata*)." This pun is often invoked by locals criticizing the Palestinian Authority and was deemed unnecessarily insulting by local authorities that otherwise supported the film. Despite Dabbour's insistence that the line merely indicted local forms of corruption, he nonetheless was eventually convinced to excise the offending word, *salata*. However, in a clever act of resistance, Dabbour chose to cut the scene in mid-sentence: just as the boy is about to finish the well-known phrase with the word "*salata,*" the scene cuts to two women having a conversation across town. One of them begins to chop a cucumber in preparation for a traditional Arabic salad. Dabbour's joke thus comes through to its intended audience. During the initial screening of the film, this moment was received with considerable laughter and applause. This moment of censorship re-inscribes the importance of the self-censorship that Nossek and Rinnawi identify, making clear that traditional forms of censorship in the Palestinian territories remain operative, if only in rather liberalized forms. In the case of *Spiderwebs*, the limitations placed on certain phrases served as a sort of rent-taking on the part of the authorities offering in-kind help for local productions in exchange for modest concessions in terms of governmental criticism.

The Pressures of the Regional TV Market:
The Team and External Expectations

Spiderwebs has not yet been introduced to the international television market; however, it is worth considering the additional levels of pressure to change content to which it will likely be subjected if it is. In order to address this aspect of the censorscape in which Palestinian media production takes place, I turn to the recently completed television serial, *The Team*. Produced as a co-production between the Ma'an Network and Search for Common Ground, *The Team* is a 40-episode soap opera following the efforts of a Palestinian soccer team to overcome its internal differences and act as a successful unit. The metaphor of the team, which, much like *Spiderwebs*, obliterates the role of Israel, is particularly poignant at a time during which Palestine is politically split between Hamas' control of Gaza and Fatah's continued reign in the West Bank. The program is part of an international series produced in cooperation with Search for Common Ground's production wing that includes similarly themed shows in Morocco, Kenya, Egypt and nearly a dozen other locations.[12]

The director of the Palestinian version of *The Team*, Nabil Shoumali, reports that he had received relatively little interference from his American supporters, with the main demand being the absence of violence. However, they did make additional specific requests. Most of these demands go back to a stance taken by the US Department of State that representations of life in the Palestinian territories should reflect how the Americans feel things ought to be, not the way they are. For example, while Palestinian society includes an enormous diversity of opinions on the ultimate answer to the conflict with Israel, characters in American-funded productions are very unlikely to question the wisdom of the two-state solution. As Catherine Joppart, one of Ma'an Network's first fundraisers, notes: "The Americans want things to reflect normalization with Israel because they think that will help make it so. But if people aren't ready for it, it just rings false."[13]

The Team was combed for anything that might be considered a statement in opposition to American policy, with even the set décor being reviewed for potential offenses. This scrutiny proved rather damaging to the production, as the presence of a simple and very common wall-decoration made a number of images taken for the program unusable. Many Palestinian homes feature a tapestry or poster representing historical Palestine. Most often, the colors of the contemporary Palestinian flag covers the land, consuming all of today's West Bank, Gaza Strip and Israel. Despite the pedestrian nature of this item in the eyes of many Palestinians, it was deemed an unacceptable provocation for a production produced with American tax dollars. A map without Israel would not be allowable, regardless of the role it plays in this story, and any shot featuring it was rendered useless and a waste of money. This mode of criticism is a mainstay of Israeli watchdog groups such as NGO-Monitor and Palestinian Media Watch, with some of their most common reports featuring talk and game shows in which Israeli cities such as Tel Aviv and Haifa are described as "Palestinian ports."[14] The influence of these groups, combined with the American position on the two-state solution, served as the impetus behind a small but costly change in the filmmaking process.

However, according to Shoumali, the Americans and Israelis hardly represent the only challenge to his work. The role that other Arab nations play is often just as restrictive and perhaps is even more damaging to the long-term commercial hopes for program such as *The Team*. For Shoumali and the Ma'an Network, pan-Arab satellite channels offer the best opportunity to find revenue beyond the purview of local or international government grants. There is interest from a variety of Egyptian, Lebanese and Gulf stations in broadcasting Palestinian programming and many of these outlets possess the resources to support regular production. However, according to Shoumali, they desire a very specific image of Palestine one that hardly fits the kind of stories he wants to tell:

> They want to see fighting, bombing, resistance. They don't want to see that we live amongst Israelis, use Israeli shekels. They don't want to see that we have middle class, that our economy isn't so terrible. They think we should be beggars, refugees and fighters and not doctors, mechanics or accountants. They don't want to see we are people who want to live.[15]

In discussing *The Team* with content-buyers from regional stations, Shoumali found them to be no less nit-picking than the Americans who tore down his tapestry. The use of Israeli currency was particularly galling to some, despite the fact that such a representation is, like the existence of Palestinian maps that ignore Israel, utterly undeniable. Much like the Americans,

Arab programmers asked Shoumali to remove those aspects of his project that failed to match up with their political objectives. What becomes clear is that Palestinians are victims, not agents, in the narrative they wish to tell and projects such as *Spiderwebs* and *The Team* run contrary to the stories potential buyers wish to see told. Of course, local viewers are likely to be bored or even offended by such reductive pictures of Palestinian life, but the current production environment makes them nearly inevitable.

Due to the lack of private investment or insulated public funding in the Palestinian territories, producers find themselves caught in a "censorscape" that extends in all directions, limiting their options for representations of local life and sometimes making contradictory demands. For example, the easiest way to procure a major budget is to go through American sources that will demand the project eschew violence and make no mention of resistance. However, in order to recoup the money invested in such a project, the best option is to turn to pan-Arab stations that tend to associate Palestinian pacifism with collaboration and will look elsewhere to fill their need for programming about Palestine. It is important to note that each of these funding possibilities, despite their obvious drawbacks, do allow Palestinian producers, artists and technicians the opportunity to practice their respective crafts. The development of local talents will ideally lay the groundwork for what may one day emerge as a self-sufficient moving-picture industry and a productive element of the public sphere. However, as of now the restrictive elements of Palestinian production are myriad and serve to exacerbate a situation in which even the simplest elements of media production are already enormously challenging.

Conclusion

In Amal Jamal's history of media and politics in the West Bank and Gaza Strip (2005), he argues that the early stages of the Palestinian media development were devoted to a battle over what would constitute Palestine's "media regime." Jamal identifies three main contenders for control of the broadcasting sphere, arguing that while the main battle was staged between the political and religious elites, there also existed voices from civil society, particularly from within women's groups, who demanded decisions not be made strictly along partisan or theological lines. While these outsider voices never threatened to dominate the new Palestinian media world, Jamal shows that they nonetheless were able to influence the culture of broadcasting in the West Bank and Gaza Strip in subtle but significant ways. Despite the authoritarian portrayals of Palestinian media in the West, media standards have nonetheless always been subject to negotiation.

The internally focused mode of analysis offered by Jamal is particularly useful in its nuanced picture of the formative years of the Palestinian television system. In the wake of the Oslo Accords, decades of debates amongst Palestinians both at home and in the Diaspora were first given concrete expression in the form of official, albeit limited, political power. Such circumstances demanded a scholarly focus on the establishment of local media rules and regulations, with the insulated nature of Palestinian broadcasting being particularly apparent in the wake of America's refusal to participate in the funding of the PBC after 1998. However, the contemporary media landscape in the West Bank requires a new, additional focus, one that takes into account the direct role that international figures and institutions play in the negotiation over what ideas, stories and images are produced and disseminated, particularly with regard media relating to conflict.

Although the concept of a "media regime" certainly remains operative within the context of the highly contentious world of Palestinian politics, it is now incumbent on scholars, critics and policy makers to understand the pressures on Palestinian media outside of a dual focus on factional negotiations and the impact of production under circumstances of occupation. Despite its continuing struggle towards nationhood, Palestine has nonetheless produced a media system that is entering the international system in a variety of complicated, and sometimes even contradictory, fashions. While producers such as Saleem Dabbour and Nabil Shoumali certainly believe in media's potential role in soothing internal Palestinian conflicts and building a nation strong enough to overcome decades of military occupation, they are also committed to finding a niche for Palestinian film and television in the global media economy. To do so requires compromises with a variety of forces, many of which have been here outlined. This industrial goal in no way minimizes the impact of Israel's unrelenting grip on the West Bank or the cultural and political battles that exist between Hamas, Fatah and other factions. It does, however, force these obstacles into an international context that refuses to localize conflicts that have, and in truth always have had, profound relationships to global political economy.

As O'Regan notes in the context of national cinema, smaller nations, if they wish to maintain modest but self-sufficient media industries, must work to establish a sense of product-differentiation that separates their work from media hegemons such as Hollywood. A means of doing this is to exploit "local specificities in domestic social events, issues, stories and myths" (O'Regan, 1996: 45). In this sense, media projects that honestly discuss both the conflict with Israel and the well-publicized internal struggles in Palestine could potentially serve the dual purpose of bolstering the Palestinian public sphere and providing a small area in which to begin selling media products that could underwrite future work. Eventually, Dabbour, Shoumali and others hope such projects would finance the infrastructure in which to create films without external funding or aspirations, allowing for the production of works that are not about conflict, but instead express more subtle elements of local life, culture and aspirations.

However, as this chapter has shown, a variety of forces work to suppress local specificities and force local Palestinian discourse to fit into international modes of discussion that tend to flatten and depersonalize conflict. Such a system, despite the efforts of talented producers, is bound to produce programming that fails either to authentically express local concerns or truly fill in a market space that other international productions focused on Palestine or the Middle East fail to address. This situation emerges not from a local media regime, nor as a mere result of Israel's role in suppressing elements of Palestinian society, although both elements remain relevant. With regards to productions such as *Spiderwebs* or *The Team*, these factors must be understood within a broader, international context in which Western funding partners work to limit what Palestinians are able to say and potential regional buyers choose to look away from aspects of Palestinian life that fail to conform to their pre-conceived notions.

Dabbour, in recognition of the "censorscape" that surrounds his work and limits its avenues for discussing the conflict, looked beyond the standard NGO-driven international system in order to finance the production of his most recent screenplay, *Beyond the Sun*. The film, unlike *Spiderwebs* or *The Team*, takes head on both the brutality of the conflict with Israel as well as the controversial issue of Palestinian collaboration with the Israeli military during the *intifadas*. Knowing that a film, which details his painful, personal experiences as a prisoner would not attract foreign money (either from NGOs or Arabic language broadcasters), Dabbour turned to the Palestinian diaspora and found an executive producer in the person of Anas Abusada, a Palestinian living in Holland. Using strictly private money, the film was produced and features many of the elements specifically prohibited in projects that emerge from the global system that supports large-scale, independent Palestinian media. However, in breaking free from the restrictions of the "censorscape," Dabbour also moved his project away from its most promising distribution network, which features small but important outlets such as the stations of the Ma'an Network. As such, the film must turn to the fickle world of international film festivals, in which it is very likely to be overshadowed by films produced by more famous directors with considerably more robust budgets. And even if it does find a place in the crowded festival market, it remains highly unlikely that Abusada could ever recoup his investment. The contrasting circumstances of *Beyond the Sun* and *Spiderwebs* bring into focus the bind created by the panopticon in which independent, local Palestinian screen media exists. If one wishes to avoid the eyes of the guards who man the international "censorscape," one most likely needs to escape the gaze of viewers as well. Until international forces, both Western and Middle Eastern, recognize the value in the unfettered expression of the complex lives that Palestinians experienced under conflict, it is difficult to foresee a true escape for independent producers such as Dabbour.

Notes

1. Matt Sienkiewicz, "Hard Questions: Public Goods and the Political Economy of the New Palestinian Televisual Public Sphere," *The Velvet Light Trap*, 66 (2010) 3–14.
2. Arjun Appadurai, *Modernity at Large: Cultural Dimensions of Globalization* (Minneapolis: University of Minnesota Press, 2006).

3. Nassar Laham, personal interview, 2007.
4. Daoud Kuttab, "The Role of Media," *Palestine-Israel Journal* 5(3–4) (1998) 29–33.
5. Muhammad Ganaiem, personal interview, 2009.
6. Lourdes Garcia-Navarro, "Palestinian TV Show Satirizes Life, Leaders," accessed November 10, 2010, http://www.npr.org/templates/story/story.php?storyId=112940559.
7. Saleem Dabbour, personal interview, 2009.
8. NETHAM "NETHAM Rule of Law Program/Justice and Enforcement" available at pdf.usaid.gov/pdf_docs/PDACO790.pdf, 2010.
9. Saleem Dabbour, "Netham Application Form," Internal Memo, 2009, p. 9.
10. Aryeh Dean Cohen, "Tube of Hatred," accessed November 10, 2010, http://www.jpost.com/home/article.aspx?id=151395 2009.
11. CSPAN *Palestinian Education* 2003, Washington: CSPAN.
12. John Bell, "Goal—Using Soccer to Ease Conflict, One Episode at a Time," accessed November 10, 2010, http://www.nytimes.com/2010/04/27/sports/soccer/27goal.html.
13. Catherine Joppart, personal interview, 2010.
14. Itamar Marcus and Nan Jacques Zilberdik, "EU Logo Prominent in PA TV Quiz in Which 'Palestine' Replaces Israel," accessed November 10, 2010, http://www.palwatch.org/main.aspx?fi=157&doc_id=2394.
15. Nabil Shoumali, personal interview, 2010.

References

Amin, Hussein (2001). "Mass Media in the Arab States between Diversification and Stagnation: An Overview." In Kai Hafez (ed.), *Mass Media, Politics and Society in the Middle East* (New Jersey: Hampton Press), pp. 23–43.
Appadurai, Arjun (2006). *Modernity at Large: Cultural Dimensions of Globalization* (Minneapolis: University of Minnesota Press).
Bell, John. "Goal—Using Soccer to Ease Conflict, One Episode at a Time." *New York Times*, April 26, 2010. Accessed November 10, 2010. http://www.nytimes.com/2010/04/27/sports/soccer/27goal.html.
Challand, Benoit (2006). "Civil Society, Autonomy and Donors: International Aid to Palestinian NGOs." EUI Working Papers: 24.
Cohen, Aryeh Dean. "Tube of Hatred." *The Jerusalem Post*, August 10, 2009. Accessed November 10, 2010. http://www.jpost.com/home/article.aspx?id=151395.
CSPAN (2003). *Palestinian Education* (Washington: CSPAN).
Dabbour, Saleem (2009a). "Netham Application Form", Internal Memo, p. 9.
——— (2009b). Interview by author. Palestine.
Downing, John D. H. et al. (2001). *Radical Media: Rebellious Communication and Social Movements* (London: Sage Publications).

Ganaiem, Muhammad (2009). Interview by author. Palestinian territories.

Garcia-Navarro, Lourdes. "Palestinian TV Show Satirizes Life, Leaders." Accessed November 10, 2010. http://www.npr.org/templates/story/story.php?storyId=112940559.

Jamal, Amal (2000). *Media Politics and Democracy in Palestine* (East Sussex: Sussex Academic Press).

—— (2000). "The Palestinian Media: An Obedient Servant or a Vanguard of Democracy?" *Journal of Palestine Studies*, 29(3): 46.

Joppart, Catherine (2010). Interview by author. Palestinian territories.

Khalidi, Rashid (2006). *The Iron Cage: The Story of the Palestinian Struggle for Statehood* (Boston: Beacon Press).

Kuttab, Daoud (1998). "The Role of Media." *Palestine-Israel Journal*, 5(3–4): 29–33.

Laham, Nassar (2007). Interview by author. Palestinian territories.

Lynch, Marc (2005). *Voices of the New Arab Public: Iraq, al-Jazeera, and Middle East Politics Today* (New York: Columbia University Press).

Marcus, Itamar and Nan Jacques Zilberdik. "EU Logo Prominent in PA TV Quiz in which 'Palestine' replaces Israel." Accessed November 10 2010. http://www.palwatch.org/main.aspx?fi=157&doc_id=2394.

Mattelhart, Tristan (1999). "Transboundary Flows of Western Entertainment Across the Iron Curtain." *The Journal of International Communication*, 6: 106–121.

NETHAM. "NETHAM Rule of Law Program/Justice and Enforcement." Accessed November 10, 2010. pdf.usaid.gov/pdf_docs/PDACO790.pdf.

Nossek, Hillel and Khalil Rinnawi (2003). "Censorship and Freedom of the Press under Changing Political Regimes." *The International Journal for Communication Studies*, 65: 194.

Al-Obaidi, Jabbar (2007). *Media Censorship in the Middle East* (Lewiston: Edward Mellen Press).

O'Regan, Tom (1996). *Australian National Cinema* (London: Routledge).

Rugh, William (1979). *The Arab Press* (London: Croom Helm).

Sakr, Naomi (2007a). *Arab Television Today* (London: I.B.Tauris).

—— (2007b). *Satellite Realms: Transnational Television, Globalization and the Middle East* (London: I.B.Tauris).

Shoumali, Nabil (2010). Interview by author. Palestinian territories.

Sienkiewicz, Matt (2010). "Hard Questions: Public Goods and the Political Economy of the New Palestinian Televisual Public Sphere." *The Velvet Light Trap* 66: 3–14.

Tawil-Souri, Helga (2007). "Global and Local Forces for a Nation-State Yet to Be Born." *Westminster Papers in Communication and Culture* 4: 4–25.

3

MEDIATING INTERNAL CONFLICT IN LEBANON AND ITS ETHICAL BOUNDARIES

ZAHERA HARB

The Lebanese media scene could be identified as polarized and diverse and is characterized by the *interwoven* relationship between the media and the politicians in Lebanon. This polarized media system went through different phases and engendered different media models since Lebanon gained its independence in 1943. The civil war (1975–1990) witnessed an influx of illegal TV and radio stations which were later regulated in the post-civil war Lebanon. The regulation mirrored the confessional political system. Even though the law specified that no political party or politician should own a dominant majority in any of the newly licensed TV station, the practice came to echo the socio-political structure of the Lebanese society (Dajani, 2001). The two periods this chapter explores are: the period following the assassination of former Prime Minister Rafic Hariri in 2005 and the period between 2007 and 2008. The first period witnessed the emergence of a media model that helped mobilize people and led them to achieve change to the political status quo, and the second is a model of confrontation that facilitated sectarian tension and hatred among the Lebanese. It is during this second period that questions and concerns are raised regarding Lebanese journalists' ethical guidelines and boundaries and aspects of moral reasoning in the Lebanese media. This chapter examines how the internal conflict in Lebanon is mediated and narrated by Lebanese media. It also explores the ethical boundaries (if any) that Lebanese journalists retain when reporting internal conflict. The chapter starts by examining the Lebanese media system and its media scene and then investigates how a polarization model has moved from being a tool of change to being a tool of confrontation. The chapter ends by assessing the ethical boundaries within which Lebanese journalists work.

Lebanese Media System

William Rugh, in his book *The Arab Mass Media* (2004), divided the Arab media into three categories:

> The mobilising media, which is characterised by the almost total subordination of the media system to the political system; the loyalist media system, which is privately owned, but follows the line of governments, as those regimes can still control their resources (like paper or transmission rights) and persecute journalists through legal systems; the diverse media system, where the press is described as free, and the transitional system, where the media begin to move from the mobilised and loyalist systems to being diverse. (Rugh, 2004)

This chapter is not concerned with critiquing Rugh's categorizations. What is of relevance here is that the Lebanese media system, according to his classification, is described as diverse, which he also identified as "free." However, I would argue that Rugh's categorization is not fully representative because while the Lebanese media system is diverse and free from government and state control, it is not free from political and economic affiliation. This makes it closer to what Hallin and Mancini (2004) identified in their book *Comparing Media Systems* as the "Polarized Pluralist Model," which applies in the Mediterranean countries of southern Europe and is characterized by a politically polarized media, closely associated with political parties and a plurality of media, representing the diversity of political interests. According to Hallin and Mancini, the media of the Mediterranean countries in many ways, seem close to "Curran's (1991) model of 'radical democratic' public sphere," in which the media function as a "battleground between contending social forces" (ibid.: 29). The media in Lebanon follow closely these function patterns. Within the pluralist polarized media module, there seems to be a tendency towards low levels of professionalism. Hallin and Mancini (2004) argue that a high degree of professionalism in journalism means that journalism is differentiated as an institution and form of practice from other institutions and forms of practice—including politics (ibid.: 38). They go on to say that:

> Where political parallelism is very high, with media organisations strongly tied to political organisations and journalists deeply involved in party politics, professionalization is indeed likely to be low: journalists are likely to lack autonomy, except to the extent that they enjoy it due to high political positions, and journalism is likely to lack a distinct... sense of social purpose, apart from the purposes of the political actors with which the media are affiliated (ibid.).

This lack of autonomy tends to be a dominant feature among Lebanese journalists as this chapter will demonstrate; journalists became tied to the political actors with which they are affiliated. To borrow Hallin and Mancini's term, the media in Lebanon became "instrumentalized." According to them, "instrumentalized" media is controlled by outside actors, parties, politicians, social groups or movements, or economic actors seeking political influence (ibid.: 37). Journalists in Lebanon during the two periods under investigation identified themselves with particular points of view, which meant not serving the public (even though they claimed they were), contradicting their own standards of practice as specified in the Code of the Profession ratified in 1974 and adopted by the Press Federation in Lebanon, and which will be presented later in the chapter.

The Lebanese Media Scene

Lebanon was the first Arab country to permit private radio and television stations. Commercial stations kicked off TV broadcasting in Lebanon (Harb, 2011). Compagnie Libanaise de Télévision launched in 1959 backed by the French and was followed in 1962 by Télé Orient, backed by the US network ABC (Boulos, 1995). Lebanon's broadcasting scene is well-developed, lively and diverse, reflecting the country's pluralism and divisions. Lebanese media feature diverse opinion, aggressive question-and-answer television shows with government officials and politicians, and lively criticism of authorities and policies (Dajani, 2001). However, political affiliation, thus self-censorship, remains a problem. Authorities, owners and editors are quick to clamp down on journalists who cross both un-stated and stated boundaries on sensitive topics. There always existed an *interwoven* relationship between the media and Lebanese politicians. Politicians had a strong appetite for owning and even running media organizations. Many prominent politicians own shares in private broadcasters and publications. The map of TV ownership is as follows.

LBCI was founded by the Lebanese forces, a right-wing Christian militia, and its ownership passed thereafter to its chairman Pierre Daher and to several politicians and businessmen including Prime Minister Najib Mikati, former Deputy Prime Minster Issam Fares and its Satellite branch LBC SAT to the Saudi prince Al Walid bin Talal. Future TV was owned by late former Prime Minister Rafic Hariri. The ownership has passed to his successor, his son, Saad Hariri and the family, including his wife Nazek Hariri. Al Manar TV (part of Lebanese Media Group LMG) is owned by members and close allies of Hezbollah (the Lebanese Party of God). New TV (Al Jadid) is owned by Lebanese businessman Tahseen Khayat, seeking a political role in Lebanon and a close friend to former Prime Minister Omar Karami and former-house speaker Hussein Husseini. NBN is affiliated with House Speaker Nabih Berri; some of its shares are owned by Berri family members and relatives. Murr TV, known as MTV, was put off air in September 2002. For the first time in Lebanon history, the Lebanese publications court ordered the closure of MTV and Jabal Lubnan Radio for breaching Article 68 of the Electoral Law which bans the promotion of parliamentary candidates on a religious or ethnic basis.[1] Télé Liban, the state run TV station, was closed for three months in 2001 after suffering from massive financial debts and being plagued with cash flow problems, ranging from overstaffing to inadequate equipment. OTV, a newcomer to the media scene, is the voice of General Michel Aoun's party Free Patriotic movement (see Bontems, 2007 and Khatib, 2007).

During the civil war (1975–1990), the radio and TV market was unregulated, with more than 100 stations on the air. With the introduction of the 1994 Audio-Visual Law 382, the government restrained the media and licensed a smaller number of private radio and TV stations in 1996. The law legalized channels already being broadcast illegally and introduced new ones, handing out licenses on a confessional, political and geographic basis (Harb, 2011). Audio-Visual Law 382 set certain principles broadcasting media should consider while operating. Among those were the preservation of public order, the needs of national defence, and the requirements of public welfare. Journalists should avoid inciting religious hatred, threatening national security, and disturbing relationships with friendly countries, mainly Arab countries. However, Journalists abide consciously and sometimes un-consciously with the political agenda of their media organization (ibid.). In terms of ownership, the law compels institutions to have nominal shares and prohibits any natural or legal person from owning more than 10 percent of the company's equity (Boulos, 1995: 308). In February 1996, the government issued a complementary Decree No. 7997 based on Audio-Visual Law 382.

> It was considered by many to be a restrictive law that banned stations from broadcasting news deemed to rouse sectarian or religious tensions, as seen in the eyes of the authorities, while others deemed it necessary considering the confessional and sectarian feuds in the country. (*IIM*, issue 5, November 2002)

Two years later, in accordance with the Audio-Visual Law 382, the Cabinet decided on September 17, 1996 to legalize the most prominent of these television companies and grant them the special licence needed to broadcast news (Fontan, in Sakr 2004: 167). Four stations were legalized besides TL: the National Broadcasting Network (NBN), Future Television, Murr Television (MTV) and the Lebanese Broadcasting Corporation International (LBCI). The others were given a time limit of two months to liquidate their business. As Naomi Sakr notes, confessional thinking (based on sectarian loyalties and divisions) and the minimum number of constituencies that the government felt it needed to satisfy determined these decisions. Confessionalism in broadcasting became institutionalized:

> Thus, besides Télé Liban, Maronite Christians were supposed to content themselves with LBC, Sunni Muslims with Future TV, Christian Orthodox with Murr TV and Shia Muslims with NBN. (Sakr, 2001: 51 cited in Harb, 2011: 108)

A sixth license was eventually awarded to Al Manar TV, affiliated with Hezbollah, the Lebanese Shi'i political group dedicated to resisting Israel's occupation of south Lebanon. This license was granted to Al Manar as a "resistance channel," which meant its license would expire when the occupation ended. However, Al Manar was granted a full license to operate as a national television station in 1997 after it was able to match the requirements mentioned in Audio-Visual Law 382. According to Sakr, this was only conceded after a political struggle in which Télé Lumière, an unlicensed Christian religious station, was allowed to continue broadcasting, "supposedly to restore the delicate sectarian balance by providing a counterweight to Al Manar" (ibid.).

In 1999 the new government reconsidered the applications rejected by the previous government and consequently three more licenses were granted. The stations receiving the new licenses were ones that had opposed the former prime minister, Rafic Hariri. These were: New Television (NTV), in June, and the Independent Communication Channel International (ICNI) and United Television (UTV), in September. Both of the latter channels had not resumed operations after they stopped transmissions in 1996 (Dajani, 2001). The political and sectarian affiliation of the broadcast institutions in Lebanon mirrored that of the Lebanese press and matches Hallin and Mancini's (2004) polarized pluralist media system discussed earlier.

In his book *Disoriented Media in a Fragmented Society: The Lebanese Experience,* Dajani concluded that the 15 years of civil war in Lebanon (1975–1990) represented an abnormal time for the Lebanese press in which the content and uses of the media were subjected to severe strains (Dajani, 1992). In analyzing the content of three newspapers during "relatively quiet periods of the civil war," he noted that both news and views were mixed up in Lebanese press stories and revealed that the "letters to the editor that express opinions are scarce or non existent:"

> While the three papers under study ran feature stories most of these features were generally superficial. More interpretive reports, though scarce, followed the line that agreed with the views of the political forces in control of the area where the paper is published. A noticeable deficiency in the Lebanese press is the absence of investigative reporting. (ibid.: 128)

According to Dajani, the Lebanese press was characterized by a general tendency to oppose the national government. However, "this did not mean that it played the 'watchdog' role safeguarding public interest." Its opposition to the government, the analysis revealed, was usually a result of its support for, or bondage to, another authority that was "politically and/or militarily active on the Lebanese scene" (ibid.: 127). In addition, the fact that a Lebanese media supported a particular authority did not necessarily mean that it would continue in its support for this authority. The country went through a long period of civil war, "during which new political authorities appeared, and several others changed positions" (ibid.: 127).

This situation did not change much in post-civil war Lebanon. Newspapers still carried political allegiances. Despite the fact that newspapers readership is not as widespread in Lebanon or the Arab world as Dajani (2001) suggests, some journalists and writers are viewed as "opinion leaders," while their ideas and writings are used as starting points during several political or social debates. In Lebanon, being a journalist and a political activist at the same time are functions that complete each other and do not contradict each other. There are several examples of journalists who pursued political careers after working in journalism for several years. Journalism has turned out to be a route to becoming MPs or Cabinet Ministers (for example Jubran Twiani and Bassem Al Sabeh to name few).

Media Diversity and Polarization: A Model for Democratic Change

Hallin and Mancini (2004) argue that polarized pluralist societies have been characterized historically by sharp political conflicts. For them, the media typically are used as instruments of struggle in these conflicts and by contending parties in periods of democratic policies. Lebanon, in this case, abides by the rule. The Lebanese media scene can thus be identified as *polarized* and its dominant feature is the interwoven relationship between the media and the politicians in Lebanon.

The 2005 independence movement and the way it was covered provide proof of this interwoven relationship and the influence it has over audiences. The slogan itself and the emblem that represented it was introduced by journalist Samir Kassir of *An-Nahar* newspaper who was assassinated on June 2, 2005 and labeled as "the martyr of Independence Intifada" being one of its main activists. However, during this period, the Lebanese media avoided inciting sectarian hatred. On the contrary, national unity was what different rival parties were calling and standing for and the media followed that line. Nevertheless, this demonstrated a clear example of "instrumentalization" of media institutions in Lebanon explained in the previous section.

On February 14, 2005, Lebanese Prime Minister Rafic Hariri was assassinated in a tragic way. Hundreds of thousands of mourners took part in his funeral. Future TV (FTV) borrowed a helicopter from Dubai TV to be able to provide a bird's-eye view of the proceedings, and all Lebanese and Arab television stations broadcast the event live, including images provided by Future TV. Future TV had established an outdoor studio near the grave and planted a huge screen in Martyrs' Square in Beirut. It was broadcasting images of masses visiting the grave. Soon demonstrators from different Lebanese sectors and factions filled Martyrs' Square, chanting slogans of "truth, freedom and national unity." One of these slogans, "the truth for Lebanon," was first introduced by Future TV. Shortly, it was produced on T-shirts caps and repeated by the protestors in Martyrs' Square. People's reaction at the beginning was spontaneous. Muslims and Christians were standing by Hariri's grave holding the Qur'an and the Cross emphasizing the "National Unity," a picture captured and promoted by most Lebanese dailies and TV channels.

This triggered opposition parties to take their protest a further step. They called upon the Lebanese people to keep demonstrating in Martyrs' Square till the complete withdrawal of Syrian forces and Syrian intelligence services from the country and resignation of key intelligence and security officials in Lebanon whom the opposition held responsible for Hariri's death. They called upon Lebanese youth to hold an open protest in the square till the demands were fulfilled. The Lebanese youth representing opposition parties set up a camp in the square with TV cameras surrounding them. Encouraged by TV coverage of peaceful demonstrations that filled the square, it is said that some of the Lebanese living abroad flew back to participate in the events, or organized and managed protests in the cities in which they live.

Soon the political scene in Lebanon was divided into two, one identified as anti-Syrian and the other identified as pro-Syrian. The two were also labeled as "opposition to Syrian regime, the government and Lahoud presidency" and the other as "loyalist to the Syrian regime, the government and Lahoud presidency." The opposition formed a political forum and so did the loyalists. The opposition had their TV channels and media outlets and so had the loyalists. The opposition unified their slogans, flags and emblems for the cameras and so did the loyalists. The movement was soon labeled by media scholars as the made-for-TV *Intifada*, as if slogans were written for the cameras. Cameras were the medium demonstrators from both sides use to communicate with each other (see Khatib, 2006 and Abu Fadil, 2005).

Studies showed that Lebanese turned to their own media to make sense of the historic moment their country was experiencing. They had a choice of channels offering competing interpretations, coverage and analyses (Abu Fadil, 2005). Future TV dedicated most of its coverage locally and via satellite to opposition rallies and activities in addition to programs on Hariri's life and accomplishments. FTV became the voice of the opposition and the advocate for an international inquiry into the explosion that killed Hariri and 18 other people. LBCI also dedicated most of its air time locally and via satellite to covering anti-government/anti-Syrian rallies. Pro-government/Syria rallies and activities were given prominent coverage on NBN and Al Manar. NTV and ANB[2] were in the middle between the two parties, even though ANB seemed to be keener into covering the opposition activities.

On March 5, 2005, President Bashar al-Assad of Syria announced that Syrian troops would withdraw from Lebanon by the end of April. During his speech in the Syrian Parliament, he referred to the anti-Syrian rallies in Beirut, saying that they did not represent the majority of the Lebanese. He made a clear reference to the role of TV in these rallies by saying: "if they zoom out their cameras, you would be able to identify the small number of protesters." On March 8, loyalist forces (with Hezbollah as their driving force) organized a pro-government/pro-Syria rally in Riyad Al Solh Square, which is adjacent to Martyrs' Square in Beirut's central district. It was the loyalists' first main rally. The rally was covered by NBN and Al Manar which reported the crowds totalled up to 1.5 million, which was disputed by the opposition. Future TV had experts presenting in detail how many persons could inhabit each meter square in the city center and they concluded that the number of the participants could not have exceeded 275,000.

LBCI and Future TV had limited the number of hours dedicated to airing the loyalist show of force. Future TV and Al Manar were on opposite ends. Future reported that the Riyad Al Solh rally's numbers were inflated by Syrians who had been brought in on busses in the night before and early morning. Al Manar was insisting on denying that, addressing what it called "Future TV claims." Sayyed Hassan Nasrallah, the secretary general of Hezbollah, commented indirectly on what President Assad said and called upon all cameras to zoom out and show who has more of a crowd. Slogans in this rally were written to address protesters on the other side of the spectrum. Catchphrases carried were political messages sent through TV cameras. Slogans like "Hey you Fu Fu and Nu Nu [names used to call 'camp' people in Lebanon], we liberated the land [referring to liberating south Lebanon from Israeli occupation forces]" and "we are not Ukraine or Georgia, we're Lebanon". Accusing the opposition of being influenced by the Americans and the French, the demonstrators carried banners like "Thank You Syria" and "No to American Interference" (Abu Fadil, 2005). Two things unified the loyalists with the opposition. They also waved the Lebanese flag and they also raised the slogan "the truth" in reference to who killed Hariri. NBN and Al Manar dedicated all their air time for the demonstration and its build up.

On March 14, the opposition hit back. Protesters from all over Lebanon filled Martyrs' Square and the adjacent Riad Al Solh Square, with the crowd swelling to 500,000 people, but the opposition was talking about one million protestors. The demonstrators waved Lebanon's cedar-tree flag and thundered, "Syria out!", "Freedom, Sovereignty and Independence" and "Truth, Freedom and National Unity." The banners carried direct messages to both the loyalist protesters and to the Syrian leadership such as "This Crowd is Made in Lebanon", "Zoom in, We are All Lebanese", "Zoom Out and Count", "Do You See What Fu Fu and Nu Nu Can Do?", "The Truth Hurts, Moo (Syrian for right)?" "We Surprised You Moo" and "Can't You See?" [to ophthalmologist Bashar al Assad], "Better Keep Swimming and Not Talking" (in reference to President Lahoud, a devoted swimmer) (ibid.). Future TV and LBCI dedicated all air time to the demonstration and its build up. It was labeled as "Independence 05 Intifada (uprising)" and "Loyalty for Hariri demonstration".

LBCI commented on what was happening in the square on that day by announcing: "Spring has come early to Lebanon this year." Future TV and LBCI brought in Cranes to guarantee the "zoom out" shots and most Arab and international channels operating at the scene were using the two stations' images for free. There were no financial obligations here; it was a political battle the two channels were fighting. The events that took place in Lebanon on February 14 and after drew the attention of regional and international media outlets. However, the Lebanese media were the key player on the national level, while international and regional media—mainly Al Jazeera, Al Arabiya and CNN—were used by the Lebanese to address Arab and international communities and leaderships.

Nevertheless, it should be mentioned that the division between pro- and anti-government/Syria camps in Lebanon had its impact on both pan-Arab Satellite channels Al Jazeera and Al Arabiya. Al Jazeera dedicated more of its coverage to the pro-government/Syria camp while Al Arabiya gave more air time to cover the anti-government/Syria camp.[3] The events that followed brought the Lebanese media to prominence, but showed at the same time that the Lebanese media act as a mirror of the political scene in Lebanon and follow its narrative line. The question here: was it the media who helped in mobilizing demonstrators and political movements or was that related to people's political loyalty?

The answer is both, again reflecting the interwoven relationship. There were hundreds of people who joined the March 14 demonstration without being loyal to any of the opposition parties. They were driven by the sentiments of the messages the opposition media were transmitting day and night. And the same applies to the loyalists. Were the media institutions in Lebanon a tool used by political parties or were they generators of a public mood that politicians gripped and based their political strategies upon? The media in Lebanon generated a mood that made it easier for opposition politicians to take their political demands a step further and be able to achieve some of what they was calling for, mainly the withdrawal of Syrian troops from Lebanon. The polarized diverse media system has generated a mood of political change.

Media Diversity and Polarization: A Model for Confrontation

This mood of change that the media helped generate during and following what came to be known as the "*independence intifada*" was later on, mainly in the months and years that followed, manipulated into disseminating an environment of political and sectarian hatred that led to deadly clashes in the streets of Beirut and in north Lebanon was named as Black Tuesday, Black Thursday and Black Wednesday on May 7, 2008. The polarized pluralist media system engendered a model of media confrontation between the March 14 camp and the March 8 camp led by the two main parties, Future Movement (Sunni dominant) and Hezbollah (Shi'i dominant), which changed positions as loyalists and oppositions.

The political confrontation was fought on the screens that are affiliated mainly with the two parties, Future TV and Al Manar, and the other TV stations were divided in support of one over the other. Journalists became clear about their religious and political affiliations, and news programs were produced and set to serve directly this camp or the other. Stories started emerging on religious-based attacks against one group of people and retaliation would take place in no time. During the clashes, claims were made that a group of people in a Christian suburb was targeted with mortar fire from the Shi'i resident area. This was later found to be untrue, but reprisal left many casualties.[4] The journalists did not just wear the colors of their political parties or the movement they were affiliated with, but became almost military spokesperson, going beyond being embedded to being a mouthpiece of this political and religious group or the other.

Journalists and media institutions lost their diversity as they soon became involved in the campaigns of hatred and divisions in the post-civil war Lebanon. Lebanese media stations became tools used and abused by political parties and nothing was done to draw a fine line that would prevent them losing their professional integrity, autonomy and social responsibility. The Qatari foreign minister, whose country was involved in brokering the Doha agreement that put an end to street clashes in Beirut, even said that the problem lay with the large number of TV stations that could not be controlled. One of the Doha agreement clauses was related directly to stopping media campaigns and preventing the language of hatred (Al Jazeera May 21, 2008).

The problem does not lie with diversity; diversity that is ruled by chaos becomes a force of destruction. Diversity can only be protected by journalists themselves. There is an ongoing discussion about what went wrong. The ministry of information has suggested a code of practice for media institutions which calls for the protection of civil peace in Lebanon, but some see this as constraining freedom and others see this as a necessity. The code never saw light. Jaafar Al Attar, a journalist for the Lebanese daily *Assafir*, believes that the code of practice didn't see light because it didn't achieve consensus.[5] Hassan Illaik, a journalist for the Lebanese daily *Al Akhbar*, saw in the code a constraint to his freedom of expression.[6] Both journalists started working in journalism after 2005 and have been involved in covering events that followed the assassination of former PM Hariri. They both believe that fellow TV journalists have been showing their real political affiliations during their coverage. Attar witnessed a TV reporter telling people to praise the political group his TV station is affiliated with after Bourj Abi Haidar clashes that took place in 2010, while Illaik admits that journalists who think about ethics are few.

It is important to point out that publishing ratifications is an action mostly adopted by the press, while TV stations rarely take that route. Press in Lebanon is governed under the 1962 Press Law that was amended in 1977 by a decree-law[7] known as Number 104. Journalists were threatened, in the 1962 law and its amendment, with prison if they misreported anything that had to do with "public safety" and "national security".[8] In 1994 the law was amended for a second time, withdrawing the prison penalty and multiplying the fines incorporated in Decree-Law 104 by twenty.[9] Lebanon is also one of the few Arab countries to have ratified a code of ethics for its journalists to abide by. The Press Federation in Lebanon (which combines both the publishers and the journalists' syndicates) adopted the code in 1974. It was drafted with print journalists in mind, but could be applied to both print and broadcast journalists. However, none of the two journalists interviewed here is familiar with the code or has heard of it. The following section will demonstrate that Attar and Illaik are not the only two journalists in Lebanon who do not know of the existence of such document.

Lebanese Journalism Ethical Boundaries

According to the data derived from a study conducted by this author,[10] which included a survey of 100 Lebanese journalists, a debate with five mid-career journalists and several phenomenological and in-depth interviews, it seemed clear that reporting in Lebanon lacks the basis of a firm ethical foundation and that formal ethical guidance for most Lebanese journalists barely exists.

Most of the journalists interviewed for that study confirmed they did not have any ethical guidance, and those who took part in the debate also pointed to the same problem. The results also showed that journalists lacked sensitivity to the quantity and quality of harm their acts might cause to the people on whom they were reporting—levels of harm described in sometimes heart-rending terms. None of the journalists seemed to be familiar with the ethical code (or what is known as "the honor of the profession") ratified by the Lebanese Press Federation in 1974 and their decisions were based mostly on what they called "personal conscience." Others, as the survey results showed, variously cited editors, families, colleagues, or religious leaders as points of reference when faced with an ethical dilemma. As mentioned above, a firm foundation for shared ethical values on the particularistic moral problems raised by journalistic activity was missing.

Most of the journalists did not believe that participating in political or commercial activities would affect their integrity, and—particularly importantly in the context of Lebanese journalism—that this might lead them to play a partisan role, representing one or other party or interest group in their papers or media organizations. While it may be argued that total impartiality is impossible to attain—and even that in some circumstances it is undesirable—there are grave dangers in underestimating how far an abandonment of this principle can rebound on other ethical issues. Commitments to accuracy and fairness, for example, may be considerably subverted by demands to downplay or ignore salient information in an effort to promote a particular cause. Just as importantly, perhaps, partisanship can undermine the public's trust in journalism as a "truthful" account of events in general. As Day (2000: 21) puts it:

> [Journalists] stand at the crossroads between... citizens and their political, economic, and cultural institutions. Accurate and reliable information is the lifeblood of the democratic process, whether it be political intelligence offered up by journalists or the economic messages of advertisers.

Once journalists lose sight of this responsibility, there is a very real risk that they will do their readers a serious disservice.

> Maintaining a sense of integrity and following our conscience may finally be the best alternative in many situations. However, careerism is a serious professional problem and often tempts us to act out of our self-interest while we claim to be following our conscience (Christians et al., 1991: 21).

Most of the journalists made informal comments about ethics, the consensus seeming to be that ethical decisions depended mostly upon matters of personal "principle" or "conscience." On the face of it, they were articulating—albeit loosely—a deontological (duty based) line of moral reasoning in which emphasis is placed on the principles underlying an action and not on "the consequences that might result" (Day, 2000: 59). A useful summary of those journalists' general position is that "it is with the individual journalist that lies the responsibility—or, it might be said, the agony—of deciding what is right or wrong, ethical or unethical" (Fink, 1988: 1). Years later the same line is presented by the two journalists interviewed for this chapter and by several informal chats with Lebanese journalists during the time of the events mentioned above.

Lebanese Code of Ethics

The notion of public safety has been endorsed in the Lebanese press ethical code ratified by the General Assembly of the Press Syndicate during an extraordinary session held on February 4, 1974, a year before the civil war started. The code opens with an ideological, statement:

> The Lebanese press has always been proud of its honourable history, which is full of struggle and martyrdom for the Nation and the Citizen; a history that has intermixed with liberal thought the national and popular struggle.
>
> Therefore, the Lebanese press has the pleasure to declare in the code of ethics of the profession all principles of behaviour inspired by the pioneers who established its disciplines, laws and traditions. (*Al Sahafah Al Loubnaneih* issue 7, 8.84)

In pointing out that the principles which the codes embodies are the same as those to which the press has adhered since its establishment, we are assured that these principles are stronger than the laws. It asserts that the Lebanese press affirmed these principles spontaneously to put an end to the controversy concerning the rules for its practice (ibid.). The code describes a newspaper as an institution, which offers a public service (cultural, social, national, humane) despite its commercial and industrial aspects. It adds that "a newspaper is committed to its own freedom while defending public freedom." The code also makes it clear that press responsibility is not restricted to abiding by the law only, but also to "professional conscience" and the reader, and that the press is bound to principles of truth, loyalty, accuracy and discretion. It states:

- The press is a platform for the readers who have there the chance to express their opinions and the right to reply and rectify.

- The press has to mobilize public opinion to defend the country and justice and to confront injustice and oppressive powers.
- The press must avoid fanaticism, religious contempt, defamation and vilification.
- The press must avoid invented and distorted news, which is not fit for publication.
- Accusation without proof is harmful to the press.
- The press must avoid uncertain news. However, if published, the newspaper must indicate their uncertainty.
- The press must avoid the publication of any materials that could encourage crime and vice (ibid.).

All of this is left dependant on the "professional conscience," which has been lacking ethical consideration mainly by inciting religious and sectarian hatred and rushing into judgment and causing harm to innocent people.

Conclusion

There is an urgent need in Lebanon for both public debate and guidance about media ethics. That urgent need still stands now and it is even more urgent. Internal conflict in Lebanon is mediated and narrated through the prism of political affiliation and that is difficult to change without introducing new regulations that organize private ownership and give full support to Télé Liban as a public service institution that should speak for all the Lebanese citizens whatever their religious or political affiliation. In a country where the media is owned and controlled by politicians and political parties and affiliated with religious sects, it is up to the journalists themselves to protect their professional standards and to act in a socially responsible manner. Abiding by certain ethical boundaries might be the answer to that.

Notes

1. There were serious claims that the Syrian regime had put pressure on Emile Lahoud, the Lebanese president at the time, to close the two stations down. It is believed that the Syrian regime had expressed its deep concerns to the way that MTV was speaking against the Syrian military presence in Lebanon.

2. A relatively new channel at the time that broadcasts only via satellite and that is not registered as a Lebanese station.

3. Both channels were acting according to the political positions of their sponsors, the Qatari and Saudi governments (Harb, 2011). In January 2011, one of Al Jazeera's outside broadcast van (SNJ) was burned down by anti-Syrian/pro-Hariri protestors in Tripoli. Al Jazeera was accused by the protestors of supporting the March 8 camp against March 14 camp (Robertson and Husseini, CNN, January 26, 2011).

4. See LBCI news 8pm January 27, 2008.

5. Interview with author (2010).

6. Interview with author (2010).

7. In the late 1970s and because of the civil war, the government was given exceptional authority by the Parliament to issue laws having the name "Decree-Laws" to differentiate between them and the laws issued by the Parliament.

8. This is based on a draft published in the Lebanese *Official Gazette* (19. 5. 94). According to the Lebanese constitution, all the laws should be published in the *Official Gazette*. It is where all laws are documented.

9. The current press law 330 spans 11 chapters and includes themes such as Malicious or false news; prohibited information; blackmail; defamation and libel; injurious acts against heads of states; seditious libel and compromise of state security; censorship; and control of publications' revenues (Article 2, 1994: 7). Perpetrators of false news that may compromise "public safety" are liable to a fine. A publication suspension of 15 days may also be ordered and in cases where the offence is repeated, the period of suspension can be for three months. It should be noted that "public safety" as mentioned several times in the law, includes any statements which bring into contempt any of the religions acknowledged in the country or any seditious libel "that may excite any religious or racial conflicts or disturb public safety or compromise the security, sovereignty, unity or borders of the State or its foreign affairs" (Article 25, 1994: 7).

10. Harb Zahera (2000), *Moral Reasoning in the Lebanese Press*, Cardiff School of Journalism.

References

Books and journal articles

Abu Fadil, Magda (2005). "Live From Martyrs' Square: Lebanon's 'Reality TV' Turns Coverage of Peaceful Protests into a Media Battle", *TBS, 14*, Spring 2005. URL: http://www.tbsjournal.com/Archives/Spring05/abufadil.html. Accessed April 10, 2010.

Boulos, J. Claude (1995). *Television History and Stories*, FMA, Lebanon.

Christians, Clifford, Kim Rotzoll, and Mark Fackler (1991), *Media Ethics: Cases and Moral Reasoning* (New York and London: Longman).

Dajani, Nabil (1992). *Disoriented Media in a Fragmented Society: The Lebanese Experience* (Beirut: American University).

———(2001). "The Changing Scene of Lebanese Television," *TBS Electronic Journal*, No. 7 (Fall/Winter). URL: www.tbsjournal.com/Archives/Fall01/dajani.html. Accessed January 9, 2005.

Day, Louis (2000). *Ethics in Media Communications: Cases and Controversies* (UK: Wadsworth).

Fink, Conrad (1988). *Media Ethics in the Newsroom and Beyond* (New York: McGraw-Hill).

Firmo-Fontan, Victoria (2004). "Power, NGOs and Lebanese Television" in N. Sakr, *Women and Media in the Middle East* (London: I.B.Tauris), pp. 162–79.

Hallin, D. and P. Mancini (2004). *Comparing Media Systems: Three Models of Media and Politics* (New York: Cambridge University Press).

Harb, Zahera (2011). "Arab Revolutions and the Social Media Effect." *Media and Culture Journal*, 14 (2) (May 2011).

Khatib, Lina (2007). "Television and Public Action in the Beirut Spring," in Naomi Sakr (ed.), *Arab Media and Political Renewal: Community, Legitimacy and Public Life* (London: I.B.Tauris), pp. 28–43.

Rugh, William (2004). *Arab Mass Media* (London: Praeger).

Sakr, Naomi (2001). *Satellite Realms: Transnational Television, Globalization and the Middle East* (London: I.B.Tauris).

Codes and Articles

Al Jazeera, "Doha Agreement Main Points," May 21, 2008. URL: http://www.aljazeera.net/news/archive/archive?ArchiveId=1091172. Accessed October 10, 2010.

Al Sahafa Al Loubnania, (1984). "Present Lebanese Newspapers," 7 (August): 16.

———(1984). "The Honour of the Profession," 7 (August): 5.

An-Nahar, (2008). "Media Hatred Incitement is Affecting All." June 7, 2008.

Assafir, (2006). "Incidents from Bshamoun to Aramoun Proceeded by Media Campaigns," June 6, 2006.

BBC News. "Lebanon Country Profile." June 14, 2011. URL: http://news.bbc.co.uk/1/hi/world/middle_east/country_profiles/791071.stm#media. Accessed June 14, 2011.

Bontems, Natalie (2007). "People Power?" *Communicate.ae*, June 1, 2007. URL: http://www.communicate.ae/node/122. Accessed October 11, 2010.

IIM [Information International Monthly] (2002). "Grey Areas in the Audio-Visual Law," Issue 5 (November). URL: http://information-international.com/iimonthly/issue5/editorial.html. Accessed January 6, 2005).

Official Gazette, (1994). "Press Law No. 330," May 19, 1994, issue 7.

Robertson, Nic and Nada Husseini (2011). "In Lebanon Protests Erupts as Prime Minister is named," *CNN World,* January 26, 2011. URL: http://www.cnn.com/2011/WORLD/meast/01/25/lebanon.protests/index.html. Accessed January 26, 2011.

Interviews with the author

Attar, Naji, journalist, *Assafir Daily,* Lena's Café Hamra, September 12, 2010.

Illaik, Hassan, journalist, *Al Akhbar Daily,* Lena's Café Hamra, September 13, 2010.

4

NEGOTIATING REPRESENTATION, RE-MAKING WAR: TRANSNATIONALISM, COUNTER-HEGEMONY AND CONTEMPORARY ART FROM POST-TAIF BEIRUT[1]

HANAN TOUKAN

There is this famous text of Kant, Critique of Judgment, saying that aesthetic judgment asks us only to be sensible of form. When standing in front of a palace, it does not matter that it was built out of the sweat of the poor people; we have to ignore that, says Kant. I think Kant was right. At the same time I came upon a text written by a joiner, a floor-layer, and he explains precisely what he sees as he is laying a floor in a rich house. He decides to acquire an aesthetic perception of the room, of the garden, of the whole perspective. So he decides to do as if he had a disinterested gaze and could get an aesthetic judgment, notwithstanding the fact that he is poorly paid, that he works for a boss, and that he works for the rich. For me this was important. It reminded me of my view of aesthetics—aesthetics not being a sociology of art but as being a form of experience. That is, an experience of disconnection. This has been conceptionalized by Kant and Schiller in terms of disconnection: there is something that escapes the normal conditions of sensory experience. That is what was at stake in emancipation: getting out of the ordinary ways of sensory experience. This thought has been important for my idea of politics, not being about the relations of power but being about the framing of the sensory world itself.

Jacques Rancière[2]

This chapter discusses the local and international perceptions of "representations" circulating in and about post-war contemporary art from Beirut. It evaluates what has become known internationally as "post-war contemporary art from Beirut" to demonstrate that what is portrayed on the global arts circuit as counter-hegemonic artistic production consumed with deconstructing representations of the Lebanese civil war cannot be evaluated without a comprehensive reference to the politics of transnationality, locality and temporality. Specifically it interrogates the dynamics by which a group of artists and artist-supporting organizations that set out in the 1990s to present the "un-representability" of the civil war, arguably and quite ironically, became representatives of yet another Middle Eastern conflict when propelled onto the "global" art arena. Hence, an examination of the complex relationship between neo-liberalism, funding sources and the politics of cultural practices is central to the main arguments made here. The issues that the chapter raises are reflected in a succession of conversations relayed among artists, art critics, curators and academics both internationally and locally. The anxieties some actors express concern some of the most urgent questions that impact the way in which "representations" are read, processed and articulated. Some of these include the practice, production, exhibition, reception and circulation of contemporary art from Lebanon. Accordingly, the chapter makes Foucaultian claims that even seemingly "progressive" discourses of knowledge about art, resistance and counter-representation in Middle Eastern cultural production can sometimes be embodiments of power relations in society and in international relations.

The chapter begins with an analysis of the rise of contemporary artistic practices in Beirut. In the 1990s, contemporary Lebanese artists and their supporting networks and organizations working in Beirut reacted to a very specific post-civil-war scenario which propelled them to subvert understandings of how the history of the Lebanese civil war might be read and narrated; interrogate and challenge the traditional role of cultural institutions and the commercial gallery system in the circulation of civil war related art; and probe prevalent and accepted understandings of hegemony and ideology in post-war identity formation. They did so through an introspective turn which entailed a move away from what they saw as their predecessors' tendency to 'write back to the empire'. More specifically, the particular body of work and the processes that gave rise to them and which are the focus of the chapter may be read as a re-visualization of the post-colonial entity of its own self, rather than a statement forged in response to the former "empire", so to speak. The chapter then moves on to analyze the development of the Lebanese contemporary art scene within the realities of the neo-liberal paradigmatic shifts Lebanon was undergoing at the time. It draws on Sarah Rogers's (2008) meticulous portraiture of the post-war Beiruti contemporary art scene and its move into the global art circuit[3] to argue that that by the early 2000s, the scene was growing in par with international funding organizations operating within the rubrics of Washington's "civil society and democratization" programmatic framework in the region. This reality, which in part enabled the internationalization of that same scene—particularly from 2002 onwards—raises urgent questions regarding the politics and power of the image.

These questions largely challenge political and visual theorist Jacques Rancière's (2004) articulations of politics as revolving around what is seen and what can be said about it, around who has the ability to see and the talent to speak, and around ways of doing and making as a shared sense of the "common" (Rancière, 2004).[4] Within this framework, he argues, the image and the potential it holds for engaging spectators and artwork in a dialectical exchange of reconceptualizing the world as it has been ascribed to them is tantamount to explicating art's role as politically counter-hegemonic. On the one hand, this formulation offers the possibility to deconstruct the challenging paradoxes associated with the traditional understanding of the artistic avant-garde's role as utopian and resistant to capitalist hegemony through the consistent negation it could perform. On the other, however, it may render the viewer of the image incapable of recognizing or deeming relevant the very same violent relations of power between geo-politics and capital that enable the circulation of certain images and not others in transnational spaces of production. It is in thinking about the dialectical tensions flowing between these two scenarios that this chapter is framed.

Deconstructing War: The Politics of Memory, Historiography and Art

> You're still thinking with the logic of the enemy. The enemy
> thinks that our work is provocative. They accuse us of
> being influenced by the West. Of being cerebral. Formalist.
> There's no story here...no actors.... We have suffered and
> are still suffering from the homogenization of the Arab and
> Islamic identity. But in reality people are not all proud of
> this identity. This is our reality; and what I did was attempt
> to tell the truth. We don't remember that we're Arabs until
> the Americans and the Israelis bomb Beirut, the West Bank,
> or Iraq...in times of crises....It's only when things like
> this happen that this instinct in us is stirred. Our loyalty is
> instinctive; therefore it's not positive. In this context, the
> Arab identity can be considered an issue or matter, which in
> itself imposes upon us the inevitability of fate and destiny.[5]

The end of the Cold War coincided with the end of Lebanon's
15-year-old civil war and the signing of the Ta'if Accord in 1989, which
opened up a world of possibilities seemingly unfathomable in the
preceding period. Artists who lived this period often cite a number of
reasons for this, including the reopening of the eastern and western
parts of Beirut to each another, investments in audiovisual media,
with which the government of late Prime Minister Rafic Hariri was
most consumed, and exposure to ideas brought with returnees
from abroad, including various artists. These factors all provided
much of the impetus for the changes in the contemporary cultural
production scene. Conscious of their city's legendary dynamism
and their place in it, young Beiruti cultural actors did not set out to
revive what they perceived of as the old terms of ideologically-driven
political and cultural references in any way, as they were under no
illusions as to what they understood the impact on their society to
have been. Both realistic and cynical about Beirut's regional status
as cultural center, and continued efforts to market it as a tourist and
business destination within the post-war reconstruction process,
these young men and women chose to express their manifold
perspectives openly. Such sentiments are well articulated in artists
and filmmakers Joana Hadjithomas and Khalil Joreige's *Wonder
Beirut* project (1996–ongoing) where they purposely corrupt classic

images of the city. The project includes *Postcards of War* and *Novel of a Pyromaniac Photographer* both of which are consumed with the power of the image of Beirut as the Champs-Élysées of the East.[6] Hadjithomas and Joreige's works, however, highlight the absurdity of the lingering image of Beirut maintained by a prevalent attitude which regarded the 15-year-old civil war as a mere "disruption"—a stand-alone event with no repercussions for the essentialized image that has been created. In this context, it is relevant to ask the question: "If it was all so rosy in Beirut before the war, then how the hell do we explain the war?" a question posed by many of those I interviewed for the research project on which this chapter is based. The notion of Beirut's glorious past as marketed in the spiffy logo by the Hariri firm Solidere: "Beirut: Ancient City of the Future" became the inspiration for much of the critical artistic work I studied.

At least initially, young artists expressed in extra-institutional settings, as well as outside the regulations, guidance, and even sometimes the finance normally provided by conventional cultural institutions to support the arts. What was unique to this generation of cultural actors were the frames of reference they employed. Actors within Beirut's field of cultural production set out to work on addressing what they perceived as Lebanon's post-war ills in much the same way that many young, secular members of civil society did, attempting to make sense of the new boundaries drawn up by the Ta'if Agreement and reinforced by Hariri's neo-liberal economic and reconstruction policies (Makdisi, 1997).[7]

Akram Zaatari, artist and co-founder of the Arab Image Foundation, said artistic work was produced out of a sense of urgency, and not in response to an art market (see Wright, 2002).[8] For young artists at the time, this included coming to grips with a public space largely defined by an enterprise-driven restructuring process embedded in a campaign of rent seeking, patronage, and nepotism (Becherer, 2005).[9] Yet, in early 1990s Lebanon, there was virtually no public infrastructure for the arts, no contemporary art museums, and no official institutions of culture that might have been prepared to sponsor and advance contemporary art practices.[10] Artists, filmmakers, architects and writers thus understood an ill-defined and ill-structured world of contemporary art as a strategic entry point for intervening in an established, official war narrative and the popular discourses surrounding it, by confronting it on two levels. First, they did so by addressing common understandings of "shared" public space in a traditionally divided city, and second, by deconstructing conventional forms of historiography of the war by delving into the notion of the archive.[11] Consequently, a hybridization of installations, urban interventions, video, photography, image-text collages, performances and encounters fused with historical and philosophical speculation, research and theory became the main media through which much of this contemplation and, to some extent, disruptive thinking was relayed.

Concurrently, cultural actors grappled with the apparent demise of Arab and other nationalisms, the increasing marginalization of leftist political movements and the ascendancy of Islamism in the region. At the domestic level, Lebanon was the only sovereign Arab country on whose soil the war with Israel was still being fought, but like other countries in the region, it suffered from rising economic inequalities in an increasingly globalized market. Understandably, notions of war, its memory and what was often termed as associated 'trauma', and how to look at and archive it featured quite prominently in most of the works. While approaches to archival as well as public space could be read as "political" statements which combined performance, documentation and critical thinking, the aim of the art production in this period was to make sense of the subjectivities of various histories of the war within the field of contemporary art as opposed to representing any sort of objective history through the medium of artistic practices. This understanding constitutes the basis of much of the new generation's take on the role of art in the post-war era as opposed to how some members of the older generation took it to mean.

Bilal Khbeiz, poet, essayist and journalist, states that there existed prior to the war a *total* subservience of the arts to the politics of the Arab liberation movements: "Where a poem may resemble a tear, a painting may amount to a scream, and a novel may exceed expectations, the arts were always successful in communing with their audience. In that context, the artist was like Rilke, the person most capable of expressing general and common emotions" (Wright, 2002: 68). Khbeiz here sees the pre-war generation in a certain light, emphasizing its link to "out-and-out" ideology particularly because, as he says, the arts today have managed to "escape the edict of politics." While his words were relayed in 2006, they also apply to the 1990s, and are central to understanding how Beirut's role as a major cultural hub in the Arab world might be perceived by its post-war generation of cultural actors. What is of significance in this approach are the subjectivities of the post-war actors—in other words, how they came to read their place in history as antagonistic and distanced from what preceded them.

Explicitly, artists saw themselves as making art *politically* rather than making political art. Political art in this purview is that which is associated—in the context of the region—with what is understood to be art funded by political parties and bureaucratic state structures as part of the nation-building process and subsequent identity formation in the post-colonial years and then as a form of resistance after the colossal losses of the 1967 war with Israel. Very much like social realism, such art is perceived as "socially grounded" working in politically conscience styles. Of course, this logic is a reference to Walter Benjamin's "politicization of aesthetics" where visual form is seen to define the models of speech and action and vice-versa. Social experiences in this sense become the direct sum total of affective perceptions. In line with Derridian deconstruction, post-1990s art, in contrast, is represented as having responded to what preceded it by deriving its new style from the more complex subjective experience and embodying it in contemporary forms. Accordingly, the former art form became contaminated by the clichés of popular political art to the extent that today's generation of Arab artists express clear discomforts with having their work labeled "political art" or the cruder "*l'art militant*" as the artists I interviewed in Beirut often termed it.

Reiterating Khbeiz's position, Lina Saneh, one of Lebanon's best-known contemporary post-war artists, explains how the pre-war cultural scene, which continued to dominate the early post-war years, was articulated by an older mindset and ideology that refused to acknowledge the changing of the guard, both literally and also in terms of the role of art in society which she and her contemporaries "were trying to break out of."[12] Saneh elaborated that the change in mind set influenced how each generation reacted to the war, partly referring to the "*auto-critique*" that was carried out differently across generations. For her, the older generation focused on descriptive analyses of the effects of the war, but "we were more introspective."[13] This introspection is aptly demonstrated in the excerpt from her play with Rabih Mroue with which this section opens, about the positioning of theater, sexuality and censorship. This piece "Biokhraphia" touches on crucial issues regarding an artist's position in the era of globalization by confronting the role of certain political taboos rooted in Lebanese society and attacking norms and conventions and teases out the seemingly hypocritical in Lebanese and Arab society at large.[14]

As Ibrahim Abu-Rabi' (2004: 186) has argued, contemporary Arab thinkers are grappling with questions of modernity, post-modernity and globalism with a twofold purpose:[15] They seek to reflect upon the challenges the phenomenon of globalization has posed to the Arab world and to assess the overall progress of the Arab world over the past century or so (ibid.). Hence, Mroue and Saneh's piece begs a deconstruction of Arab society's overall relationship to modernity. Yet what seems to be left out of such new reformulations is a direct questioning of what exactly has taken the place of the old and, specifically, how the world of art is located within it.

Perhaps most symbolic of Beirut's contemporary artists' severing of their identity from that of their predecessors is the way in which painting as a medium became somewhat suspect. In one exhibition catalogue, contemporary artist Tony Chakar relays the story of his father's murder on Beirut's Green Line in 1975 as he went out to buy his young son some underwear.[16] Deliberating on the killing, Chakar commissioned a portrait of his father from one of Hezbollah's official painters, who transposed his father into an improbable Christian martyr by adding cedars, an image normally associated with Christian aspects of the Lebanese republic's identity and rarely seen in the south of Lebanon, from which many Shi'i martyrs hail. The unlikelihood of this depiction of the artist's father emanates a certain distrust of painting associated with its historical use, especially during the civil war.

It was through the early efforts of independent non-profit cultural and arts organizations and initiatives—Ashkal Alwan, the Ayloul Festival, the Arab Image Foundation and Zico House—as well as a loose network of artists, architects, writers, filmmakers and self-styled curators and cultural managers that channels for the production and presentation of new works became possible.[17] It was within these initiatives that young Lebanese cultural actors found and provided a platform to push what is generally described in international art writing as critical and cutting-edge production in the arts, addressing issues sidelined by the political and economic forces playing the field (Wilson Goldie, 2007).[18] Hence, as a temporal and spatial concept, the contemporary art scene in Beirut (as in much of the Arab world) has since the early 1990s operated largely outside the system of commercial galleries and those public institutions supporting the arts. Instead, in the 1990s, the focus was site-specific and ephemeral works in public spaces rather than in the more traditional venues of galleries and museums.[19]

On the political front, and in line with the bulk of recent literature that analyzes the dismembered Arab Left's alliance along with the "liberal" project of pluralism, human rights and civil society, on the one hand, or active Islamic movements, on the other, secular cultural actors comprised largely of ex-leftists and newly avowed neo-liberals by and large found themselves functioning in what Samah Idriss, writer and editor-in-chief of the cultural magazine *al-Adab,* terms the "Hariri industry" (Idriss, 2007: 2).[20] Capitalizing on its tradition as a service economy, its economic and cultural openness, entrepreneurial spirit and relatively well-educated, cosmopolitan work force, Lebanon's post-war generation (sometimes dubbed the "Hariri generation") was thrown into a pool of jobs within civil society and NGO projects, media, advertising, graphic design and public relations, as well as a host of other posts tied to transnational markets and networks.[21] Future TV, Hariri's television station founded in 1993, was particularly active in recruiting young people trained in film, theater, and graphic design, providing them with the technical capacities to develop skills which many used in their art work. What is described here in some sense laid the groundwork for civil society's increasing dependence on international organizational funding for some of its work.[22]

While the rest of the region experienced a neo-liberal turn in the post-Oslo and post-Cold War era, Lebanon was busy rebuilding what it had destroyed of its pre-war economic history of *laissez-faire.* Its increasing dependence on foreign funds, which had started during the civil war and solidified with Washington's drive for democratization in the Middle East, along with its concomitant emphasis on liberal understandings of citizenship and civil society, accentuated its already existing neo-liberal order. This crescendo of neo-liberal values prompted many to question the depoliticizing effects of the "NGO-ization" of society and the professionalization of activism as a clear manifestation of a new take on institutionalism as traditionally understood in the new global order.[23]

In 1995, the then-young contemporary arts organization Ashkal Alwan organized a group exhibition that was held in the Sanayá Garden in Beirut, during which artist Ziad Abillamá staged a disruption within what was already perceived as a disruption of young contemporary artists probing the notion of "public" space in post-war Beirut. Abillamá provoked other artists by handing out a questionnaire asking each if they would allow him to sequester 30 centimeters of each of their allocated spaces and proposed that in any space granted to him by his contemporaries he would exhibit what he wanted as long as he complied with the agreement he made with the respective artists. His request was unanimously refused. But, in many ways, his request became his contribution to the exhibition. Abillamá explained:

> The piece was saying: 'What do we do when as artists we are invited to behave as liberal democratic [beings]?' You have your own space, each has their own little house, we can all live together; does this not sound like the idea of a Lebanon of all the different mosaics and cohabitation—the cohabitation that failed us during the war? I was asking: 'What is the connection with that model not only as a failure but as an idea that was refused by different actors of the Lebanese civil war?'[24].

Abillamá's discomfort at the time stemmed from what he saw as a formal change to the way contemporary art was lived and experienced, yet without the difficult feat of actually addressing it conceptually. By interrogating the notion of territoriality, he provoked crucial questions. Art came to be displayed in public spaces—something young contemporary artists saw as a new phenomenon associated largely with their efforts in post-civil war Beirut—but the question is what conceptual reworkings were simultaneously occurring in what Jacques Rancière refers to as the "distribution of the sensible"

(Rancière, 2004). Perhaps in a premonition of what was to come, Abillamá's effort seemed to suggest that if, as per Rancière's logic, the political's role in the aesthetic lies in disrupting the space designated and naturalized by the "police," then meanings of an art show allotting artists space in a city divided and split into military checkpoints for so long had to be unpacked. Indeed, when looking at developments after the early 2000s, the need to question what makes contemporary cultural production and art practices necessarily counter-hegemonic becomes more pressing.

From War to the World

As the global mushrooming of art events took place amidst a media revolution and the consequent decentralization from Western art capitals in arts production in the post-Cold War era, artists of developing nations, of so-called different "ethnicities" and "cultures" long marginalized in the Western mainstream art world, were for the first time acknowledged by Western critics and able to enjoy commercial success through multicultural exhibitions and group shows.[25] The latter became directly relevant to Lebanon's post-war contemporary art scene, especially towards the end of the 1990s.

Lebanese Artist, scholar and critic Walid Sadek cites the first edition of the *Ayloul Festival* in 1997 as the turning point in the post-war contemporary art scene:

> In 1997 when Pascale [Feghaly] took the initiative and found the necessary funds from the first edition, it [the Beirut post-war contemporary art scene] was at a crossroads. I think for many of the artists who had been working since 1992 and even before—of course I'm speaking retrospectively here—it was a time when many had to almost graduate from being local amateurs but producing interesting work precisely because they are local and because they are "amateurs," in the sense that they really were not as yet contemplating the possibility of becoming artists who have mobility in the international arts circuit. Retrospectively, I think 1997 was a moment when the internationalization of Lebanese art was quickly felt not as an invitation, but rather as a havoc, almost like an interpellation—like you have to in a sense do that and I think that that impacted the work of many.

Some really took on the challenge and began to organize and present their work in ways which allow it to travel, others were reluctant to do so and preferred to remain to a certain extent more bound by the context, even bound by the language and continued to work mostly in Arabic rather than translate their work.[26]

The *modus operandi* of this graduation from the local to the international is reflective of a formulaic misperception that from early on framed, shaped and processed the local expression found in contemporary Lebanese artistic production. These early misperceptions became endemic, especially within the circuits of international observers. Relevant here is Sadek's interpretation that a lot of these artists were already working in a language that Western art historians understood:

Another remarkable thing about post-Ta'if Lebanese art is that most artists were very conversant with contemporary Western art. So the form and not necessarily the content was often the forum for a Western audience. I know a few instances where the familiarity of the form allowed a kind of interpretation [that] is completely irrelevant to the work and the context in which it was made.[27]

Similarly, in 2002, Sonja Mejcher, assisted the House of World Cultures in Berlin with the preparations of their project *DisORIENTation* by researching the art scenes in both Damascus and Beirut.[28] Reinforcing Sadek's interpretations, Mejcher relayed how representatives of the House of World Cultures made it clear that despite being impressed with the rich body of art work that existed in Damascus, and which remained mostly hidden in small ateliers, these works were nonetheless not the sort that could be showcased in Berlin, due to the dominance of what (at the time) was seen as the more "traditional" art forms, such as painting.[29] To Mejcher, this demonstrated the degree to which the show was already loaded with pre-conceived ideas about how to frame contemporary art practices from the region. Confirming Mejcher's observation, Beirut-based gallery owner Saleh Barakat asks: "Isn't it telling that there is not a single curator or funder who has come from abroad who is interested in painting?"[30] Such observations shed light on the way in which particular formal prejudices may have colored Western curators and critics' understandings of the multi-faceted context in which production was taking place. They might also help in explaining how and why the counter-hegemonic was framed and focused on, even after the early 2000s, when it continued to be the trope defining the post-war contemporary artists' works despite the fact that artists began to "receive mainstream recognition on both the local and international scene" (Rogers, 2008: 44).[31]

Most of the contemporary art practices that emerged out of Lebanon in the period under study were consumed with the civil war and post-war reconstruction, national identity dilemmas and the violence of regional politics. The documentation and archiving of the war, its memory and its associated trauma were always subsumed within these practices. Combined with the new media that was used in breaking with the past, the contemporary art scene offered an exciting new terrain for curators interested in the region. Symbolically speaking, it is almost as if, through Lebanon, the Western art world would have a slice of the Arab world in order to feed the former's new emphasis on multiculturalism. The content and the form of what was coming out of Beirut was something foreign curators could understand and respond to. The works emerging explained a lot about the history of the region in an aesthetic language that interested foreign parties could understand. The political content, therefore, continued to signify a counter-hegemonic location even when it was incorporated into the global arts circuit on terms that, one might argue, conflicted with such a standing.[32]

The 1990s was a decade during which much of the post-war contemporary scene began to take shape. Sadek gives credence to the ability of what was being produced then to intersect with politics and consumerism so that one did not need to defend one's work solely through an art discourse. According to him, however, the construction of a form of institutionalism through funding and infrastructural development changed the context for artists in Lebanon. "It's not because I make a painting and place it in a gallery that it (becomes) relevant. It's not the gallery that makes it relevant. Neither is it the institution that makes it relevant. You have to find an argument without appealing to the authority of the art institution."[33] Herein lies the counter-hegemonic, an argument this chapter puts forth, because in reality, as some argue, the "art institution" is laden with paradoxes and, depending on the context, the political could become gestural, lending itself to manipulation.[34] Indeed, as Brian Holmes demonstrates, the political in art wears a dubious mask when exhibited in mainstream channels, as the picture of excluded people's politics is worth a lot to the included. Holmes's point is that as long as such works remain within the bounds of conventional art-world logics of display and critiques, then works will always contain self-evident contradictions that weaken their potential power.

Internationalization and its Discontents

Toward the end of the 1990s, and especially since 2002, several well-known Lebanese artists participated in international biennials, gallery shows and festivals for film, theater, video and performance art.[35] Many continue to have their works featured in various art journals that had dedicated special issues to Beirut. Much of the work exhibited abroad was displayed under the rubric of group shows (sometimes among a larger group of Arab artists) aimed at exposing Western audiences to what came to be understood as contemporary post-war art from Beirut. Titles such as *Tamás: Contemporary Arab Representations* (2002), *DisORIENTation* (2003), *Out of Beirut* (2006), *Art Now in Lebanon* (2008), *Les Inquiets: 5 artistes sous la pression de la guerre* (2008) contain some examples of terminology that immediately places the artists in pre-conceived frameworks of identity and locality and highlights the ongoing difficulty of penetrating the white cube (walls) of established venues in Western art capitals outside of such structures.[36] Other examples include *Images of the Middle East* (Copenhagen, 2006), *Arabise Me, V and A* (London, 2006), *In Focus* (London, 2007) and *Unveiled: New Art from the Middle East*, (Saatchi Gallery, 2009). Some shows, like *Les Inquiets*, have been accused of reducing artists to mere chroniclers of war.[37] Others, like the long-term project *Contemporary Arab Representations* as well as *DisORIENTation* are perceived as homogenizing the region's cultural production, highlighting a certain type of scene or art at the expense of diversity.[38] In a powerful critique of the logic that predetermines such shows, Ramadan (2009) makes the case that the end result is an objectification of artists whereby they are reduced to representing the "collective" or the "community" to which they belong.[39]

Some artists took personal stands against partaking in some of these exhibitions at different points in their careers.[40] The decision to exhibit work is generally regarded as one involving a simultaneous process of reflection and negotiation between the artist as well as the curator of the show and the host institution. Accordingly, for some artists, if the show is deemed too "orientalist" or seemingly bent on showcasing artists from Beirut in a certain light, they can choose to opt out.[41] For others, the notion of a group show is not seen as a result of a power-free dialogue between two equal partners. Significantly, as Ziad Abillamá points out, some of these shows can be equated with the notion of humanism, which is in and of itself problematic when viewed especially within Western civilizational history. Abillamá questions humanism's implications in the Second World War and its role in discourses that eventually fuelled a consensus behind the establishment of the state of Israel.[42] Hence, the notion of humanism in this perspective is tied inextricably to imperialism, which he sees as never a solely violent experience, but rather one that simultaneously, and perhaps controversially, possesses a humane face that teaches, educates and restructures. "We see here a productive process that has led to certain [cultural and political] practices in the last two centuries and the question I ask is, 'How have those practices been reshuffled in the past two decades in Lebanon?' "[43]

Commonly, the debate on the politics of representation at the level of the international arts circuit was amiss in discussions carried out with artists and the organizations supporting them, for participation in such exhibitions is not seen as necessarily promulgating a distorted politics of "representation." The logic behind this, as Lina Saneh says, is that "modernity has no nationality."[44] Subsequently, contemporary art discourse and theory do not yield to the *passé* ideological arts of national representation.[45] Yet while participating artists and organizations have specifically written off *national* identity, some sort of identity (specifically a new globalized and post-local ideological one) continues to bring Lebanese (and other Arab artists) together at group shows for Western audiences. This identity is not national, but rather one specifically consumed with all levels of Beirut's war-related realities. This new articulation of identity prompts us to question the complex ideological shifts at play in the realm of contemporary art whereby an object and project ripe for consumption may also lead to rarefied conceptions and fetishizations, depending on context.

It is a truism that the position of the contemporary art scene in Lebanon is especially precarious because it operates amidst a maze of identity politics and contested understandings of modernity and post-modernity, all constrained by implicitly conditional funding and all functioning against a backdrop of neo-colonial tension. Relevant here is the view held among the Beiruti cultural elite not directly involved in the post-war contemporary arts scene which posits that despite the structural challenges facing that sector and despite the success it has had in putting Lebanon on the global contemporary art map, the works that came to represent the country's war and memory are generally neither exhibited nor debated locally—a phenomenon that could culminate in the re-representation of the "Orient" back to itself once it is confirmed as acceptable by international art standards outside of Lebanon.[46] The prevalent sentiment shared by many of those interviewed for this research demonstrates an unease with civil war-related works on exhibit on the global arts circuit, even if they were inspired by the local and by the imperatives within which the local exists— war, memory and the narration of history. One work that attracted attention was contemporary artist Rabih Mroue's *I, the Undersigned*[47] which he bases on the story of a former militiaman who makes a public apology for his actions during the war. Explaining that no one took the apology seriously, Mroue proceeds to poke at the possibilities and limits inherent in a public apology by apologizing for a series of personal faults he himself committed. Critiques of this piece revolved mostly around the anxieties triggered by questions concerning the logic of a discourse which leaves unquestioned the continued relevance of representations of lived experiences of the war without the consideration of the politics of time, place and space. The question most critics seemed to be concerned with was related to the implications of aestheticizing imaginings of the war and a historically exotic Beirut in the realm of the European art museum or gallery space (with its particular audiences). Of prime concern here are the politics of *locality* (in which institution the artwork is exhibited as well as next to whom the work is displayed) and *temporality* (the reason a specific work is exhibited at a particular moment in history).

A new generation of "globally" oriented artists in Lebanon as well as other Arab countries appear to be contesting the weight given to official versions of history and prevalent imaginings of it.[48] In a sense, they are the latest in a set of critiques of Orientalism and post-colonial theory perceived to be as far too focused on binaries such as colonizer versus colonized, and East versus West. If we take the conventional definition of post-colonialism as dealing with cultural identities in colonized areas in addition to the dilemmas of developing a post-colonial national identity, then the ways in which the pre-war generation of Lebanese writers and artists articulated and celebrated that identity are bound to be at odds with those of today's generation, or the post-war generation. It is precisely the post-war generation's logic of deconstruction tied to the the post-modern idea that sees language as inherently unstable and shifting, and that the "reader" rather than the "author" is central in determining meaning, that is sometimes contested by the older generation of artists and critics. But to frame such differences solely within the binary of two different generations is misleading not only because it reduces the value of the rationale employed by each generation, but also because in reality the various dialectics can sometimes bridge these divides.

Novelist, playwright and cultural critic Elias Khoury, speaking of the post-war generation's claim that the pre-war generation finds the form and content of the new work intimidating, says: "It's not the content, nor the form that I have a problem with; rather, it's the *approach*. Much more profound than content, there is an *approach* that I am very hesitant to deal with."[49] Khoury is not alone in taking this position. Others of his generation, as well as young cultural actors not directly involved in the post-war contemporary art scene, spoke of what they saw as a characteristically unquestioned "post-modern" phenomenon in the debates around the contemporary cultural scene in Beirut. This phenomenon is reminiscent of Baudrillard's notion of "transaesthetics," which relates to similar phenomena of "transpolitics," "transsexuality," and "transeconomics," in which everything becomes political, sexual and economic. These domains, in turn, very much like art, lose any boundaries or specific characteristics they might have, resulting, as Baudrillard has argued, in a confused condition where there are no more criteria of value or judgment and in which the function of the normative collapses into a "morass of indifference."[50] One effect of this phenomenon is made clear by the director of Ashkal Alwan, Lebanon's internationally foremost contemporary arts organization:

> [T]oday there is clearly not a center and a periphery. There's one center: the interconnected, global art world, and we are all influenced by it and have access to it, whether one is in Shanghai, Beirut, or London. Increasingly, there is no Arab world, or Third World, either. Yes, there are differences between countries, but there's one center, and it's a kind of reservoir for all of us.[51]

Paradoxically, the "local" for some members of the pre-war generation and for certain post-war actors, still exists beyond representations of lived experiences in artworks exhibited on the global art circuit and is still consumed with issues of local regime–corruption, poverty imperialism, ongoing colonialism in Palestine and civil strife accentuated by the United States, Israel and their allies in the Arab world. Manifestations of the latter, in turn, are deemed part and parcel of the same paradigm of power within which contemporary cultural production is being produced, accessed and represented in Lebanon and on the global arts circuit. For according to this logic, contemporary production of the post-war generation became inextricably tied to foreign aid and soft power upon its internationalization.[52] This means that access to the "global" art world that the director of Ashkal Alwan speaks of does not exist independently of positionality *vis-à-vis* the various hegemonies and ideologies at play, both regionally and internationally. Curator and critic Nav Haq, referring to funding structures for Middle Eastern art, notes that work is being undertaken as part of a structure which predetermines contemporary ideas on the very meaning of what constitutes the "critical" and the "international" in art (Haq, 2006: 37).[53]

Rancière's discussion of the potential and possibility of a reconceptualization of the senses innate to the image in an artwork is worth returning to as it allows for the visibility of marginalized historical subjects, which broader homogenizing (and vulgarly materialist) meta-narratives had rarely allowed, to emerge. Rancière's theory of politics *being* artistic production is based on art's ability to make visible those issues and peoples made invisible by the system that determines who is to be seen, what is to be said and how it will be heard—or the process that he terms the "police".[54] Consequently, the understanding that those who are designated marginal or having no spaces at all by the "police" may reclaim what is theirs through the aesthetic act's ability to reframe the sensory world is a novel reformulation of how art burdened by questions of representation, power and agency such as in post-colonial contexts like Lebanon's, may overcome them when exhibiting internationally and even locally. Yet such an approach simultaneously carries in it polarizing conceptions which enable structural historical dynamics, such as disparities in power, the inequalities of class and the violent persistence of geo-politics and their cultural materializations to be elided. In such formulations, internal art world "policing" that occurs under the guise of neutral funding and curating as well as the ethically-driven practices of powerful institutions of culture with their specific audiences are rendered irrelevant to how and why an image is contextually framed and articulated—a quagmire in which artistic production consumed with deconstructing representations of the Lebanese civil war plays out. If anything, this is a somber reminder of the difficulties of globally circulating and reflecting on contemporary art-making embedded in post-structuralist discourses in post-colonial contexts. It is also a reminder of what writing, processing and then representing about the resistant act in art actually entails.

Notes

1. This chapter is adapted from an article published by the author titled "On Being the Other in Post-civil war Lebanon: Aid and Politics in Processes of Contemporary Cultural Production" in *Arab Studies Journal*, 18(1) (Spring, 2010): 118–161.
2. Sudeep Dasgupta, "Art is Going Nowhere and Politics has to Catch it. Interview with Jacques Rancière" in *Krisis*, 1: 70, 2008.
3. Sarah Rogers, "Post-War Art and the Historical Roots of Beirut's Cosmopolitanism," PhD dissertation (Massachusetts Institute of Technology, 2008).

4. Jacques Rancière argues that politics involves a "distribution of the sensible," understood as a legitimization of ways of seeing, feeling, acting, speaking and being in the world with one another. For Rancière, aesthetic practices are political to the extent that they play a key role in what he terms "distribution of the sensible." See Jacques Rancière, *The Politics of Aesthetics*, trans. Gabriel Rockhill (London: Continuum, 2004).

5. "Biokraphia," by Rabih Mroue and Lina Saneh, which was performed as part of *Home Works: A Forum on Cultural Practices in the Region* in Beirut in 2002.

6. The subtitle of the first part of the project "Wonder Beirut", "The Story of a Pyromaniac Photographer" is about the fictive photographer Abdallah Farah who was commissioned by the Lebanese Tourist Office to make a series of 24 postcards of Beirut (some of which are still on sale today) as well as 12 images for the official calendar of 1969. The idea was to represent the modern aspects of the city and its Riviera, its luxurious hotels. These same postcards are still on sale today in bookshops even if the places represented were almost totally destroyed during the civil war. When the war started, Farah burnt his negatives progressively as the destruction of the city between 1975 and 1990. He tries to update them to reflect the present, the events that are happening and to the bombardments that deface or destroy the photographed buildings.

7. Saree Makdisi, "Laying Claim to Beirut: Urban Narrative and Spatial Identity in the Age of Solidere," *Critical Inquiry*, 23: 661–705 (Spring 1997).

8. Zaatari's full comment is quoted in Stephen Wright, "Like a Spy in a Nascent Era: On the Situation of the Artists in Beirut Today," *Parachute* 108 (2002): 13–31.

9. Richard Becherer, (2005) "A Matter of Life and Debt: The Untold Costs of Rafiq Hariri's New Beirut." *Journal of Architecture*, 10(1): 1–42.

10. Masrah Beirut (The Beirut Theater) is regarded by many cultural actors as one of the earliest institutions to accommodate post-war contemporary artists. Its role proved pivotal mostly from the mid-1990s onward when young actors like Rasha Salti and Pascale Feghali worked to advance the interests of the younger generation.

11. For a thorough review of some of the works produced in the period of the 1990s as well as the early 2000s in public spaces, see Walid Sadek, (2007) "Place at Last," *Art Journal* 35–47, Summer. Regarding the archive, the *Atlas Group* was founded in 1999 to research and document the contemporary history of Lebanon through locating, preserving and producing audio, visual, literary and other artefacts which shed a light

on Lebanon's recent history. The work is presented in mixed-media installations, screenings, visual essays and performances.

12. Interview with the author, Beirut, 9 July 2009.

13. Ibid.

14. Since the mid-1990s, Rabih Mroue and Lina Saneh have been interested in the evolving meaning of the physical body in theatre. Specifically, by questioning the absence of the body, they tackle the complexities of the role of the individual in the community, a phenomenon prevalent in Lebanon's confessionally-organized society. For more, see the appendix to Lina Saneh, *Lina Saneh Body Parts* (Lebanese Association for Plastic Arts, Ashkal Alwan and Le Festival d'Automne à Paris).

15. Ibrahim Abu-Rabi', (2004) *Contemporary Arab Thought: Studies in Post-1967 Arab Intellectual History* (London: Pluto Press), 186.

16. Tony Chakar, (2001) "4 Cotton Underwear for Tony." Postcard, (Townhouse Gallery and Ashkal Alwan, Cairo).

17. This list is by no means exhaustive, but Beirut DC, Né à Beyrouth, BiPod an international dance platform, Espace SD, and now the Beirut Art Center are just a sample of the many organizations and initiatives established in the decade following 1999 and the entry of various international developmental funders such as the Ford Foundation, the Heinrich Böll Foundation, the Open Society Institute, and the European Cultural Foundation.

18. See Kaelen Wilson Goldie, (2007) "On the Margins," in *Pavilion of Lebanon Forward: Fifty-Second Venice Biennale* (Beirut: Alarm Editions). See also, Goldie in Darat al Funun, Khalid Shoman Foundation (Art Now in Lebanon). http://www.daratalfunun.org/main/activit/curentl/art_lebanon/b.htm. Accessed March 8, 2010.

19. Examples include the Sanayeh Project (1995), the Sioufi Project (1997), the Corniche Project (1999) and Hamra Street Project (2000).

20. Samah Idriss, "*al-Makina al-Haririya*," *al-Adab* 5: 2. On the Arab left's alliance with the liberal project, see Michaelle Browers (2004) "The Civil Society Debate and New Trends on the Arab Left," *Theory and Event*, 7(2), (2004).

21. I use "Lebanon" sparingly here. For the post-war generation in the country as a whole were surely affected as young people emerging out of a war in different ways that are also largely dependent on geographical location, class, and, to a large extent, confession. For the purposes of this article, the post-war generation refers to those who belonged broadly speaking to the upper middle classes, who came of age during the years of Lebanon's civil war, and conglomerated in Beirut at the end of the war. Regarding Hariri's role in Lebanon's post-war

reconstruction, see Volker Perthes, (2007) "Myths and Money: Years of Hariri and Lebanon's Preparation for a New Middle East" *Middle East Report* 203: 16–21, Spring. See also Michael Young, (1998) "The Two Faces of Janus: Post-War Lebanon and Its Reconstruction," *Middle East Report* 209: 4–7, 44, Winter.

22. Some of the organizations involved in funding civil society projects include the Ford Foundation, the Open Society Institute of George Soros, the Dutch Prince Claus Fund for Culture and Development, as well as more traditional bilateral funding bodies such as Germany's Goethe Institute, the British Council, Spain's Cervantes Institute, and the French Cultural Center. The USAID, through its Office of Transitional Initiatives and Ambassador's Fund for Cultural Preservation, also took part in funding.

23. There is ample evidence from the cases of Palestine and Egypt to illustrate that under the impact of donors' criteria and priorities, NGOs evolved into professional organizations redesigning their projects to complement the new international development agenda. In many cases, they shifted from grassroots programming to professionalized advocacy. Escobar calls this process the "professionalization" of development, where it becomes possible "to remove all problems from the political and cultural realms and to recast them in terms of the apparently more neutral realm of science." For more, see Arturo Escobar, *Encountering Development: The Making and Unmaking of the Third World* (Princeton, NJ: Princeton University Press), 45. See also Rema Hammami (1995) "NGOs: The Professionalisation of Politics," *Race and Class,* 2(37): 51–63. For general reading on the development of NGO discourse, see Dorothea Hilhorst (2003) *The Real World of NGOs: Discourses, Diversity, and Development* (London: Zed Books), and Partha Chatterjee (2004) *The Politics of the Governed: Reflections on Popular Politics in Most of the World* (New York: Columbia University Press). Chatterjee, in particular, discusses the notion of "political society" as opposed to the professionalized "civil society," a space historically occupied by elites in post-colonial settings, thereby illustrating his uneasiness with the universal applicability of the "civil society" tool.

24. Interview with the author, Beirut, June 17, 2009.

25. For more on de-politicization in the art world, see Julian Stallabras (2004) *Art Incorporated: The Story of Modern Art* (Oxford: Oxford University Press). On multiculturalism, see Olue Oguibe (2004) *The Culture Game* (Minneapolis: University of Minnesota Press).

26. Interview with the author, Beirut, February 17, 2009.

27. Interview with the author, Beirut, February 17, 2009.

28. Sonja Mejcher Atassi is Assistant Professor in the Civilization Sequence Program at the American University of Beirut. The show she contributed to was *DisORIENTation, Contemporary Arab Art Production from the Near East-Egypt, Palestine, Lebanon, Jordan, Syria, and Iraq,* exhibited in the House of World Cultures from March–May 2003.

29. Interview with the author, Beirut, June 11, 2009.

30. Interview with the author, Beirut, August 5, 2008. Also see Miriam Cooke (2007) *Dissident Syria: Making Oppositional Arts Official* (Durham, NC: Duke University Press). Cooke gives an account of the ways in which dissidence in the arts continues to be embedded in what might be viewed as more traditional and formal practices.

31. Rogers, "Post-War Art and the Historical Roots." Rogers details international exhibitions and journals which covered the works as evidence of their mainstreaming into the global arts circuit.

32. Some examples include the comments of Laura U. Marks. "Indeed, the independent artists' scene in Beirut is one of the strongest critical voices in the contemporary Lebanese political scene." Marks (2004) "The Ethical Presenter or How to Have Good Arguments Over Dinner," *The Moving Image* 4(1): 34–47. See also Stephen Wright: "In as much as political activism is not currently a viable option, you tend to intervene in the realm of ideas, which is in itself a relatively autonomous sphere." Wright, *Out of Beirut*, 58. Catherine David also noted: "In a sense what has been occurring here for the past ten years is an antidote against despair, a hope in the political and cultural potential of the aesthetic act" ("Learning from Beirut: Contemporary Aesthetic Practices in Lebanon: Stakes and Conditions for Experimental, Cultural, and Aesthetic Practices in Lebanon and Elsewhere," paper presented at "Home Works: A Forum on Cultural Practices in the Region, Egypt, Iran, Lebanon, Palestine, and Syria," Beirut, April 2–7, 2002). For a more journalistic representation, see Morgan Falconer, "The Long and Wounding Road," *Times* (London), May 2, 2006. Falconer refers to the contemporary art scene and specifically what curator Suzanne Cotter found in the research prior to mounting the 2006 *Out of Beirut* exhibition as "the city's rather underground scene."

33. Interview with the author, Beirut, February 17, 2009.

34. For more on the place and use of politics in the arts, see Paul Virilio, (2003) *Art and Fear,* trans. Julie Rose (London: Continuum).

35. Rogers, "Out of History." She lists these artists as Tony Chakar, the partners Joana Hadjithomas and Khalil Joreige, Bilal Khbeiz, Bernard Khoury, Rabih Mroue, Walid Raad, Walid Sadek, Lina Saneh, Jalal Toufic, and Akram Zaatari. Occasionally they are joined by Ziad

Abillamá, Ali Cherri, Nadine Touma, Marwan Rechmawi, Jayce Salloum, and the partners Paola Yacoub and Michel Lasserre.

36. Writing in the *Guardian*, Antonia Carver, editor of *Bidoun* magazine, a quarterly forum for Middle Eastern art, stated, "Only a handful of Middle Eastern artists have had the privilege of seeing their work defined by terms other than its, or their, geographical origin." Carver lists Walid Raad, Akram Zaatari, Joana Hadjithomas, and Khalil Joreige. Antonia Carver, "Don't Force Artists into an Identity Straitjacket," *Guardian*, September 6, 2006.

37. Nikki Columbus (2008) "Past Imperfect; Nikki Columbus on 'Home Works IV' in Beirut," *ArtForum*, (Summer). *Les Inquiets* brought together a group of five Israelis, Lebanese, and Palestinians in an exhibition that explored aspects of life amidst the Arab-Israeli conflict.

38. Nat Muller, "Reciprocal Collaborative Gestures: Of Different Voice, Of Different Eye," in *An Alternative Gaze: A Shared Reflection on Cross-Mediterranean Cooperation in the Arts*, http://medreflection.eurocult. org. Accessed February 12, 2009. See also an interesting discussion with Catherine David and others on the Contemporary Arab Representations project in Sandra Dagher, Catherine David, Rasha Salti, and Christine Tohme, with T.J. Demos, (2007) "Curating Beirut: A Conversation on the Politics of Representation," *Art Journal* (Summer 2007): 109–112. For the general frameworks within which these described experiences fall and for other examples see for instance, Matthew Rampley (2007) "Assessments" in James Elkins (ed.), *Is Art History Globa?* (New York and London: Routledge).

39. For example Dina Ramadan, "Regional Emissaries: Geographical platforms and the Challenges of Marginalisation in Contemporary Egyptian Art". Proceedings of Apex Conference 3. Honolulu, 2004, http://apexart.org/conference/ramadan.htm.

40. See, for instance, the notes of Jack Persekian, curator of *DisORIENT-ation*, which speak of artist Walid Sadek's declining to partake in the show. For more on this see House of World Cultures: http://archiv.hkw. de/en/dossiers/disorientation/kapitel9.html. Accessed March 2, 2010.

41. Interview with Lamia Joreige, Beirut, July 7, 2008.

42. Such logic fits squarely into Jessica Winegar's "humanity game." See Winegar (2008) "The Humanity Game: Art, Islam, and the War on Terror," *Anthropological Quarterly* 81(3) (Summer): 651–681. Winegar critiques universalist assumptions about humanity and the agentive capacity of art to build bridges of understanding in contexts of so-called civilizational conflict.

43. Interview with the author, Beirut, June 17, 2009.

44. Interview with the author, Beirut, July 9, 2009.

45. Zolghadr, *Bidoun*, 64–66.

46. Writers such as Elias Khoury and Samah Idriss indicated that cultural producers looking for a stamp of approval at the international level and, in specific, the West is a phenomenon prevalent across the board in the domain of cultural production. Hence it is not related only to the visual arts. It is, if anything, further reinforcement of the idea that "globalization" is not after all so "global."

47. Rabih Mroue, *I, the Undersigned* (Video/film) (2008).

48. Kaelen Wilson Goldie (2009) review of *Palestinian Art from 1850 to the Present* by Kamal Boulatta, *Art Magazine* (April).

49. Christine Tohme, Interview with the author, Beirut, June 4, 2009.

50. Douglas Kellner (2009) "Baudrillard and the Art Conspiracy," in David B. Clarke, Marcus Doel, William Merrin, Richard G. Smith, (eds), *Jean Baudrillard: Fatal Theories* (London: Routledge), 95.

51. Dagher et al., "Curating Beirut," 114.

52. Hanan Toukan, "On Being the Other in Post-Civil War Lebanon: Aid and the Politics of Art in Processes of Contemporary Cultural Production." *Arab Studies Journal* XVII(1) (Spring 2010): 118–161. See especially pages 141–44 for the relationship between international funding organizations, local cultural organizations and the transnationalism of the contemporary post-war art scene.

53. Nav Haq (2006) "Pashmina Power: Class Structure in International Arts Funding," *Bidoun* (Winter), 37.

54. For Rancière's definition of the police see *Disagreement: Politics and Philosophy*, University of Minnesota Press (1999), 29. Rancière does not identify the police with what is conventionally understood as the "state apparatus" and its associated disciplinary structure. For Rancière the "state apparatus" is implicated in a presumption of an opposition between state and society in which the state is portrayed as a machine that imposes rigidity on society. Thus "policing" is not so much the "disciplining" of bodies as it is a set of established regulations that govern the appearance of these bodies and the characteristics of the spaces they are to occupy and the patterns by which they are to be distributed.

References

Abu-Rabi', Ibrahim (2004). *Contemporary Arab Thought: Studies in Post-1967 Arab Intellectual History* (London: Pluto Press).

Badiou, Alain (2005). *Metapolitics*, trans. Jason Barker (London: Verso).

Becherer, Richard (2005). "A Matter of Life and Debt: The Untold Costs of Rafiq Hariri's New Beirut." *Journal of Architecture*, 10(1): 1–42.

Carver, Antonia (2006). "Don't Force Artists into an Identity Straitjacket," *Guardian*, September 6.

Chakar, Tony (2001). "4 Cotton Underwear for Tony." Postcard. Cairo: Townhouse Gallery and Ashkal Alwan.

Chatterjee, Partha (2004). *The Politics of the Governed: Reflections on Popular Politics in Most of the World* (New York: Columbia University Press).

Columbus, Nikki (2008). "Past Imperfect; Nikki Columbus on 'Home Works IV' in Beirut," *ArtForum* 46(10): 179.

Dagher, Sandra, Catherine David, Rasha Salti, and Christine Tohme, with T.J. Demos (2007). "Curating Beirut: A Conversation on the Politics of Representation: A Roundtable Discussion," *Art Journal*, 98–119.

Dasgupta, Sudeep (2008), "Art Is Going Elsewhere. And Politics has to Catch It", an interview with Jacques Rancière in *Krisis*, Issue 1.

David, Catherine (2002). "Learning from Beirut: Contemporary Aesthetic Practices in Lebanon: Stakes and Conditions for Experimental, Cultural, and Aesthetic Practices in Lebanon and Elsewhere," paper presented at "Home Works: A Forum on Cultural Practices in the Region, Egypt, Iran, Lebanon, Palestine, and Syria," Beirut, April 2–7, 2002.

Escobar, Arturo. *Encountering Development: The Making and Unmaking of the Third World.* (Princeton, NJ: Princeton University Press) p. 45.

Falconer, Morgan (2006). "The Long and Wounding Road," *Times* (London), May 2, 2006.

Hammami, Rema, (1995). "NGOs: The Professionalisation of Politics," *Race and Class*, 2(37): 51–63.

Haq, Nav (2006). "Pashmina Power: Class Structure in International Arts Funding," *Bidoun*, 37.

Hilhorst, Dorothea (2003). *The Real World of NGOs: Discourses, Diversity, and Development.* (London: Zed Books).

Kellner, Douglas (2009). "Baudrillard and the Art Conspiracy," in David B. Clarke, Marcus Doel, William Merrin and Richard G. Smith (eds). *Jean Baudrillard: Fatal Theories* (London: Routledge).

Makdisi, Saree (1997). "Laying Claim to Beirut: Urban Narrative and Spatial Identity in the Age of Solidere," *Critical Inquiry*, 23: 661–705.

Marks, Laura U. (2004). "The Ethical Presenter or How to Have Good Arguments Over Dinner," *The Moving Image*, 4(1): 34–47.

Mroue, Rabih (2008). *I, the Undersigned* (Video/film).

Mroue, Rabih and Lina Saneh (2002). "Biokraphia," performed as part of *Home Works: A Forum on Cultural Practices in the Region* in Beirut in 2002.

Muller, Nat (2009). "Reciprocal Collaborative Gestures: Of Different Voice, Of Different Eye," in *An Alternative Gaze: A Shared Reflection on Cross-Mediterranean Cooperation in the Arts*, http://medreflection.eurocult.org. Accessed February 12, 2009.

Oguibe, Olue (2004). *The Culture Game* (Minneapolis: University of Minnesota Press).

Perthes, Volker (1997). "Myths and Money: Years of Hariri and Lebanon's Preparation for a New Middle East." *Middle East Report*, 203: 16–21.

Ramadan, Dina (2004). "Regional Emissaries: Geographical Platforms and the Challenges of Marginalisation in Contemporary Egyptian Art". Proceedings of Apex Conference 3. Honolulu, 2004, http://apexart.org/conference/ramadan.htm

Rampley, Matthew (2007). "Assessments" in James Elkins (ed.), *Is Art History Global?* (New York and London: Routledge).

Rancière, Jacques (2004). *The Politics of Aesthetics*, trans. Gabriel Rockhill. (London: Continuum).

Rogers, Sarah (2008). "Post-War Art and the Historical Roots of Beirut's Cosmopolitanism," PhD dissertation (Massachusetts Institute of Technology).

Stallabras, Julian (2004). *Art Incorporated: The Story of Modern Art* (Oxford: Oxford University Press).

Toukan, Hanan (2010). "On Being the Other in Post-Civil War Lebanon: Aid and the Politics of Art in Processes of Contemporary Cultural Production." *Arab Studies Journal*, XVII(1): 118–161.

Wilson Goldie, Kaelen (2007). "On the Margins," in Pavilion of Lebanon Forward: Fifty-Second Venice Biennale. Beirut: Alarm Editions. See also, Goldie in Darat al Funun, Khalid Shoman Foundation (Art Now in Lebanon).

———— (2009). "Review of Palestinian Art from 1850 to the Present" by Kamal Boulatta, *Art Magazine*.

Wright, Stephen (2002). "Like a Spy in a Nascent Era: On the Situation of the Artists in Beirut Today," *Parachute*, 108: 13–31.

Young, Michael (1998). "The Two Faces of Janus: Post-War Lebanon and Its Reconstruction," *Middle East Report*, 209(44): 4–7.

Winegar, Jessica (2008). "The Humanity Game: Art, Islam, and the War on Terror," *Anthropological Quarterly*, 81(3): 651–81.

Zolghadr, Tirdad (2005). "The Forward Thrust of Christine Tohme," *Bidoun*, 64–66.

5

NARRATIVES IN CONFLICT: EMILE HABIBI'S *AL-WAQA'I AL-GHARIBA* AND ELIA SULEIMAN'S *DIVINE INTERVENTION*

REFQA ABU-REMAILEH

Threat to Existence: Present but Absent

"The Palestinian people truly appeared in the mid-1960s to be facing an existential crisis of daunting proportions," writes the historian Rashid Khalidi in *The Iron Cage*, "and to be in serious danger of disappearing from the political sphere, just as their country had disappeared from the map, and indeed from public discourse" (Khalidi, 2006: 164–165). This threat of disappearance that Khalidi refers to in fact extends further back to 1948 when the state of Israel was created, and the first to encounter this threat were the Palestinians who had remained in their towns and cities, and found themselves within the borders of an alien state, sealed off from other Palestinians and the rest of the Arab world and caught between two narratives competing for the same land. The Israeli-Zionist narrative is one of exclusion, which tells history "as a sequence in which the Zionists took root in, developed, and built an empty and desolate territory [...] to present a social totality that excludes Palestinians" (Khleifi, 2008: 63). This narrative of denial has meant that the production of a standard "official" Palestinian narrative was never really possible and it has "jeopardized the Palestinians' historical patrimony," (Khalidi, 2006: xxxvi–vii) as Khalidi suggests.

This continuous conflict over history and narrative forms the backdrop to the novels of Emile Habibi (1922–1996) and the films of Elia Suleiman (1960–), whose works will be the focus of this chapter. This experience was more pronounced for them growing up as Palestinians inside Israel than it was for Palestinians who lived in the Occupied Territories or the diaspora. In light of this state of imposed historical, political, cultural and geographical absence they found themselves in (despite their physical presence on the land), writers and artists took it upon themselves to document and record their existence in order to assert their presence. Haim Bresheeth (2007: 183–4) describes it as living between:

> ...fact and fiction, between narrative and narration, between the story and its telling, between documentary and fiction, not to mention between Israel and Palestine, and between life and death.

As Palestinian citizens of Israel, Habibi and Suleiman narrate a conflict that, though no longer as visibly militaristic as it once was, is ongoing on a deep and disturbing psychological level, facilitated by a labyrinthine and discriminatory legal system. In an interview, Elia Suleiman refers to the "psychological" occupation of Palestinians inside Israel:

> The occupation of 1948, is no longer militaristic, there's no longer a military government with tanks and soldiers in the streets and all that. It's become psychological, economic, denial of rights, humiliation in all its forms [....] In the 1967 territories, obviously, the occupation is overt. It's as blunt and pornographic as it was for the 1948 Palestinians, but with the difference of time.[1]

The military rule imposed on the Palestinians inside Israel— despite the fact that they were formally declared citizens of the state in 1948—lasted till 1966. The lifting of the military rule meant an easing of the tight physical control the state of Israel exerted on all aspects of life for the Palestinian minority, but the physical separation transformed into systemic and institutionalized discrimination thereafter, under the pretext of a "strategic and demographic threat" that the Palestinian citizens of Israel were assumed to pose to the state of Israel. With the suppression of Palestinian/Arab identity in most aspects of daily life, narratives and images—even if silent such as in Suleiman's films—became a place of refuge and an alternative venue for expression.

The Impulse to Document

The conflict over history is also a conflict over narrative. In Habibi's and Suleiman's work, there is a process of documenting and historicizing that is used to compensate for the failure of the chronological, linear narrative of history to account for the Palestinians' interstitial state of living between the cracks. Even the titles of their works are clues to a creative fascination with recording and documenting. For example, the first word of Habibi's most famous novel *al-Waqa'i' al-ghariba fi ikhtifa' sa'id abi al-nahs al-mutasha'il* (1974), has been translated as "truths," as in, *Strange Truths Concerning the Disappearance of Sa'id Abi Nahs Mutasha'il*,[2] or using the word "history," as in: *The Strange History of Sa'id the Pessoptimist, the Luckless Palestinian* (LeGassick, 1980: 215). Words related to chronicling and record-keeping also feature in the title of Suleiman's fiction films. In *Yadun ilahiyya* (*Divine Intervention*, 2002) the word *yawmiyyat* features in the subtitle of the film, *yawmiyyat al-hubb wa-l-alam*, which has been translated as "chronicle" in the English title of the film *A Chronicle of Love and Pain*, and also refers to a diary form and the recording of daily occurrences.

Through a close reading of Habibi's *al-Waqa'i' al-ghariba* and Suleiman's *Divine Intervention*, this chapter will address a number of questions: How is presence documented/recorded in the face of the threat of imposed disappearance? What techniques do Habibi and Suleiman use to reflect the absurd lives of the Palestinians inside Israel? How do these works situate themselves in relation to the historical narrative of the conflict, and how do they reflect on their own construction as fictional narratives?

The basis for selecting the novels of Emile Habibi and the films of Elia Suleiman for comparison, and their appeal to this chapter, lay initially in the fact that there was no direct relationship between these works, especially not one of novel/film adaptation. In the absence of pre-conceived notions and hierarchies based on different media, a number of striking overlaps emerges from the two bodies of work. Habibi's and Suleiman's works share an experimental, innovative spirit that strives to reflect the absurd reality of their historical, political and cultural situation. I will explore how this impulse manifests itself in works of fiction and how it is treated in different media.

Biographies

When Habibi appeared on the Arab literary map, he did so with a remarkable and unusual work. In this chapter, I will focus on Habibi's debut novel, *al-Waqa'i' al-ghariba fi ikhtifa' sa'id abi al-nahs al-mutasha'il* (*The Strange Truths of the Disappearance of Sa'id the Pessoptimist*, 1974), which took the Arab literary world by storm when it was first published. Habibi began writing literature later in his career, spurred by a statement made by the Israeli politician Yigal Allon after the Arab defeat of 1967 in which he claimed that the Palestinians no longer existed, and, if they did, they would have produced their own literature.[3] Habibi took this on as a personal challenge, recognizing the importance of literature not just as a form of resistance, but also a document of existence.

Habibi, who was born in Haifa in 1922 during the period of the British Mandate of Palestine, found himself an Israeli citizen after 1948. He rose to public prominence as a politician; a leader of the Communist party and a three-term member of the Israeli Knesset. For his literary achievements, Habibi was awarded the al-Quds Prize by PLO Chairman Yasser Arafat in 1990. This was followed by a more controversial award that provoked a strong reaction from across the Arab world and in Israel. Two years later, in 1992, Habibi was awarded the Israel Prize—the state's highest honor—by Israeli Prime Minister Yitzhak Shamir for excellence in Arabic literature.[4]

Elia Suleiman was born in 1960. He grew up not in British-ruled Mandate Palestine as Habibi did, but in a Nazareth that had become part of the new State of Israel. In his early twenties, Suleiman left Nazareth for New York where he began to experiment with filmmaking. Even though Suleiman may have been influenced by the cultural and intellectual life in New York, the fact that he never trained as a filmmaker imbues his films with a kind of naive simplicity, reminiscent of silent era films. Suleiman moved back and settled in Jerusalem in 1994, where he re-worked a script that he had begun writing in New York, eventually securing enough funding to make his first long fiction film, *Chronicle of a Disappearance* (*Sijill ikhtifa'*, 1996). In this chapter, however, I will focus on his second fiction film, *Divine Intervention* (*Yadun ilahiyya*, 2002), the more mature evolution of his style, and for which he won the Grand Jury Prize at the 2002 Cannes Film Festival.

History and Territory

One of the most obvious documenting techniques in Habibi's novel, *al-Waqa'i' al-ghariba*, is the interjection of non-fictional material into the fictional text. This technique takes on two forms: the direct historical/non-fictional interjection into the main body of the narrative text, and the use of footnotes, which are appended to the main body of the text.

Habibi's novel, *al-Waqa'i' al-ghariba*, is written in the form of a long episodic letter, and has no central, connected plot, but is rather an arrangement of short actions, events, histories, commentaries in chapter form, making up three "books" or parts. It spans the life of a lowly character named Sa'id who, like Habibi, is born in Mandate Palestine and recounts his life and experiences through both the *Nakba* (catastrophe) of 1948 and the *Naksa* (setback) of 1967. The epistolary nature of the work allows numerous digressions and the freedom to create a non-linear narrative peppered with interjections from a variety of different sources, including classical and modern Arabic literature, history, and travel literature. There are a number of ways in which direct interjections appear in Habibi's novel. *Al-Waqa'i' al-ghariba* records names of Palestinian villages destroyed in 1948, as lists of names with some description. It also includes detailed non-fictional historical information mostly about the city of Acre, but also on Haifa and Jerusalem. This "orientation to place" is distinctive of Palestinians who lived on the land pre-1948 and emphasized by Lila Abu-Lughod and Ahmad Sa'di in their book on *Nakba* narratives and memories:

> If the most distinctive feature of Palestinian social memory is its production under constant threat of erasure and in the shadow of a narrative and political force that silences it, one of its most characteristic qualities [...] is its orientation to place. (Sa'di and Abu-Lughod, 2007: 13)

When a young Sa'id is told to wait in the al-Jazzar mosque after he "infiltrates" back into his country, the newly established state of

Israel, he meets ghost-like refugees-to-be who bombard him with questions about whether he has met anyone from their villages. They begin naming their villages and how they were destroyed:

> "We are from Kwaykaat. They demolished it and evicted everyone. Did you meet anyone from Kwaykaat?"
>
> [...] "I am from al-Manshiyya. There's not a stone left standing there except tombs. Did you meet anyone from al-Manshiyya?"
>
> "We are from Amqa. They plowed all its houses under spilled its oil onto the ground. Did you meet anyone from Amqa?"
>
> "We over here are from Berwah. They forced us out and obliterated it. Did you meet anyone from Berwah?"[5]

Sa'id's answer to all these questions is "No", and it appears that he has never heard of any of these villages before either. However, that does not put a stop to the incessant questioning, and a whole list of villages is recited: al-Ruwais; al-Hadatha; al-Damun; al-Mazra'a; Sha'b; Mi'ar; Wa'rat al-Saris; al-Zib; al-Bassa; al-Kabri; Kufr Bir'im and Iqrit. After the questions cease, Sa'id admits that:

> We of Haifa used to know more about the villages of Scotland than we did about those of Galilee. Most of these villages I have never heard mentioned except for that one evening.[6]

Sa'id's statement combined with the fact that none of these villages appears on any maps of Israel raises the question as to whether these village names were invented or really did exist. One does not have to look far to confirm that these villages did indeed exist, and that Habibi's purpose in recording their names is to remind those Palestinians who have forgotten and those who simply do not know, what was lost and intentionally destroyed in 1948. Walid Khalidi's volume on Palestinian villages occupied and depopulated by Israel in 1948 (1982) reveals the history of these villages, their locations, descriptions, topographies, populations and how they were destroyed and/or occupied. The villages Sa'id was asked about, Khalidi's volume reveals, were small villages surrounding Acre and Haifa, with the exception of al-Hadatha, which is in the Lake Tiberias district, and al-Mazra'a, in the Ramla area.

History of Palestinian Cities

In a number of instances Habibi interjects non-fictional information about the city of Acre, some of which is inserted in dialogue between characters in *al-Waqa'i' al-ghariba*. These factual interjections draw attention to the construction and interpretation of historical narratives. During the same stay at al-Jazzar mosque, and while waiting for his fate to be settled with other refugees-to-be, Sa'id has a conversation about history with an old school teacher he meets in the mosque. The teacher tells him that the Israelis are but one of many successive occupiers in the history of the land: "The truth is, son, that they are no worse than the others like them in history."[7] The teacher, however, goes further in claiming that, ironically, the Israelis are more merciful than previous occupiers:

> It's true, they did demolish those villages the others mentioned and did evict their inhabitants. But, my son, they're far more merciful than the conquerors our forefathers had years before.[8]

He continues, using the history of Acre as an example:

> Take Acre, for example. When the Crusaders conquered it after a three-week siege in 1104, they slaughtered the people wholesale and confiscated their property. And Acre remained in their hands for eighty-three years, until Saladin freed it after the battle of Hittin, the history of which I taught you in school. [...] Then the Crusaders besieged it again for two years, from August 1189 to July 1191, when hunger forced its people to surrender on very harsh terms. When they were unable to meet those terms, the king of the Crusaders, Richard the Lionhearted, ordered the heads of 2,600 hostages to be chopped off. So Acre remained in their hands for another century, one hundred years, my son, until it was liberated by the Mamluk leader Qalawun, in 1291.[9]

What the teacher relates is that these cities have a history that predates that of their current occupation by Israel, but that that history had been obscured and eschewed over time: "So Haifa, you see my boy, is not a new city. The point is that after every massacre there was no one left to tell the new generation about their origins."[10]

The teacher's comments and explanations suggest an alternative history, a history of these ancient cities which remains unwritten; one of *sumud* (steadfastness) and resistance through the ages regardless of the identity of the occupiers and the length of their occupation. In that sense, the teacher takes the long view of history, from which his interpretations of historical fatalism follow, and in which he seems to seek comfort.

Beyond the Text: Footnotes and Fiction

The third example of interjections is an indirect one, which sits alongside the main body of the text. The use of these footnotes can be seen as a process of documentation, used most often in scholarly and academic writing as a method of verifying information and pointing to sources used in shaping the arguments of the text. Footnotes are not commonly appended to fictional texts and this is a distinct feature of Habibi's works, highly unusual, if not unique, in modern Arabic literature in general. Unlike direct interjections, footnotes make up a body of text that exists outside the main narrative, supplementing and commenting on it. The Egyptian literary scholar, Sabry Hafez, comments on the presence of the footnotes in Habibi's novel as a "secondary text":

> *The Pessoptimist* is full of footnotes creating a secondary text which serves as the cultural context of the novel and roots every aspect of the narrative in the historical and geographical reality of Palestine. The detailed information provided in these notes generates an elaborate, internal memory which serves as a counter argument against any denial of the existence of Palestine and its identity.[11]

Habibi makes use of these footnotes as a liaison between the fictional text and external reality to reach out and draw on various types of sources. Asked about the extensive use of footnotes, Habibi responds:

> I wish to enrich the reader with information, so that he doesn't feel that he wasted his time reading [...] I prepare extensive notes, facts, and sources before I begin to write a new novel, so why shouldn't the reader himself benefit from this too?[12]

The presence of footnotes in *al-Waqa'i' al-ghariba* means that a large amount of text exists outside the main frame of the fictional text. By blurring the genre between fiction and non-fiction, footnotes imbue Habibi's works with a strong impulse to verify, validate, authenticate and historicize fictional narrative. Indeed, much of the rewriting and commenting on history and non-history (fiction) takes place within the footnotes in Habibi's text. Maintaining a link with the *turath* (heritage) is seen as an important function of footnotes in Habibi's works. Just as Habibi uses the *turath* stylistically, with footnotes harking back to the classical tradition of *istitrad* (digression), he also uses the *turath* to interpret the Palestinian tragedy and transmit it through literature, recording that very cultural heritage that Israel has been trying to obliterate.

Not only does the use of classical sources give Palestinian literature credibility, but it also gives Palestinian literature the status of Literature, reevaluating the classical heritage and moving from a general "Arabness" to a more specific "Palestinianness" of identity and literature (Sessona, 2001: 220). It becomes evident that footnotes in Habibi's works not only highlight Palestinian history and its relation to pre-modern and modern history of the region, but also bring alive the geography and toponymy of the area.

Habibi's process of historicization begins in *al-Waqa'i' al-ghariba*, especially evident in footnote #34, which is an explanation of an abbreviation Habibi uses in the main body of the text.[13] A number of footnotes refer to events in modern Palestinian history in *al-Waqa'i' al-ghariba* but the reference in footnote #34 is to a term that is unique, and coined by Habibi. In the main body of the narrative, Sa'id tells the story of a woman called Thurrayya who returns to Lydda after the June 1967 war to uncover the treasure she had buried in the walls of her home before she fled her hometown in 1948.

In re-narrating this story, Sa'id refers to 1967 using special acronyms: "For on the tenth day of September, in the fifth year *ba ha* – *ba'd harb huzayran* (after the June War), that is, and therefore 1971 [...]."[14] Since letter abbreviations do not commonly exist in Arabic, Sa'id's historicization of events following the June War as the letter *ba* and the letter *ha* (b.h.) can be seen as both an imitation and a parody of the use BC (Before Christ) and AD (Anno Domini) to demarcate the two distinct epochs of history as related to the birth of Christ. Thus, Saʿid uses it to create a new historical boundary, hailing a new period in Palestinian history, except in this case this new period does not mark a new dawn on humanity. It is in fact even worse than the period that preceded it, as the story of Thurrayya later indicates.[15]

The footnote alone does not achieve a sense of irony, but it certainly contributes to the overall effect. Thus, in this example Saʿid switches historical perspectives through the use of terminology and language, raising questions about the process of historicization, giving names to historical events, and its relationship to the perspective from which it emerges. Saʿid therefore is capable of historicizing events from both the Israeli and Palestinian/Arab perspective which reflects his in-between and precarious identity and existence as a Palestinian living in Israel.

In *al-Waqaʾiʿ al-ghariba,* only two footnotes make reference to modern Arab literary figures, both of which are Palestinian citizens of Israel: Mahmud Darwish and Tawfiq Zayyad. The poets are not named in the main body of the text, but are instead referred to through the names of places from which they come. For example, Darwish is referred to in relation to the village of al-Birwa,[16] and Zayyad in relation to the Galilee.[17] The footnotes (footnotes #7 and #9 respectively) then reveal the names of those poets for those who do not pick up references to them in the text.

Literary references in *al-Waqaʾiʿ al-ghariba* range from the classical/medieval to the modern. Most modern literary references, however, relate to contemporary Palestinian literature, for example Mahmud Darwish and Tawfiq Zayyad, both Palestinians from inside Israel, just like Habibi. Habibi's impulse to document, elaborate or even digress is not done for mere display of literary skill or breadth of knowledge, but rather because of the existential threats that haunts much of Palestinian life and literature. Those living inside Israel feel their conditions as much as those who have been refugees for more than sixty years. To counter that threat, external reality and history come into play. Furthermore, to get direct access to external reality through indirect means (because of the fictional nature of the narrative), Habibi uses footnotes, which serve both the text and the meta-fictional needs of the author. Footnotes are a clear sign of a process of documentation and serve to verify, authenticate and historicize the fictional narrative. Their liaison position helps ground the fictional text in socio-politico-historical reality, but at the same time serve as tools to comment on and rewrite history.

A De-territorialized Cry

Habibi's impulse to document grounds his work both in terms of place as well as historical and literary narratives as related to Palestinian history. A few decades later, in the post-Oslo era of the 1990s when Suleiman begins to make his film, instead of a grounding in the face of disappearance, the conflict is presented through a fragmented de-territorialized lens that appears to be ahistorical.

While Maher Jarrar argues that the geography of the Arabic language in Habibi's literature is one of "de-territorialized Arabic" (Jarrar, 2002: 22), I have shown that *al-Waqa'i' al-ghariba* can be an example of a text placed within a grand historical tradition, asserting the continuity of Palestinian presence on their disputed homeland by using classical/medieval literary and historical references and allusions, rather than a de-territorialized Arabic. Furthermore, there is a direct association between history, territory and language in *al-Waqa'i' al-ghariba*. On the other hand, a deep de-territorialization and fragmentation of Palestinian geography and (lack of) language is reflected in Suleiman's semi-silent *Divine Intervention*, where the dissociation between history and territory is apparent. Instead of a smooth flowing storyline and a transparent, inconspicuous editing style, there is narrative and visual discontinuity in the structure of the film that obscures the connections between events and the spaces in which they are set. Gertz and Khleifi write about a process of the reduction of space in *Divine Intervention* where "landscape still existed and one could travel through them from one place to another" (Gertz and Khleifi, 2008: 178). However, they continue, this landscape slowly disappears and trips across the country no longer reveal it:

> In *Divine Intervention*, even those subdued landscapes have vanished. The first part of the film is reduced to the narrow and enclosed streets of Nazareth, shown as a place choked by courtyards crowding each other, occupied parking spots, neighbours who violently infringe on each other's territory. (ibid.)

The atmosphere of fragmented spaces with no continuity between them reflects a daily life that seems to provide no outlets for enquiry and has become a claustrophobic space where people unleash their frustrations on each other. Suleiman's documentation of the landscapes is a drawing of maps of fragmentation, not maps of historical and cultural continuity as in the case of Habibi. The fragmentation of Palestinians continues with the physical and political separation of the West Bank, Gaza, the Palestinians inside Israel, Palestinian refugees, and Palestinians in the diaspora. The dissociation between history and territory in Suleiman's *Divine Intervention* and the fragmentation of spaces and landscape is a reflection of the post-Oslo reality of division and sub-divisions of Palestinians and their geography. It is also a reflection of another sentiment, a disillusion with the collective nationalist vision and a reluctance to narrate a collective chronological tragedy. The fragmentation of territory has also meant a loss of the grand vision of an all-knowing omniscient narrator in Suleiman's films. This loss is translated into a preoccupation with the day-to-day, the routines, the *yawmiyyat* of tragedy rather than a tragic collective history. In fact, the title "Divine Intervention" could be read as a call for a vision that transcends the claustrophobic ghettos of Nazareth, the political quagmire of Jerusalem, and the idea of Palestinian statehood, held under occupation, struggling to be born in the West Bank.

Epistolary and *Yawmiyyat*

The chosen structures of Habibi's novel and Suleiman's film highlight the desired effect they each want to achieve with regards to situating their works, whether in the long view of history or the minutiae of everyday life. The titles of Suleiman's films give away the intended structure of the film. The word *yawmiyyat* refers to a daily record of events, appearing as ES's observations recorded and chronicled in film, and which Suleiman takes to its extreme banal depths. Hamid Naficy writes that many exilic filmmakers emphasize the day-to-day through the "performative expression of dailiness" (Naficy, 2001: 117). The "documentary-like" descriptions of mundane routines slow the film's pacing, Naficy continues, but they are important because these routines and details "carry with them highly significant cultural, national, and critical import; they are not empty gestures or bad filmmaking" (ibid.).

Linking the fictional with an autobiographical framework and the *yawmiyyat* structure is a way to stress the day-to-day over grand historical or political narratives. *Divine Intervention* makes no direct references to any of the major events in Palestinian history that continue to plague and shape Palestinian lives today and are a constant topic of debate among people and in the media. The deep silence in his films allows the viewer to see beyond the supposedly mundane acts of parents lying in front of TV, and the neighbor throwing out the garbage. The slow-paced Nazareth scenes in *Divine Intervention* can be tedious viewing for some, but it is these slow repetitive vicious cycles, of neighbors lashing out at each other, that build up and give the film its claustrophobic ghetto-like atmosphere. These seemingly banal scenes are in fact psychological explorations of the depths of the indirect occupation—the occupation of the mind—that Palestinians in Nazareth suffer from.

In *al-Waqa'i' al-ghariba*, Sa'id uses the epistolary form, which Peter Heath sees as a framing device that allows the creation of a narrative that is less bound to laws of linearity and temporality:

> The epistle's open-endedness provides ample opportunity
> for anecdotal asides, cultural and historical interjections,
> and topical political observations, all of which permeate the
> work. (Heath, 2000: 159–160)

This flexibility of the epistolary form is important as it allows Sa'id and Habibi to include information, footnotes and digressions that would have been difficult to include in a more traditionally fictional narrative. The use of the epistolary form is given further significance as a response to the epigraph that prefaces *al-Waqa'i' al-ghariba*. The epigraph quotes an extract from the poetry of Samih al-Qasim, which is a call to action to all those who have waited in vain too long for "those letters for which they so yearn," insisting that they write those letters to themselves. LeGassick sees that it is no coincidence that "this work is in the form of a long, episodic and anecdotal letter, a conscious attempt to respond to the poet's challenge" (LeGassick, 1980: 216).

Both Habibi and Suleiman choose forms that allow them to represent a kind of fictionalized reality, not distinguishing or marking the real from the fictional. Such choices for fictional narratives are no doubt deliberate techniques to blur narrative and structural genres, as Naficy maintains:

> Despite these and other autobiographical and authenticating elements, the film is neither truly autobiographical, nor documentary, nor fictional, as it contains elements of each type without specifying which is which. (Naficy, 2001: 236)

With their works set in the post-1967 "disturbance of spirits" period, in which the knowability and representability of reality came under intense scrutiny, Habibi and Suleiman challenge known forms of genre and authority, especially narrative authority. What Habibi and Suleiman are interested in is finding forms that can reflect the complexities of their lives and are flexible enough to cater to their particular needs, whether it is in being able to include digressions, historical interjections, or mix autobiographical material with myth or fantasy. The effect is one where the line between any known narrative categories and genres are blurred.

Self-reflexivity and Truth

More than documenting their personal narratives, Habibi and Suleiman use a self-reflexive narrative, one that meditates on and draws attention to its medium and its own construction. Since the narratives of history and politics are not seen to have satisfied Palestinians in their national struggle, Habibi and Suleiman expose mechanisms of fictional construction that allow the reader to question the makings of other narratives, especially those of historical narrativeness, the linearity, assertiveness and myths which have both failed and occupied them.

An important aspect of the autobiographical façade of Habibi's and Suleiman's works is the process of reflecting on the work within the work, drawing attention to the writing and filmmaking processes. Self-reflexivity can be defined as the texts' (and this can also apply to film) "metafictional awareness of its own constructedness and textuality."[18] Such "self-reflexive utterances," as Ansgar Nünning and Birgit Neumann (2009: 204) describe them, are "comments referring to the discourse rather than to the story." Sage Hamilton Rountree, in her analysis of Woody Allen's films (a prime example of self-reflexivity in American cinema), writes that self-reflexive films consistently draw attention to the means by which they are created by foregrounding form, and thus forcing the audience to consider "not only the technical aspects of filmmaking but also the motivations that lead to the production of a film" (Rountree, 2001: 21).

The violation of "poetological norms" through use of self-reflexive techniques such as intrusive narrators, authors directly addressing readers, or drawing attention to the technical aspects of filmmaking, lead to questioning "how literary assumptions and conventions transform and filter reality, thus trying to ultimately prove that no singular truths or meanings exist" (Huber, Middeke and Zapf, 2005: 9). This resonates strongly with Suleiman's views on narrative perspective in his own films:

> Every center point has a narrative, but I want to create an image without a specific center. In the case of Palestine, my challenge is to avoid a centralized, unified image that allows only a single narrative perspective, and on the contrary, to produce a kind of decentralization of viewpoint, perception, narration. (See Bourland, 2000: 97)

Divine Intervention and the Self-reflexive Storyboard Scenes

Suleiman, in a less direct and informative effort than Habibi's in his footnotes, draws attention to the process of filmmaking and narrative construction. Instead of using self-reflexive film techniques such as having the characters look directly into the camera or describe the film they are in, Suleiman uses a combination of structural and narrative techniques to draw attention to the film within the film. Even though Suleiman's self-reflexive techniques differ from Habibi's, the examples will highlight that they also result in creating an effect of immediacy in the experience of viewing the films.

Since the relationship between Suleiman's character, ES, and filmmaking is more ambiguous in *Divine Intervention*, I will examine more closely the three scenes that feature the yellow sticky notes. In these scenes, ES appears standing between two walls in his Jerusalem flat which are lined with well-ordered yellow notes. The notes appear to relate to the scenes we see or are about to see in the film and can be thought of as the equivalent of a text-based storyboard. The storyboard scenes appear in the second half of the film, and unlike *Homage* and *Chronicle*, there are no direct references to ES being a filmmaker or having a link to the film during the film (there are no interviews that point to that). Only the storyboard scenes suggest a clue to a possible association between ES, the titles written on the yellow notes, and the scenes we see in the film.

The first of the storyboard scenes shows ES standing facing a wall lined with well-ordered yellow notes in the corridor between his kitchen and living room (Figure 1). He takes one of the notes off the wall (which I will call Wall 1) and looks down to read it. The note is located three rows down, in the second column of notes. The camera then cuts back to a black title card to show us what we assume is the text on the note: *yamrad al-ab* (father falls ill). The camera cuts to a different angle, revealing that the opposite wall (which I will call Wall 2) is also lined with well-ordered yellow notes, to which ES turns and sticks the note he had just picked up from Wall 1. ES sticks the note on an empty spot on Wall 2 that is at the parallel position: third row down, second column. The text on the note, announcing that the father falls ill, is in fact retrospective; we

Figure 1   Stills and title card from the Post-it scene, *Divine Intervention*.

Figure 2   Still and title card from second Post-it scene, *Divine Intervention*.

had already seen the father fall ill and be hospitalized in previous sequences.

The second storyboard scene begins with ES facing Wall 2: we see ES take a note off the wall and look down to read it (Figure 2). In fact, the note ES picks up from Wall 2 is from the same spot he had placed the note in the first scene. This time, however, the title card reads: *ana majnun 'ashan bahibbek* (I am crazy because I love you). ES does not stick the note back on the wall, but instead the note makes an appearance in the next scene when ES drives to the checkpoint to meet with his girlfriend. As he parks his car next to hers, he rolls up the window with the note stuck on it. The woman gets into his car, after which ES embarks on the only courageous act he takes in the film by taking the risk of crossing the checkpoint with the West Bank woman without the proper permits, taking her with him back to Jerusalem (Figure 3).

Even though in this context the note can be seen as prospective in announcing the next scene, the text that is written on it appears in an earlier scene in the film. In fact, it appears in the Nazareth section as an explanation for the scenes of the man waiting by a

Figure 3   Stills of the phrase "I am crazy because I love you" appearing in other scenes, *Divine Intervention.*

deserted bus stop, knowing very well that no bus passes by there. The last of the man-waiting-at-the-bus-stop scenes finally resolves the mystery of his waiting: the wall next to the bus stop has the sentence "*ana majnun 'ashan bahibbek*" (I am crazy because I love you) spray-painted on it, facing an apartment building where a young woman, his love interest no doubt, lives and is seen peering from the balcony (Figure 3).

The final storyboard scene follows an intense action scene where the female protagonist appears as a *fida'i*. It opens with a medium shot of ES chopping onions in the kitchen, with tears in his eyes. The camera then cuts from the kitchen to a shot of the corridor, where we see ES standing between the two walls of Post-it notes. First ES takes a row of about five notes off Wall 1, the same row he had previously taken notes off. He stops, looks down at the notes, and turns to look at Wall 2. The camera cuts again and we see ES walk over to Wall 2. He no longer has the other notes in his hand, and instead, walks up to the wall and removes one of the notes (yet again, it is the note three rows down, second column).

He looks down at it, and the title card reads: *yamut al-ab* (father dies). The camera cuts back to ES's profile holding the note. He then tears it up (Figure 4).

The storyboard scenes are, if anything, ambiguous. The notes and their related title cards correspond to a number of scenes in the film, either retrospectively or prospectively. The retrospective notes give the sense that ES, a character in the film, is reflecting upon earlier scenes of the film within the film, while the prospective notes imply that he has control over the progression and content of the scenes. Even though ES's relationship to the film as a whole remains ambiguous, the film is imbued with the effect of immediacy and existing in the present.

What is curious about the second Post-it scene and the sentence "*ana majnun 'ashan bahibbek*" is how it came to be in ES's possession as a sticky note after we had seen it written on the wall in the scene of the man-waiting-for-the-bus. Even though the film has a voyeuristic feeling to it, the collection of disparate sequences in the Nazareth section are narrated by an omniscient narrator rather than from the perspective of any particular character. In fact, ES does not

Figure 4   Stills and title card from the final Post-it scene, *Divine Intervention*.

make an appearance in the Nazareth section until after his father falls ill. So if ES was not observing the Nazareth sequences, one interpretation of how he comes to be familiar with the sentence *ana majnun* is if he is already familiar with the film that we are watching. In other words, there is an element of premeditation and the character of ES appears to have a prior relationship to the film. This ambiguity in the narrative raises questions about who or what it is that is generating the narrative.

Based on the presence of the character of ES in his earlier films, the viewer can assume to a certain degree that Suleiman's on-screen persona in *Divine Intervention* is also a filmmaker. Taking this interpretation further, and seeing that the storyboard is flexible in nature, narratives and story lines change spots during the course of the film, dependent, it seems, on external factors. Since the dedication at the end of the film reads *ila dhikra abi* (in memory of my father), and two out of the three Post-it notes relate to the father's illness and subsequent death, it is not difficult to see that the film reflects the process of being at the mercy of a real-life trajectory of events, and thus the clear parallels to events in Suleiman's own life. In other words, Suleiman exposes the process of filmmaking as a construction, but the effect he achieves is not one that stresses: "this is a film – not reality," on the contrary, the construction of the film appears to be constrained and influenced by real events.

In Suleiman's film self-reflexive elements reveal the influence of real-life events on the narrative structure and how autobiography and fiction intertwine and coexist. In both cases there is a desire to resolve the dichotomy between fiction and reality by using self-reflexive techniques to raise questions about how narratives are constructed, to make autobiographical references, and in Habibi's case to ground the work in a socio-political and historical context directly.

Conclusion

This chapter looked at the narration of the Palestinian-Israeli conflict over history, territory and narrative in the works of two Palestinian citizens of Israel whose absurd lives are reflected in non-linear, multi-layered, fragmented, but rich narratives. I looked at a number of documenting techniques used primarily by Habibi to assert presence in the face of imposed absence. Two examples of direct in-text interjections were the recording of names of Palestinian villages destroyed in 1948, and the long view of the histories of Palestinian cities, such as the city of Acre. A unique example of indirect interjection of non-fictional information on Palestinian history and culture is Habibi's use of footnotes as a parallel text that comments on and rewrites history.

The association between history and territory is a corner stone to Habibi's *al-Waqa'i' al-ghariba*, while a sense of de-territorialization and fragmentation is characteristic of Suleiman's *Divine Intervention*, where spaces do not connect and journeys across a Palestinian geography become impossible. Suleiman's narrative structure of the *yawmiyyat*, embedded with the intense observations of the everyday and the minute details of life imbues his film with the sense of ahistoricism, and the dissociation of territory from history. This is a characteristic of a number of narratives that have emerged in the post-Oslo era which saw the collapse of an overarching grand view of history and adherence to a national project.

A sense of disillusionment but also an awareness of the creation and manipulation of narratives, especially historical narratives, is reflected in the Habibi's and Suleiman's self-reflexive narratives. These narratives expose the mechanics of each of their media and draw attention to how narratives are constructed, questioning, ultimately, where truth lies amidst conflictual layers of narrative.

Notes

1. Linda Butler, (2003) "The Occupation (and Life) through an Absurdist Lens: An Interview with Elia Suleiman," *Journal of Palestine Studies*, 32(2): 70, 2003: 70.
2. Edward Said, (1980) *The Question of Palestine* (London and Henley: Routledge & Kegan Paul), p. 153.
3. Sabry Hafez, (1996) "Obituary: Emile Habibi," *The Independent*, 1996, http://www.independent.co.uk/news/obituaries/obituary-emile-habibi-1345602.html. Accessed June 23, 2006.
4. Many in the Arab world castigated Habibi for accepting the prize, while right-wing Israelis were hostile to Israel's most prestigious award going to a Palestinian. Habibi, on the other hand, saw it as recognition

of Palestinian national culture, and having accepted the prize donated it to a Palestinian charity.

5. Emile Habibi, (2003), *The Secret Life of Saeed the Pessoptimist*, trans. Salma Khadra Jayyusi and Trevor LeGassick (Moreton-in-Marsh: Arris Books), p. 21. Emile Habibi, *al-Waqa'i' al-ghariba fi ikhtifa' sa'id abi al-nahs al-mutasha'il*, 2006 edn. (Amman: Dar al-Shuruq, 1974), p. 41.

6. Habibi, *Saeed the Pessoptimist*, p. 22. Habibi, *al-Waqa'i' al-ghariba*, p. 33.

7. Habibi, *Saeed the Pessoptimist*, p. 23. Habibi, *al-Waqa'i' al-ghariba*, p. 35.

8. Habibi, *Saeed the Pessoptimist*, p. 23. Habibi, *al-Waqa'i' al-ghariba*, p. 35.

9. Habibi, *Saeed the Pessoptimist*, pp. 23–24. Habibi, *al-Waqa'i' al-ghariba*, pp. 35–36.

10. Habibi, *Saeed the Pessoptimist*, p. 24. Habibi, *al-Waqa'i' al-ghariba*, p.37.

11. Hafez, "Obituary: Emile Habibi."

12. Habibi as quoted in Muhammad Bakr al-Buji, *Imil Habibi bayn al-siyasa wa-l-ibda' al-adabi* (Gaza: 2000), p. 209. My translation.

13. The footnotes in the original Arabic text have unfortunately not been included/translated in the English translation of *al-Waqa'i' al-ghariba*. The examples here are based on the original Arabic text.

14. Habibi, *al-Waqa'i' al-ghariba*, p. 129.

15. Another example of a tongue-in-cheek historicization is Habibi's reference to the "Tripartite Aggression" of Britain, France and Israel against Egypt in 1956 following the nationalization of the Suez Canal as *"amaliyyat qadesh (al-muqaddasa) muthallathat al-rahmat"* [Ibid., p. 65] (the holy al-Kadesh Operation of Triple Mercy). The sense of irony of using this phrase can be extracted from the combination of the footnote and the textual context.

16. Ibid., p. 24.

17. Ibid., p. 33.

18. Werner Huber, Martin Middeke, and Hubert Zapf, "Introduction," in *Self-Reflexivity in Literature*, ed. Werner Huber, Martin Middeke, and Hubert Zapf (Würzburg: Königshausen & Neumann, 2005), p. 8. Huber, Middeke and Zapf cite Shakespeare's *Hamlet*, Cervantes's *Don Quixote*, Laurence Sterne's *Tristram Shandy*, the writings of the Romantics, and the what they refer to as "the inflationary appearance of metafictional texts and genres" (p. 8) in the late twentieth century as examples of works with metafictional traits. A simple definition from the *Penguin Dictionary of Literary Terms and Literary Theory* defines the self-reflexive novel as "a novel in which the author calls the reader's attention to the fact that he or she is writing (or has written) a novel" J.A. Cuddon, *The Penguin Dictionary of Literary Terms and Literary Theory*, (4th edn.; London: Penguin Books, 1998), p. 735.

References
Primary Sources

Habibi, Emile (1974). *al-Waqa'i' al-ghariba fi ikhtifa' sa'id abi al-nahs al-mutasha'il.* 2006 edn. (Amman: Dar al-Shuruq).

—— (2003). *The Secret Life of Saeed the Pessoptimist.* Trans. Salma Khadra Jayyusi and Trevor LeGassick (Moreton-in-Marsh: Arris Books).

Suleiman, Elia (2002). *Yadun ilahiyya: yawmiyyat al-hubb wa al-alam (Divine Intervention).* Humbert Balsan. 90 mins. France/Palestine/Morocco/Germany.

Secondary Sources

Bourland, Anne (2000). "A Cinema of Nowhere: An Interview with Elia Suleiman." *Journal of Palestine Studies,* 29(1): 95–101.

Bresheeth, Haim (2007). "The Continuity of Trauma and Struggle: Recent Cinematic Representations of the Nakba." In *Nakba: Palestine, 1948, and the Claims of Memory.* Ahmad H. Sa'di and Lili Abu-Lughod (eds) (New York: Columbia University Press), pp. 162–83.

al-Buji, Muhammad Bakr (2000). *Imil Habibi bayn al-siyasa wa-l-ibda' al-adabi* (Gaza).

Butler, Linda (2003). "The Occupation (and Life) through an Absurdist Lens: An Interview with Elia Suleiman," *Journal of Palestine Studies,* 32(2): 63–73.

Cuddon, J.A. (1998). *The Penguin Dictionary of Literary Terms and Literary Theory* (4th edn.; London: Penguin Books).

Gertz, Nurith, and George Khleifi (2008). *Palestinian Cinema: Landscape, Trauma, and Memory* (Edinburgh: Edinburgh University Press).

Hafez, Sabry (1996). "Obituary: Emile Habibi," *The Independent.* http://www.independent.co.uk/news/obituaries/obituary-emile-habibi-1345602.html. Accessed June 23, 2006.

Heath, Peter (2000). "Creativity in the Novels of Emile Habibi, with Special Reference to Sa'id the Pessoptimist." In Kamal Abdel-Malek and Wael Hallaq (eds), *Tradition, Modernity and Postmodernity in Arabic Literature: Essays in Honor of Professor Issa J. Boullata* (Leiden, Boston: Koln: Brill), pp. 158–72.

Huber, Werner, Martin Middeke, and Hubert Zapf (2005). "Introduction." In Werner Huber, Martin Middeke and Hubert Zapf (eds), *Self-Reflexivity in Literature* (Würzburg: Königshausen & Neumann), pp. 7–10.

Jarrar, Maher (2002). "A Narration of 'Deterritorialization': Imil Habibi's The Pessoptimist." *Middle Eastern Literatures,* 5(1): 15–28.

Khalidi, Rashid (2006). *The Iron Cage: The Story of the Palestinian Struggle for Statehood* (Boston: Beacon Press).

Khalidi, Walid (1992). *All That Remains: The Palestinian Villages Occupied and Depopulated by Israel in 1948* (Washington, DC: Institute for Palestine Studies).

LeGassick, Trevor (1980). "The Luckless Palestinian." *The Middle East Journal*, 34(2): 215–23.

Naficy, Hamid (2001). *Accented Cinema: Exilic and Diasporic Filmmaking* (Princeton and Oxford: Princeton University Press).

Nünning, Ansgar, and Birgit Neumann (2009). "Metanarration and Metafiction." In Peter Hühn, John Pier, Wolf Schmid and Jörg Schönert (eds), *Handbook of Narratology* (Berlin, New York: Walter de Gruyter), pp. 204–211.

Rountree, Sage Hamilton (2001). "Self-Reflexivity in Woody Allen's Films." In Kimball King (ed.), *Woody Allen: A Casebook* (New York; London: Routledge).

Sa'di, Ahmad H., and Lila Abu-Lughod (2007). "Introduction: The Claims of Memory." In Ahmad H. Sa'di and Lila Abu-Lughod (eds), *Nakba: Palestine, 1948, and the Claims of Memory* (New York: Columbia University Press).

Said, Edward (1980). *The Question of Palestine* (London and Henley: Routledge & Kegan Paul).

Sessona, Anna Zambelli (2001). "Intertextual Strategies and the Poetics of Identity in Imil Habibi's Literary Works." PhD thesis (University of Oxford).

II

DISCOURSES

6

ISLAM IN THE NARRATIVE OF FATAH AND HAMAS

ATEF ALSHAER

Every discourse is situated in language, located in a space and bounded by the conditions of its time, a view espoused by the French thinker Foucault and which has methodological consequences in several fields of study. In the history of the Palestinian national movement, which emerged in the late 1950s to resist and counter Israel, particular discourses with various degrees of hegemony emerged, reflecting the philosophy and politics of the party in power. When Fatah was the key movement in the PLO in the 1960s, 1970s, and to a lesser extent, the 1980s it held sway over other Palestinian discourses, mainly those espoused by the Left, rendering them less visible, therefore, following Foucault, contributing to the institutionalization of power relations and to the diverse levels of representation that undergo discursive shifts as congruent with structural changes.[1] However, power in the context of Palestinian history remains fluid, and even fragmented, given the lack of a state and the long-term conflict with Israel. This conflict, and therefore the history of the Palestinian national movement, cannot be discussed without reference to its aim to challenge the Zionist narrative about Palestine and the entitlement of the Palestinians to it as their land. Simply put, these two discourses, one colonialist and another liberationist, have evolved with time, but have mostly remained unchanged, as the conditions of power and resistance that gave rise to them continue. However, in so far as the liberationist Palestinian side of the discourse is concerned, it had come to acquire new dimensions, as dictated by the emergence of Islamic movements in Palestine and their own discourses equipped with epistemological roots that differ from those which Fatah championed.

Discourse is a source of representation, but it also sets in motion a state of delineation, as it marks out different paradigms of knowledge and authority. Thus, the secularist nationalism that largely defined Fatah is paradigmatically different from Hamas' Islamist-nationalism. Yet, as I have argued elsewhere, both movements have a shared culture of communication and language which propels them to draw on similar historical sources and occurrences in ways that befit their understanding of their past, their involvement in the present and the future path they intend to pursue.[2] Foucault's idea that different discourses mark individual periods of history and are underpinned by political and social discursive shifts is insightful in discussing these two movements and their discourse, but lacks rootedness in history as a continuum with solid basis. Hamas' discourse in the current stage of the Israeli-Palestinian conflict differs notably from the one it put forward when it declared itself officially in 1987, yet it has always drawn on Islamic resources to legitimate and authenticate its views and political stands. Islam therefore is epistemologically essential to its politics. However, Fatah's decline in popularity, as opposed to the rise in Hamas', is grounded in changes in the relations of power, which in return gave rise to particularly corresponding discourses to the new states of power each movement occupies locally, regionally and internationally.

This chapter does not propose to examine the discourses of Hamas and Fatah in their entirety, but aims to focus on one central element defining these discourses, the role of Islam in the history of Fatah and Hamas, within the context of Palestinian politics and the conflict with Israel. Drawing on Foucault's reflections on discourse as a stream of discursive formations, it will highlight the shifts in the discourse of Hamas and Fatah regarding Islam and their relation and interaction with it. Therefore, the chapter aims to answer a set of related questions: to what extent does Islam have a decisive role in the Palestinian public sphere? How influential has Islam been in the formation of politics in its official and everyday sense for both movements? What are the shifts that happened in the discourse of both movements regarding Islam? To engage with these questions, the chapter opens with remarks on discourse and its relevance to the historical and present dimensions embodied in the political evolution of Hamas and Fatah.

The Call of Politics: Islam in a Dynamic Perspective

Islam has never been absent from the history of Fatah, a secular movement which emerged in the heyday of Arab nationalism in the 1960s. Indeed, Yasir Arafat, Fatah leader and later the first Palestinian President, used it constantly to draw connections between the Palestinian struggle and past Islamic struggles and causes (see Johnson, 1982). There has been repeated drawing on Islamic history and its foundational frame of reference, such as Jihad, by the traditional Palestinian leadership, so as to widen the scope of the Palestinian struggle and rally Muslims around the cause (Pappé, 2010). Johnson explicates the use of such concepts in Islamic and secular contexts in revealing ways:

> At the lexicographic level, the key symbol jihad has clear metonymic links to the other terms in its semantic field. But the way it exists in Palestinian political culture is ambiguous, allowing it to also occupy the secular-nationalist field and, for example, be linked to such symbols as *thawrah* (revolution) and *isti'mar* (colonialism).
>
> In other words, the neat lexicographic semantic fields collapse and as they use key symbols are seen to form a tightly interwoven pattern of metaphor, cross-meanings and oblique references in addition to their metonymically structured formal lexicography. (Johnson, 1982: 74)

Johnson's analysis suggests that Islam serves multiple purposes through the use of key symbolic semantic fields with extensive historical and social dimensions. This was, in fact, the case with Fatah and other secularist-nationalist movements in the Arab world: the use of Islam was restricted and limited to occasions, places and contexts where it added to the political capital of Fatah. Thus, we find the concept of Jihad or *istishhaad* (martyrdom) being used by Arafat during his pilgrimage to Mecca in 1974, his visit to Iran in 1980 (where the word *Mujahideen* was used), but not in the United

Nations General Assembly when Arafat gave his famous speech "The Gun and the Olive Branch" in 1974.[3] Therefore, historically, in the case of Fatah, Islam was narrowly channeled into areas where there is a fitting context in the sense of a tangible political gain, such as in the presence of Islami/c/st-minded-groups or countries, like Iran.

However, with the emergence of the Palestinian Islamic Hamas, the use of Islam changed fundamentally, so that Islam has become associated more with a political gain or with the aim of evoking the sympathy of fellow Muslims. For Hamas, Islam is not only a religion, but a basis on which to build its ideology while projecting it on the people as integral to their identity. What had changed fundamentally with the establishment of Hamas was that Islam had become "officially" determinant of life, used not merely tactically here and there to galvanize support and stir emotions; it was at the core of what Marx considered the base-structure of life, where a society can be explained by the fundaments of its beliefs and culture, which he (narrowly) referred to as subservient to the economic mode/s in question. But Hamas' version of Islam, as Lybarger (2007) insightfully explained, took notice of nationalism and the concept of the nation-state, integrating its discourse into an Islamist paradigm with the theme of national inclusiveness at its heart:

> This shift required a reinterpretation of core ideological principles, strategy, and tactics among the new generation of Islamist activists. The most important ideological shift was to subordinate the goal of reviving the *umma*, worldwide Islamic community, to a seemingly more limited objective— the retrieval of the nation's patrimony...that gave Islamist credibility within the wider society. (ibid., 2007: 9–10)

Thus, every shift in Hamas' ideology was/is constituted within an Islamic discourse that justifies and concretizes it. From its very inception, Hamas was conscious of Islam, in which it wanted to mould the Palestinian identity. The Islamic University in Gaza, the Islamic society center which it ran and later gave way to the name "The Islamic Resistance Movement Hamas," the various statements it released at the beginning of the *Intifada* of 1987, the proliferation of concepts such as "Islamic project" and "Islamic awakening," all these had political roots and associations with Islam at their heart; all allude to a state of resurrection of an Islamic identity championed by Hamas on behalf of a people long dominated by secular nation-statist (and leftist) approaches. An examination of the early communiqués of Hamas, the principal means by which Hamas disseminated its ideology to people, reveals the concerns and attitudes of Hamas. These include the liberation of Palestine, its Islamic reclamation and redemption from the Zionists who are portrayed as desecrators of *al-Aqsa* mosque and other Islamic shrines in Palestine, the regulation of behaviors such as the necessity of decorum in women's dress, the holding of prayers in public and exhortation for alms-giving, the extensive use of Qur'anic verses and Islamic sayings from the traditions of the Prophet, which cover various topics such as "martyrdom," "fighting," "steadfastness," "unity" and "decorum," etc. (see Legrain and Pierre, 1991). All these aims signaled an Islamic beginning to an Islamic movement which had gradually thrust itself into Palestinian politics through documents, statements and communiqués, interrelated aspects with what can be called coherent regularity which furnished what Foucault (1969: 41) tentatively defined as a discursive shift: "Whenever one can describe, between a number of statements, such a system of dispersion, whenever, between objects, types of statement, concepts, or thematic choices, one can define a regularity (an order, correlations, positions, and functioning, transformations), we will say, for the sake of convenience, that we are dealing with a discursive formation...".

However, though skilful and resilient in reiterating its principled views, Hamas had shown signs of change, which to some observers seem radical and far-reaching enough to qualify as inimical to the values it had initially stood by. Most notably, they point to the fact that eminent Hamas leaders had come to accept United Nations Resolutions 242 and 338, which call for the withdrawal of Israel to 1967 borders, thus following on the footsteps of its rival Fatah, which had officially recognized these resolutions in 1988 during the declaration of Palestinian independence from Algeria (see Said, 1994, Hroub, 2006/2000). This process of change within Hamas with respect to fundamental aspects of the Israeli-Palestinian conflict has important connotations. Hamas seems to have moved away from its early uncompromising position which linked the land of Palestine to Islam in such a way that it considered the perseveration and liberation of land as a matter of theological importance, an Islamic obligation over which no concessions can be offered, though such a position had never disappeared from Hamas' discourse.

As Hamas embraced a solution along 1967 borders, it adopted a discourse which to some extent is reminiscent of the discourses of the Palestine Liberation Organization (PLO) in the 1970s and 1980s, a discourse in which symbolism is more important than concrete political practices and convictions. The position and practices of Hamas reveal that, on the one hand, it is steadfast on its pledges and positions, and, on the other, it is adaptive and flexible with the evolution of times, as will be explained further in this chapter. Given the expansiveness of Islam in terms of the textual and rhetorical canon, the incidents and interpretations within which it is constituted, Hamas has at its disposal a rich heritage with historical depth which can be drawn on at various junctures and different contexts. As such, linguistically, Islamic movements, and Hamas is no exception in this regard, tend to be ambiguous as to what their real objectives are, given the multiple frames of reference available to them as well as their mutability. The fact that religion, however it can be defined as, seems to be beyond definite seizure or control in so far as how people refer and use it. Thus, the transcendental is thrust into the mundane and earthly ambiguity becomes *de facto*; for the transcendental, even if historical, is marketed as a belief system with indefinite boundaries. What this means is that the Islam/s that Hamas draws on is steeped in empowering sentiments by which people can be mobilized and reassured of victory, while at the same time helping with endurance in the face of intractable and long-term conflict and violence.

Discourses in Opposition

Almost all theories of discourse highlight the point that ideologies and discourses that represent them are born of rivalry and difference with others; so each discourse stands to contrast with another to which it somehow sets itself as corrective (see McDonell

1986: passim). Since its emergence as a political party, Hamas has been a rival to Fatah, the mainstream party within the PLO. Its project, which was concerned with diverse issues other than only politics, appeared as oppositional to the PLO goal of liberating Palestine and establishing a state on a secular and civic basis. It is true that some affiliates of the PLO seemed to have come from Islamic-orientated origins that hark back to the Muslim Brotherhood in Egypt, which was founded by Hassan al-Banna in 1928. However, once the military and political powerbase of the PLO was launched and entrenched by the late 1960s and 1970s (see Sayigh, 1999), a new era of struggle with considerable more worldly overtones began to emerge as the Palestinian struggle against Israel was influenced by other struggles in Algeria, secular pan-Arabism, and anti-colonialist fights in Vietnam and other places. It is possible to find an abundance of references to these struggles and their significance in the statements and communiqués of the PLO and Fatah in the 1970s and 1980s (Legrain and Pierre, 1991). The fruits of these struggles were still ripening and offering themselves to the PLO in the form of intellectual and political solidarity from various directions with secular objectives and attitudes. Thus the late 1960s, 1970s and 1980s are periods of political and cultural cultivation that benefited from struggles that proved promising, and in certain cases, successful. In this context, Islam was relegated to minor spheres without literal impingement on the cultural and political practices.

Hamas, however, appeared within a context radically different from that within which the PLO/Fatah grew out of. Hamas was largely home-grown; its leaders, such as Ahmad Yasin, Abdel Aziz al-Rantisi, Mahmoud al-Zahar and others, found in Islam and its history an answer to long periods of struggle that stumbled upon crisis, periods during which Islam was not centrally considered in the ideological and intellectual milieu of the PLO (see Tamimi, 2007).[4] In particular, the departure of the PLO from Lebanon in 1982 appeared to have opened a political opportunity, which Islamists were conscious of seizing. None of the movements that rivaled (and intermittently fought) Fatah to that point, such as the Popular Front for the Liberation of Palestine (PFLP) and other splinter groups from Fatah and the PFLP, had formed a serious opposition to Fatah. Only Hamas, with its distinct ideology and discourse had managed to break through and upturn the picture of Palestinian politics and culture. The political climate was conducive enough for Hamas to thrive and grow. It is noteworthy in this context that the rising stock of Islamist politics in Palestine was not significantly a generational issue as some analysts put it (Lybarger, 2008: 6).[5] In fact, the leaders of Hamas, whether from Gaza or the West Bank, were of the same age group as that of the leaders of Fatah in 1987 when Hamas was officially founded. Ahmad Yasin, the founding father of Hamas, Abdel Aziz al-Rantisi, Mahmoud al-Zahar and Abd al-Fatah Dukhan, all experienced the beginning of the Palestinian revolution as young observers in the 1960s, studying at universities in Egypt and elsewhere. At that time, they did not put themselves at the forefront of the struggle, as they did later wholeheartedly. They restricted their activities to the social and cultural fields carried out in particular by the Islamic collective "al-mujamma' al-Islami" which was founded in 1974 by Ahmad Yasin (see Hroub, 2000 and 2006, Lybarger, 2008). Instead, they witnessed the rise and fall of secular movements before stepping in to effectively take a leading political role as serious leadership crisis loomed over the struggle with Israel, with visible signs of disgruntlement and suspicion from people who appeared to take a concessionary political path, namely the PLO, in opposition to which Hamas set itself up as an assiduous rival (see Lybarger, 2007: 80–85) and perhaps in time a liquidator.[6]

Regional political dynamics helped Hamas and its leaders a great deal in this respect, as did their discourse which linked Palestine with broader struggles and inflected it with a new identity that reminded Palestinians of and rallied them around a paradigm of a dignified Islamic past in which Muslims were masters of their own fate and not subjected to colonial humiliations or betrayal of their leaderships, which framed the various concessions and gestures of the PLO towards Israel and international powers.[7] In this context, Hamas' weapon consisted of words and statements which signaled a defiant continuity of the revolution which the PLO started, as was explained above. Therefore, it can be argued that there is a considerable misunderstanding on the part of analysts who downplay the role of Islam in the popularity of Hamas and the effectiveness of its Islamic discourse, giving weight along the way to the material conditions and causes against which the ideological positions of Hamas had not been questioned vigorously. Hamas was not tested on its ideas and attitudes regarding the conflict, the PLO and other secular factions, as much as on its actions and effectiveness which, given the political vacuum mentioned above, seemed robust and effective, drawing people to trust their own power and endure against odds.

Hamas took an active part in the Palestinian struggle, deploying along the way a discourse of sacrifice and selflessness which was felt all over the Palestinian territories as more Hamas cadres and members bore the brunt of the increasingly aggressive and relentless Israeli assaults during the second Palestinian *Intifada* which began in September 2000, suffering harsh fates including killing, imprisonment, exile and house demolitions. The visibility of Hamas through actions as well as defiant and powerful communication systems and practices within the context of the weakness of the PLO and Fatah had finally paid off. Hamas won the parliamentary elections in 2006 and gradually undermined its archrival Fatah's authority and power by militarily ending its rule in Gaza in July 2007 through a short-lived civil war from which Hamas emerged victorious and in sole control of Gaza. Throughout this period, Hamas painted Fatah, the PLO and the Palestinian Authority—entities which with time had become hardly distinct—as unrepentantly corrupt and untrustworthy and on occasion as renegades "*murtadeen*" and "*mushrikeen*," terms which belong to the same religious semantic field that suggests they have given up on religion and therefore they deserved the worst of punishment. Secularism, socialism and even communism, terms which once enjoyed acceptance and adoption, had become tainted with negative political and religious connotations, forcing even Fatah to lessen their use and importance. This in effect meant Fatah had to rival Hamas in its use and manipulation of Islam in order to be viewed as mindful of Islam and its alleged relevance to the Palestinian struggle. But as will be further highlighted, Fatah and Hamas operated with different fields of power, which dictated their discourses and subsequently impacted their appeal to the Palestinian public.

Ideology Practiced

Ideological discourses are reinforced through processes of reiteration, whereby the narrowly nationalist or Islamist tenets are repeatedly articulated to authenticate and ascertain the ideology in question. On its 23rd anniversary, the prominent Hamas leader and former Palestinian prime minister Ismail Haniyya (2006–July 2007) highlighted the origins of Hamas and its source of inspiration in the following terms:

> During these events [he refers to the first Palestinian *Intifada*] we resurrected and rejuvenated the vitality of this great religion (Islam) in making big events, and we interacted with this. The mosque played a big role in the Intifada of the stones: the establishment of Hamas was in the mosque, the launching of al-Qassam (the military wing of Hamas) was in the mosque, and the revolution of al-Buraq was in the mosque (1929)[8] ... Today, we recall the saying of Omar Bin Al-Khattab (the Second Caliphate of Islam, 634–644 AD), "we are a people exalted by Islam; if we search for dignity somewhere else, God would humiliate us...". (December 14, 2010)

The use of such a statement from the Islamic heritage highlights the conceptual chain to which Hamas links itself so as to display rootedness in an old culture of communication that is perceived as a standard model of governance and social organization.

Once Hamas had taken control of Gaza in July 2007, a total siege was imposed on it by Israel and regional and international powers, a siege which left Hamas in a state of isolation and rendered Gaza poorer and more destitute than ever. In this atmosphere, the levels of religiosity and piety inside Gaza increased to the point where Hamas found itself rivaling even more religious groups than itself, namely Salafi, al-Qaeda-oriented Islamists which call for the establishment of an Islamic state with strict and literal application of Sharia rule. Hamas launched massive attacks against them and their followers to the point of almost total obliteration.[9] To justify its position, Hamas used its old standing foster-mother, the Muslim Brotherhood's view, that it is moderate in its application of Islam and that those Salafi and al-Qaeda groups have deviated from the message of moderation which stands at the heart of Islam, quoting the Qur'anic verse, "And so we made you a moderate nation, *ummatan wasata"* (al-baqara/143). From such an incident, we notice the potency of Foucault's analysis regarding power and the intrinsic imperatives which it sets in motion, as it becomes an end in itself alongside it being a means to perfect the hegemonic status quo and sustain its grip on power, a practice of domination which Hamas and Fatah follow unabatedly.

Meanwhile, Hamas opted to impose stricter rules in Gaza, issuing decrees towards disallowing women from working in court as judges, closing down hair-dressers operated by women, banning women from wearing swimming suits on the beach, disallowing them from smoking water pipes outside their homes, alongside other oppressive prohibitions and practices. All these decrees were imposed on the grounds that they are not in tandem with the traditions and customs of the Palestinian people and are contradictory to Islamic norms. In this respect, Hamas has in mind a particular view of what Palestine and its people should be. To this end, its leaders have taken hold of the mosques and appear constantly in them to fend off charges and complaints against them, their movement and government, as well as to introduce new policies. Some Hamas leaders, such as Mahmoud al-Zahar, saw in their victory in the parliamentary election an embracement of their social and political views, which are regulated and bounded by religion, thus viewing it as a sign of an "Islamic awakening," *sahwa Islamiyya,* as opposed to an outcome of rotten political conditions in which people saw Hamas as an alternative to Fatah which was weakened by its own corruption, unpopular political schemes and dogged rivalry with other political forces, such as Hamas. Therefore, when Hamas was named and presented as an Islamic movement, its leaders meant that Islam will guide its politics; the past, no matter how distant or irrelevant, would be thrust into the present so as to ultimately reproduce a perceived Islamic ideal, as has been promulgated in various treatises written by Hamas leaders, most notably Mushir al-Masir (see Alshaer, 2008). The movement is referred to by its leaders as *haraka rabbaniyyah* (divine movement), and its leader Ahmad Yasin as *qaa'id rabbaani* (divine leader). Mushir al-Masri referred to Hamas on its 23rd anniversary (December 14, 2010) as "an extension to the call (meaning the founding and spread of Islam) of the Prophet Muhammad."

The mosque had always been and remains Hamas' most important center of power, where Hamas affiliates disseminate their views, defend them, create dominant cultural values and state and reiterate political positions. The mosque is the place where various practices of piety are repeatedly exhibited, as Hamas leaders lead people in prayers and dictate to them through religious discourse underpinned by a blend of socio-political views and religious attitudes. For example, as Hamas held a strong grip on Gaza, and sensed some dismay among many of the people, it paid attention to its popularity and to the importance of maintaining its socio-political stature by organizing collective visits, which set off from mosques to houses so as to give people presents (sweets), with endearing messages on them, such as "From Hamas with love." It also organized collective prayers to celebrate the "*Eid* as well as prayers to call on God for rain, *salaat al-Itstiqa*" (the rain prayer). Thus, the mosque has been central to the formation and spread of Hamas' ideology. In addition, throughout its history, Hamas has exhibited acts of violence as well as charitable kindness, being a shrewd movement, capable of defining moves with social and political effects, since hegemony, as Gramsci contends, shows itself in several terrains, social, political and legal.

Given the shared culture of communication of the Arabs, as described at the outset, Hamas has also won many supporters and sympathizers within the Arab world and abroad, who defend its positions, whether from a political or religious perspective or both, most notably Al Jazeera, which publishes articles by Hamas members, hosts its leaders and often paints them in a favorable light, namely that it is a victim of the siege, it is defiant, and that it is protective of Palestinian rights.[10] In short, Hamas has come a long way since its establishment towards becoming a major force in Palestine with a particular Islamic worldview that has supporters abroad and can be enforced inside Palestine. Therefore, it is important to explain Hamas within its various dimensions, without marginalizing or undermining its sources of inspiration and motivation which underpin its endurance and steadfastness. For example, the group makes use of old and modern Islamic sources and figures to underline rootedness and relative adaptability at the same time. To this end, it refers to figures such the theologian and writer Ibn Taymiyya (1262–1327) to reinforce its righteousness and defiance, as in the following statement of Ibn Taymiyya, which had been reproduced in various occasions: "What can my enemies do to me? My heaven and garden are in my bosom … my killing is martyrdom, my prison is a time of privacy; my exile is tourism."[11]

The relevant question at this juncture is how its archrival, Fatah, fared within the context of the ascendance of Hamas and the Islamic discourse that it championed? This question is posed with the theoretical point in mind that discourses are, more often than not, set in opposition to other views and positions. As we learn from Gramsci, Foucault, Hall and other theorists of society and politics, the hegemony of the social and political spheres established through consent is often preceded and accompanied by a discourse congruent with what the agents set themselves the objective of establishing in terms of cultural values, political views and attitudes. In addition, as has been argued elsewhere, societies differ in terms of articulating their political priorities, depending on the challenges of the present and the contingency of the past.

In Arab societies, the past has always been a pivot around which the present revolves, given the language, the shared cultural and historical heritage, the assurance and confidence embedded in past achievements, all of which ground the present, and endow it with authenticity and legitimacy (see Alshaer, 2008: 101–121). Yet, with the diversity of Arab societies and widening gaps in their economic, educational and political makeup, the degree of oscillation between the relevance of the past and the present is a space of contestation. There are some who insist on modernity and its political and social associations, secularism and liberalism, and there are others who prefer an integration of the past into the present so that the religious institutions have a say in the politics of the day. This is a contest that has not been settled in the Arab world so far and one that has roots that hark back to earlier centuries, particularly to the period which Albert Hourani described as the "Liberal Age in the Arab World: 1798–1939," a period characterized by the appeal of the nation-state and its modernist imperatives. This bears directly on the relationship between Hamas and Fatah, as two mainstream political parties, with different views as to the relevance of the past and the needs of the present as well as the form of Palestinian state and society each envisages. Given the fact that both Hamas and Fatah share a rich culture of communication, the question becomes why Hamas' discourse appeared more congruent with political facts and therefore attractive to the public while Fatah lost its historical credibility and civic credentials as opposed to Hamas' religious dimensions, as explained above?

The Long Arms of Power

Given the discussion at hand, it can be argued that movements with ties to international powers limit the discourse of their subservient supporters (or clients), aiding and bestowing legitimacy on them in return for agreements that satisfy their demands. This is so because powers such as the USA have the capacity to create realities and influence events on a global scale.[12] In so far as the notion of the culture of communication is concerned and in view of the argument that each language is embedded in a historical trajectory with particular cultural traits which differ from other cultures and languages, it can be argued that diplomacy across languages/cultures of communication, with imbalanced power relations, implies the possibility of compromise at the level of discourse.[13] In the case of the Israeli-Palestinian conflict, this has clear manifestations. Fatah's political position, and its acceptance by Western powers after the Oslo Accords in 1993, limited its discourse. While drawing on the extensive and expansive culture of communication of the Arab world, Fatah did not have as much freedom as Hamas to be ambiguous or vague in terms of its political position and "final" objectives; Fatah's position had been translated into agreements and accords with Israel, supervised and encouraged by western powers. In this sense, Fatah's secular credentials were compromised or perhaps reduced particularly because the main objective of the Palestinian national struggle since 1948, which Fatah championed, has been concerned with liberation from Israel as an occupying power. In contrast, Hamas flourished within its discourse of resistance and liberation in so far as it only seemed to answer to its principles and its supporters in the Arab world. It could draw freely on the rich Arab culture of communication, constituted within longstanding historical records expressed in cultural, political and literary dimensions. While this rich cultural background also aided Fatah, it was to a much lesser extent than Hamas.

As highlighted above, Fatah leaders always made references to Islam, but these references never developed to the point of constituting a coherent worldview, an ideology. Many Fatah affiliates come from Muslim backgrounds, and therefore, Islam was inevitably incorporated into its ambience. Fatah still presents itself as a secularist-nationalist movement; but as it competes with Hamas, Islam made headway into its discourse. President Arafat throughout the 1990s had to argue and discuss from a political, pragmatist as well as Islamic religious perspective. He intensified the use of Qur'anic verses in relation to Jerusalem, land and other political and social domains. Palestinians became accustomed to hearing verses along the lines of "be patient because Allah loves the patient," and other promising reassuring Qur'anic references: "They will enter the mosque (the Muslims, al-Aqsa), as they entered it the first time," an allusion to the Muslims who first entered Jerusalem in 637 AD and ended the Byzantine rule of the city. Also, Arafat's successor as a Palestinian President, Mahmoud Abbas denounced Hamas' actions in Gaza following its dismissal of Fatah from there, using a Qur'anic verse which suggests they have violated the conciliatory agreement that was signed with them in Mecca in 2007. He expended some time discussing how Islam divorces politics from religion in its practical and ascetic sides, how Islam is not how Hamas integrates it into its politics. Thus, one can speak of a shift during the 1990s and the first half of the decade of 2010 in the use of Islam in so far as Fatah is concerned.

Yet, to reiterate the contention above, Fatah is tied to international powers and structures, which purport to be secular. Because of its link and to some extent subservience to these powers in economic and political terms, its frames of reference are often international norms and standards. As such, its discourse on the local level remains nationalist/liberationist, flavored when necessary and appealing to local audiences with Islamic references that reinforce a modern nation-state outlook, even if such a nation-state is hardly existent. This aids Fatah, the mainstream party in the PLO, to hold discussions with international parties and bodies without Islamic theological considerations in so far as its political discussions are concerned.[14] Whereas for Hamas, politics or what had come to be known among Islamists as "Sharia-based politics," *al-Siyasah al-Shar'iyyah*—should be squared and grounded in Islam with its permissions and prohibitions. Hence publications and the use of religious figures and authorities to sanctify what sound like modern political positions with which Hamas constituents might not feel at ease, given the projection of its Islamic outlook.

Conclusion

As Foucault suggests, power is entrenched in discourses that legitimize and normalize it. Yet power as associated with political and social currents is often embedded with a fluid historical continuum, which changes in accordance with the imperatives of the present. In the context of Palestine and the Arab world, more broadly, the past and the present are not mutually exclusive; they feed into each other depending on the particular ideology and context at hand. This is true in the case of Fatah and Hamas, which were born of different historical conditions, developed in divergent ways and became attached to different powers, while acutely competing with each other to attain the ultimate power of representation for Palestine and its cause. They are the two political movements that champion the Palestinian cause against those who created it in the first place: the Zionists on whose shoulders Israel was founded in Palestine. Philosophically, however, they embrace dissimilar worldviews that stem from different consideration of the Islamic past and its present relevance, and the historical and political conditions that give rise to and sustain each movement.

The PLO of which Fatah is the chief component was vocal about its Arab credentials, emphasizing from the beginning the Arab character of Palestine, with its diverse religions, Muslim, Christian and Jewish. Therefore, Islam, in its textual and ritualistic dimensions such as the Qur'an and the Prophet's sayings, was not an integral part of its discourse. Though its leaders (and affiliates) used Islamic concepts, such as *Jihad* and *Istishhaad*, martyrdom, in the course of the Palestinian struggle, these concepts were not constituents of an ideological paradigm. They were given cultural and nationalist inflections grounded with an anti-colonial discourse for the liberation of the land and its people from the Israeli occupation. Fatah, in the character of its leader Yasir Arafat, was aware of the centrality of Palestine to the Muslim World and voiced this wherever there was an immediate political benefit, as was explained above.

However, Islam is integral to the identity of Hamas. Given the theoretical point alluded to at the outset that Islam is to some extent an ideological abstraction, Hamas appended to its Islamic identity the feature of *al-wastiyya* (moderation). Thus emerged the concept of *al-Islam al-Wasati* (moderate Islam), which is supposed to lessen the force of dogma and be mindful of the imperatives of reality. Palestine, for Hamas, is an Arab and Islamic land in which all religions can live under an Islamic tutelage of some kind. In its day-to-day politics, Hamas oscillates between pragmatic considerations and an Islamic ethos that it purports to uphold and spread. As Hamas gained popularity, culminating in its victory in the 2006 parliamentary elections and control over Gaza, it has continually attempted to reason away its actions through religious edicts and language so as to keep the link with its religious base. Meanwhile, Hamas deployed a pragmatic language which painted the Palestinian Authority and Fatah as untrustworthy in so far as the Palestinian cause is concerned and what it needs in terms of liberation and determination. Hamas convinced many people of its narrative regarding Fatah given the failure of the peace process and the frustration with its unsound premises. Fatah, on the other hand, alarmed by Hamas and its Islamic exhortations and its frequent strident religious tone, attempts to reclaim its pluralistic view of the Palestinian people, while hinting towards being mindful of Islam. And thus the battle of narratives continues between the two major political parties whose differences have driven them to costly and stifling disputes, while the Palestinians and Palestine continue to bleed under the Israeli occupation, the actions of which reinforce division and bitter disputes over strategy, tactics and the identity of the Palestinian people.

Notes

1. See Foucault (2002 [1969]) for a comprehensive explication of various fields of study, linguistics, biology, and archaeology, through the discourses and the epistemological shifts which he subscribes to their evolution.
2. See Alshaer (2008: 101–112) for an elaborate description of the notion of culture of communication.

3. The language used in that long speech was worldly in character to appeal to the world to rectify the injustice committed against the Palestinian people. It highlighted the Arab ownership of Palestine, depicted Zionism as an extension of colonialism and imperialism and called on the ex-colonized to stand by the Palestinian people in their struggle against it. There was no appeal to the Islamic world in particular, but an international one to galvanize the support of the world to turn its back on racism and Zionism, which are equated in the speech. For the full speech, see the link: http://electronicintifada. net/bytopic/historicalspeeches/305.shtml.

4. Tamimi, a Hamas sympathizer, summarizes the situation regarding Hamas' and Fatah's positions as follows: "it seems that the issue of the Hamas charter formed part of the ongoing process of competition with the PLO. The PLO charter was utterly secular, and therefore did not reflect the Islamic identity of the Palestinian people or their cause" (2006: 151).

5. In fact, it terms of its beginnings, Hamas seemed immersed in rivalry and competition with others. It nervously declared itself in 1987 after it was irked by another Islamist movement that emerged and appeared to gain momentum at the beginning of the 1980s, namely Islamic Jihad, which was inspired by the Iranian revolution of 1979 (see Lybarger 2007: 83–4).

6. In a speech in Doha on January 2009, Khalid Mashal, the chief Bureau of Hamas, announced "a surprise," which consisted of a new political body, *marji'yya wataniyya,* that he claims would represent the Palestinians inside and outside Palestine. When asked about the weak state of the PLO, he replied with a verse from the Qur'an, which implies that Hamas' time had come and the PLO had had run its historical course: "And these days (with varying conditions) we alternate among the people" (3/140).

7. The idea of Hamas as fighters who are steadfast on their principles was echoed by Sheikh Yousef al-Qaradwi, who is in the position of the president of the organization of the Muslims' scholars. He had helped in consolidating and legitimating Hamas' ideological positions to the point of discounting the PLO as irrelevant anymore. Thus, he stated, "In Gaza Strip, there is now steadfastness and diligent work. Gaza had become a banned area for the Israelis, and if they could go there, they would have gone and humiliated the mujahedeen there... The PLO had gone to perdition and it is not possible to speak about the existence of a Palestinian authority under the occupation" (Qaradwi, January 3, 2010, my trans.). Al-Qaradawi and other Muslim Brotherhood figures cement Hamas' views and positions.

8. Al-Buraq is the Muslim name given to the area (the Western Wall of al-Aqsa mosque) containing what the Jews describe as the Wailing Wall. This area triggered the Palestinian revolution in 1929 as Palestinians demonstrated against the British who gave further access to the Jews on the site at the expense of the Palestinians and in defiance of their religious attachment to this place (see Pappé 2010: 233–45). Hamas claims this revolution to be inspired by Islamic considerations and led by Islamist leaders, such as the cleric Izz al-Din al-Qassam, hence the name of its military wing after the Sheikh Izz ad-Din al-Qassam.

9. On August 24, 2009, Hamas armed members attacked a mosque in Rafah which is named after Ibn Taymiyya, ironically one of the figures that inspires and sustains its ideology. It killed Dr Abdel Latif Musa and scores of others of his Salfiyya movement who barricaded themselves in the mosque, from which they declared an Islamic state in Gaza in defiance of Hamas rule.

10. See Al Jazeera and its coverage of the 23rd anniversary of Gaza, which included a number of articles by Hamas leaders and sympathizers defending its historical record, attitudes and political positions.

11. The name of Ibn Taymiyya appears in many writings by Islamists, including Hamas leaders and intellectuals. Ibn Taymiyya's daring personality which challenged the authorities of the Tatars who ruled Baghdad in the thirteenth century and fought them in 1302 landed him in prison more than once, seven times in total. It is noteworthy that Ibn Taymiyya carried out an action which strictly speaking contradicted Islamic teachings: he exhorted Muslims to break their fast in Ramadan to enable them to fight the Tatars effectively, over which the Mamluks finally triumphed. He was also imprisoned by the Mamluks in the castle of Alexandria and the castle of Damascus where he spent the last two years of his life. His views on several issues, theological, political, literary and linguistic are constituted in various writings, one of which that finds echoes in the writings of Hamas and other Islamic movements is entitled *al-Siyassah al-Shar'iyyah* "Sharia-based politics," or "legitimate politics." He also authored a book which pays attention to language, in which he promulgates the idea that the Qur'an does not contain figurative or metaphors. By suggesting this, Ibn Taymiyya meant to halt the train of interpretations which were gaining currency and giving rise to "liberal schools of interpretation" such as al-mu'tazilla and al-ash'ariyyah and others. The statement quoted within the text is one that Hamas members are aware of and it is a source of inspiration and assurance, given the hardships

many of them faced. Thus, the pragmatic and dogmatic aspects in Ibn Taymiyya's life find echoes in Hamas' ideology and practices. See Ismail Al-Qiratli's essay on Ibn Taymiyya, "Ibn Taymiyya: Intellectual and physical battles, 'ma'arik al-fikr wa-silah'" (Al Jazeera, December 28, 2010, http://www.aljazeera.net/NR/exeres/492984D1–7FE1–4191-AEC3–754F09DE6EDC.htm).

12. See Chomsky (2003, 2006 and 1999) *Hegemony or Survival: America's Quest for Global Dominance,* and *Failed States: The Abuse of Power and the Assault on Democracy;* see also Chomsky's (1999) book documenting the dominating role of the USA in the Israeli-Palestinian Conflict, namely *The Fate Triangle: The US, Israel and the Palestinians.*

13. What has been written above goes hand-in-hand with the point that I made elsewhere, "Language is a system of communication that is affected by cultural and political structures and attitudes in so far as use is concerned. Structurally, language is capable of expressing whatever human beings will it" (Alshaer, 2012: 275–97).

14. It is worth highlighting that the secularist and pluralist face of Fatah had more or less always been tinged with patriarchal tendencies. Thus, its modernist nation-statist approach is not without serious flaws, as it panders to the patriarchal social structures to sustain its popularity. And patriarchalism, on which much of Arafat's rule was based, bred cronyism and other forms of corruption which undermined the trust in the political thinking of Fatah and its leaders, pre- and post-Arafat period (see Ghanem, 2010). It is indeed a problem in the Arab world in general that there is an entrenched lack of trust in the political systems and parties. Hence whichever discourse is adopted, whether secular or Islamic, it often conceals and justifies autocratic and dogmatic practices which are anathema to democracy and its civic and legalistic imperatives (see Arkoun, 2002).

References

Alshaer, Atef (2008). "Towards a Theory of a Culture of Communication: The Fixed and the Dynamic in Hamas' Communicated Discourse," in *The Middle East Journal of Culture and Communication,* 1(2): 101–112.

—— (2012). "Language as Culture: The Question of Arabic." In Tarik Sabry (ed.), *Arab Culture Studies: Mapping the Field* (London: I.B.Tauris), pp. 275–97.

Allen, Roger (1998). *The Arabic Literary Heritage: The Development of its Genre and Criticism* (Cambridge: Cambridge University Press).

Arkoun, Mohammad (2002). *Islam: To Reform Or To Subvert* (London: Al-Saqi Books).

Chomsky, Noam (1999 [1983]). *The Fateful Triangle: The United States, Israel and the Palestinians* (London: Pluto).

—— (2003). *Hegemony or Survival: America's Quest for Global Dominance* (New York: Metropolitan Books).

—— (2006). *Failed States: The Abuse of Power and the Assault on Democracy* (New York: Metropolitan Books).

Foucault, Michel (2002 [1969]). *The Archaeology of Knowledge* (UK: Routledge).

Ghanem, As'ad (2010). *Palestinian Politics after Arafat* (Indiana: Indiana University Press).

Gramsci, Antonio (1995). *Further Selections from the Prison Notebooks*, Derek Boothman, (ed. and trans.) (Minneapolis: University of Minnesota Press).

Hall, Stuart (2004). "Foucault: Power, Knowledge and Discourse". In Margaret W. Stephanie T. and Simon J. Y. (eds), *Discourse Theory and Practice: A Reader* (London: Sage Publications), pp. 72–82.

Hourani, Albert (1983 [1961]). *Arabic Thought in the Liberal Age, 1798–1939* (Cambridge: Cambridge University Press).

Hroub, Khalid (2000). *Hamas: Political Thought and Practice* (Washington, DC: Institute for Palestine Studies).

—— (2006). *Hamas: A Beginner's Guide* (London: Pluto Press).

Johnson, Nels (1982). *Islam and the Politics of Meaning in Palestinian Nationalism* (London, Boston: Kegan Paul International).

Keane, Webb (2004). "Language and Religion", in A. Duranti (ed.) *A Companion to Linguistic Anthropology* (Oxford: Blackwell Publishing), pp. 414–31.

Legrain, Jean-François and Pierre Chenard (1991). *Les voix du soulèvement: édition critique des communications du Commandement National Unifié du Soulèvement et du Mouvement de la Résistance Islamique VI. Centre d'Études et de Documentation Économique, Juridique et Sociale du Caire.*

Lybarger, Loren, L. (2007). *Identity and Religion in Palestine: The Struggle between Islamism and Secularism in the Occupied Territories* (Princeton: Princeton University Press).

Macdonell, Diane (1986). *Theories of Discourse: An Introduction* (Oxford: Blackwell).

Al-Masri, Mushīr (2006). *al-Mushārakah fī al-Hayāh al-Siyāsiyyah fī zil Anzimat al-Hukm al-hāliyyah*. Markaz al-nūr lil bihūth wa d-dirāsāt: Ghaza, Filistīn.

Pappé, Ilan (2010). *The Rise and Fall of a Palestinian Dynasty: The Husaynis, from 1700–1948* (London: Al-Saqi Books).

Said, Edward (1997 [1983]). *Covering Islam: How the Media and the Experts Determine How We See the Rest of the World* (London: Vintage).

—— (1994). *The Politics of Dispossession: The Struggle for Palestinian Self-Determination, 1969–1994* (London: Chatto and Windus).

Tamimi, Azzam (2007). *Hamas: The Unwritten Chapters* (London: Hurst).
Younis, Mohammad (2000). *Medieval Islamic Pragmatics: Sunni Legal Theorists' Models of Textual Communication* (Richmond, Surrey: Curzon Press).

Websites

www. Palestine-info.info
www.aljazeera.net
www.aljazeera.net/NR/exeres/492984D1–7FE1–4191-AEC3–754F09DE 6EDC.htm
http://electronicintifada.net/bytopic/historicalspeeches/305.shtml

7

AL MANAR: CULTURAL DISCOURSE AND REPRESENTATION OF RESISTANCE

ROUNWAH ADLY RIYADH BSEISO

Hezbollah is as much a producer of culture as it is a producer of guerilla warfare. Providing a narrative, a cultural narrative, and a historical narrative, and this is what Al Manar does, it represents it as an Absolute Truth. (Habib Battah, journalist and blogger[1])

Hezbollah, the key Lebanese political party in the twenty-first century, launched its television station Al Manar (the Beacon) in 1991, beginning broadcasts from the southern suburb of Beirut, and its satellite transmissions in May 2000 with the mission to promote the group's resistance against Israel as well as its integrated social strategies. Since its inception, the channel has established its own dedicated website in Arabic, and gradually introduced three languages—English, French, and most recently Spanish—commanding, on average, an audience of 200 million satellite viewers.[2] The station describes itself as a channel with a vision, qualifying itself as a "Lebanese television channel," which "stresses...the adoption of fair and just causes of the whole nation," implying (among other things) that the threat Israel poses to

Lebanon necessitates legitimate confrontation which all Lebanese should support to preserve the future of the entire nation. Furthermore, Al Manar declares itself to be a "channel of the resistance" and the "channel of the Arabs and Muslims," which means it not only has a message, but also a mission which pushes the channel beyond being a station dedicated to telling news or making programs— but one that seeks Muslim and Arab unity and cultural harmony. According to its website, the station wants to "approach Arabs and Muslims all over the world with an open unifying speech."[3]

Clearly, Al Manar does not portray itself as distant from its audience, but neither does it displace "the subject" (those it is talking about and to) in an impersonal manner. On the contrary, the channel *intentionally brings the subject in as an actor and agent* (own emphasis) in the overarching moral and cultural narrative it produces, in the process forging an intimate relationship with its audience while offering a "true reflection of what each and every Muslim and Arab thinks and believes in."[4]

Al Manar has been regularly accused of only focusing on Lebanon's Shi'i constituency, often talked of as the *de-facto* "community of resistance." However, as Anne-Marie Baylouny notes,

> the station has won acclaim by not limiting its interests to its own confessional group. According to an official at the Lebanese Ministry of Information, Al Manar has a strong community following, perhaps the strongest, because the station hosts interviews with Lebanese personalities from diverse political trends and confessions.... Al Manar compares favorably to other stations which merely advertised their own political viewpoint, excluding alternative trends from airtime. (Baylouny, 2006: 8–9)[5]

Furthermore, much of its programming is educational and modernizing, finding parallels in the ethos of Western public broadcasting systems that emerged with modern nation-states. In addition, the station regularly endorses a public role for women, within an Islamic framework, "advocates for the poor and those moderate in income, emphasizes community solidarity, lobbies government social services and solidifies the place of the resistance and its fighters in Lebanese society" (ibid.).

In Western public and official discourses, it has been customary to label Al Manar as a "terrorist television" station or a form of "jihadi media," among other labels of a similar nature. In 2004, the US government declared Al Manar a "Terrorist Organization" under US Executive Order 12334, making it the first television station ever to be legally designated a "terrorist entity" equivalent to al-Qaeda.[6] These labels have created even more devastating implications to the channel in real life, culminating in the bombing by Israel of its headquarters during the 2006 Israel-Lebanon War. Recent scholarship has moved out of these discourses, showing how Hezbollah's diverse media, and other discursive practices, help to produce a narrative of culture that is not disjointed from the group's overarching message of resistance, but that is itself a discourse of resistance that serves to "provide meaning and legitimacy to Hezbollah's discourses and worldviews" (Matar, 2008: 122). This chapter is concerned with discourses produced in the everyday. It therefore illustrates how Al Manar produces a historically-specific "cultural discourse" that underlines everyday practices and lives and their relations to the past through daily broadcasts of specific self-produced promotional videos. These videos, this chapter proposes, repeatedly depict Lebanese families and neighbors in ordinary settings and Lebanon as a unique land-scape, producing a cultural discourse that is embedded within the larger grand narrative of resistance that Hezbollah uses to legitimize its existence and its *raison d'être* as a party concerned with the pro-tection of Lebanon's sovereignty and the integrity of Lebanese culture and people. In communicating social realities, this chapter suggests that Al Manar engages in what we might call "a meta-cultural commentary" on Hezbollah's identity, and what it stands for.

The Production of Cultural Discourse

This cultural commentary (discourse) is produced in diverse ways and through diverse programs and formats, as well as through other discursive practices, in the public sphere, such as speeches, sermons and visual displays in public spaces. In this chapter, however, I am only concerned with the promotional videos that are broadcast daily on Al Manar in between programs and regular newcasts. Although at first glance these videos would seem to be solely focused on Hezbollah's worldview, I argue that they embody an embedded cultural discourse, or a practice of representation, that in effect works as a "cultural language" (Hall, 1997: 8),[7] or, in other words, *a language that means something to someone* (own emphasis). Indeed, I would go further to suggest that the ways in which these videos are created, which words are chosen and which images and clips are used are all a product of choice, and that each choice has "consequences both for [which] meanings are produced and how..." (ibid.).[8]

The videos constitute about 30 percent of Al Manar's programming and last between 3 to 7 minutes. They draw on various historical, religious, political and cultural themes—for example, they may be glorifying the resistance, outlining Israeli actions in the Occupied Palestinian Territories or calling for Lebanese national unity while drawing on a historical repertoire or language, such as the language of the Qur'an. However, these videos also evoke scenes of "normalcy", showing images of "ordinary people" in the everyday, and reinforcing in direct and indirect ways Hezbollah's self-constructed and mediated image as Lebanese, rather than a closed group sectarian party. This is achieved through the use of songs and words that are specifically about and of Lebanon or through the use of images of specific national and historical sites. Together, these images and words portray Hezbollah as an entity that *is* the people and a group that exists on and belongs to the land of the people in order to protect both the land and people.

The videos I chose for analysis here were all produced and broadcast after the Israel-Lebanon War of July 2006, during a time of renewed sectarian divisions and tensions in the country and amid accusations that Hezbollah was behaving like a "state within a state."[9] These promotional videos represent a standardized template of Hezbollah's videos, a multi-layered embodiment of images that range from social to political to religious to historical elements that, in their entirety, reflect how everyday cultural practices are intertwined with the overall ideological discourse of the party. This is a discourse that presents the party as a national group bent on defending the land and the people from the enemy, Israel, and intent on promoting resistance to Israel and its actions.

In this chapter, I draw on Carbaugh's analysis of cultural discourse (2007) in order to examine the videos and to assess different ingredients that form the cultural discourse, specifically, their functional accomplishment; structurality and cultural sequencing. As Carbaugh argues, functional accomplishment relates to issues of representation in discourse, structurality to elements repeated in the videos, such as images of men, children and women, the land as well as cultural practices and performances, while cultural sequencing helps us see how these elements are part of an overarching sequence (Carbaugh, 2007: 167–182). Indeed, in these broadcasts, after we are shown images of the land and people in these videos, we see iconic images and figures of Hezbollah fighters watching over the land and the people. It is this "finalized sequence" (in which the land and its history are combined with the people and their cultural practices, and in which the overarching image of Hezbollah fighters are depicted as the guardians of the land and the people) that I suggest entrenches and embeds cultural narratives (with text and image) within the larger overarching discourse of resistance.

As Stuart Hall has argued, "representation can only be properly analyzed in relation to the actual concrete forms which meaning assumes, in the concrete practices of signifying, 'reading' and interpretation... [which] require analyses of actual signs, symbols, figures, images, narratives, words and sounds – the material forms – in which symbolic meaning is circulated" (Hall, 1997: 10). Representation is therefore significant because it creates meaning through "shared conceptual maps" (by members of the same culture who interpret the world in roughly similar ways) and a "shared language"—the conceptual map needs to be translated into a common language (including signs and symbols)—so that members of the same culture can correlate concepts and ideas with familiar visual images, written text, and spoken sounds (ibid.: 18). In this sense, language becomes "a shared cultural 'space,' in which the production of meaning—that is, representation—takes place" and it is this meaning that helps us make sense of our identity and who we are.

All practices have a discursive aspect to them, as they are located within the Foucaultian concept of discourse. But, more significantly for the argument here, anyone (be it a person or an entity) using signifying practices to produce a discourse must position him- or herself as if he or she was the subject of the discourse in order for that discourse to be effective. Al Manar's videos arguably position Hezbollah as the subject of discourse by personifying "the particular forms of knowledge which the discourse produces...the subjects have attributes we would expect (them to have) as these are defined by the discourse [and] these figures are specific to specific discursive regimes and historical periods" (ibid.: 56). In this sense, these videos both create the subjects of discourse and are the subjects of the discourse themselves, or, put differently, the videos images, symbols and language, construct subject positions from which the overall discourse makes the most sense, "thus they have become its own subject by subjecting themselves to its meaning and knowledge. "[10] In the videos under study, Al Manar's videos depict the resistance fighter not only as a soldier with a gun, but also as the mother, the child, the farmer, etc., whose very existence on the land is in itself an act of resistance. In what follows, I look at diverse elements of Hezbollah's cultural discourse in four videos: *Harasna Hdudak Ya Blady* [11] (*My Homeland, We Guarded Your Borders*), *Libnan Al Akhdar Libnan* [12] (*Lebanon the Green*), *Watan Al-Nour* [13] (*The Nation of Light*), and *Libnan Bil Shuhada Intasar* [14] (*The Martyrs Brought Victory to Lebanon*). These videos were all released and broadcast in the wake of the Israel-Lebanon War of 2006, and have a common theme of Lebanese unity and victory.

The People

Perhaps to state the obvious, there are repeated scenes of people in the videos—not just resistance fighters, but ordinary people in everyday life (i.e. mothers, fathers, children, etc). Such scenes include elderly men smoking *arghileh* (water-pipe), fathers greeting their sons, children playing in the streets, and men of all ages praying together (Figures 1 to 4). Furthermore, when such scenes appear, for example, as men praying together in the streets, the words "We prostrate to the ground praying, elderly men and children" (specifically in the video, *My Homeland, We Guarded Your Borders*, where it is repeated several times) are shown in the background. The use of the pronoun "we" is a common feature in Al Manar's videos, as this pronoun emphasizes a sense of collectiveness and belonging while also serving to construct a subject-position in

Figure 1   Children playing in the street.

Figure 2   Little girl picking a wildflower.

which a particular cultural discourse is produced while also serving to show the people as the subject of the discourse.

These images underline the familial and community ties which bind Hezbollah with the people in order to show Hezbollah are of the people; they are the sons and fathers and neighbors of the people, who need to be protected.

Women

A prominent feature in all four of the videos examined is the regular presence of women. The woman is a key cultural marker, as she plays a significant role in the Arab household as the mother, the nurturer,

Figure 3   Elderly man standing on his farmland.

Figure 4   Young and elderly men praying together in the street.

the giver of life and the teacher of practices and traditions. The women in the videos are shown playing an integral role in carrying out their ordinary, everyday activities which are essential to the economic cycle in the area. For example, in the videos *Oh Homeland, We Guarded Your Borders* and *Lebanon the Green*, we see an elderly woman's hand kneading homemade *khubz* (pita bread), a bread common in the Arab world. In *Lebanon the Green*, there are women pounding grain and sorting out olives. The women, as well as the familiar tasks they are undertaking, produce an emotive feeling of familiarity, as if to tell us that these women could be our own mothers and grandmothers and daughters doing their daily chores. This contrasts with widespread portrayals of Hezbollah members as shadowy al-Qaeda-like figures, with no culture or family or background. The presence of women (mothers, daughters, grandmothers) preparing food—which is a normal, everyday task—serves to provide an identity to Hezbollah as being ordinary, and its fighters as having mothers, thereby identifying them as having roots and connections, not isolated beings with no meaningful connections. The images below (Figures 5 to 9) are taken from all four videos.

Figure 5   Woman pounding grain.

Figure 6   Women sorting tobacco.

Figure 7   Woman kneading dough to make *khubz*.

Figure 8   Women ploughing the land.

Figure 9   Woman ploughing the land.

Moreover, the woman has a highly respected and revered position in Lebanese (and Arab and Muslim) society, which is why women's appearance (be they cooking, farming, or welcoming their men home) is so prominent in all four of the videos. Their importance stems from their role as the caretakers of new generations; however their reverence is also due to their importance in Islam which is highlighted in the Qur'an ("And for women are rights over men similar to those of men over women" Al-Qur'an 2:226).While women have an equal and protected status in Islam, it is especially the mother who has an esteemed place. In a well-known *hadith*, a follower asked the Prophet to whom he should show kindness, and the Prophet had replied: "Your mother." He asked who came next and he replied: "Your mother." He asked who came next and he replied for the third time: "Your mother." He again asked who came next and he replied: "Your father, then your relatives in order of relationship" (Dori, 2002).[15] This emphasis on the mother is an attribute to her sanctity in Islam and within the family which is revered throughout the Arab and Muslim world. Depicting such images in the videos serves to illustrate that Hezbollah are also people with a traditional family life who revere their women for their strength and compassion. Indeed, as Amal Saad-Ghorayeb notes, historically Hezbollah, like many Islamist organizations, is very much a male-dominated party:

> However, I think we should view the role of women outside of the Western conventional lens. Women in Hezbollah, as in other Islamist organizations, play a very important social role at the grassroots level, much more than a political role if you like, so while you won't find many women represented in Hezbollah's political ranks, you'll find that they play an extremely important role in so far as they are mothers of fighters, wives of fighters, and so forth, so I think their role would be best characterized as one of political socialization and support in terms of nurturing a resistance culture. They are entrenched in this resistance culture because women, like men, suffer the same consequences of injustice and oppression.[16]

That aside, the women in Al Manar's videos represent strength. In the video *Lebanon the Green,* the words "You stand strong in the face of your enemy, with your head held high, and all good things

Figure 10   An elderly woman gripping on to her cane, a defiant look on her face.

come to your footsteps" (author's translation) is accompanied by the image of an elderly woman holding her cane, beginning with her feet and going upwards toward her face, with a firm look of determination that she will not move from her land (Figure 10). The use of Lebanon in the first person, as though Lebanon is also the woman with the determined face, is intended to connect the strength of women with the strength of Lebanon and its fighters.

These same lyrics are repeated in another scene in the same video; the image is of an elderly woman walking with her cane, slowly but surely, past the remnants of an Israeli tank (Figure 11). Her steadfastness, as well as her indifference to the presence of the tank (as though its presence is a common state of affairs), overshadows any evident physical frailty. It symbolizes her belonging to the land, and her resolve to keep walking past the tank not only symbolizes the strength of the women, but the resolve of Lebanon (as the nation is commonly referred to as a female) as a whole to keep walking regardless of any frailty and even in the face of aggression. Repetition (*al-tikrar*) of these lyrics is a vital part of the Arabic language of poetry and song, and in Arabic poetry repetition creates the sense of pattern of form, for amplification and emphasis, as can be seen of the repetition of these lyrics and the repeated image of the elderly women standing firm and strong.

Figure 11   Elderly woman walking past an Israeli tank.

Furthermore, the repetitive use of images of women (grandmothers, mothers, daughters, sisters) happily throwing rice and greeting fighters or prisoners of war returning home (repeatedly heard shouting the phrase "May God keep you and the resistance!") to their communities further amplifies the fact that Hezbollah members are husbands, sons and fathers, not a separate entity, disconnected from the people; they are the people, and they are of the people, returning to the people. Therefore, the women serve to illustrate the connection of Hezbollah to the people, as well as a source of compassion and strength. As Rima Fakhry, a member of the political council of Hezbollah noted, "a woman is as much a part of the resistance as the men are.... [T]hey are supporters for the resistance....[W]e don't have a need for women that are soldiers because thank God the men are enough, but there is no problem if one time there will be a need for this, [as] they are ready for whatever is needed for the sake of our country and for the people".[17] The images below (Figures 12 to 14) are taken from all four of the videos and illustrate the women's support for the resistance.

The Sea, Rivers, Valleys, Mountains and Historical Sites

Lebanon is shaped by the twin mountain ranges that separate it from Syria. Its heavily inhabited, narrow coastline is lined with

Figure 12   Women throwing rice, cheering.

Figure 13   Woman seeing off the fighters before they go into battle.

Figure 14   Women welcoming their men home.

orange and banana plantations, behind which the slopes of Mount Lebanon, the range that gives the country its name, rises steeply.[18] Lebanon has plentiful supplies of water and is the only country in the region that has no desert. The Beka' Valley, which lies between Lebanon's twin mountain ranges, is one of the most fertile regions in the Middle East. Due to its natural bounty, Lebanon has always attracted outsiders, and therefore has suffered from a long history of invasions beginning with the Egyptians in the thirteenth century BC, through to the Assyrians, the Persians, the Romans, the Ottomans, the French, who withdrew in 1946, the two Israeli invasions of 1978 and 1982, and finally the Israel-Lebanon War in 2006.[19] All four videos have repeated images depicting Lebanon's landscape as well as its historical cultural sites (such as the Roman ruins in Baalbek), all serving as distinguishing symbols and identity markers representing Lebanon, suggesting that this specific cultural discourse sees Lebanon as the body politic, easily identifiable to the audience through images alone.

There is also regular language reference to the landscape in the videos, for example, in *My Homeland, We Guarded Your Borders*, the lyrics "the mountains of my homeland stand strong and challenges any danger, fenced with the fists of its men on the lines of fire" (author's translation). Not only is Lebanon's unique mountainous landscape singled out, but also the possessive pronoun "its" serves to show the belonging of the fighters to Lebanon, while also unifying the land with the resistance, as though the land itself (as the fighters) was also involved in resisting aggression. In the video *Nation of Light*, the lines "my nation of light, your soil, your stones, your crops, and your valleys and your riverbanks and your red flowers…like the lily and basil, I long for your meadows, and the *bulbul* (songbird) sang so your dawn could rise" (author's translation), all have connotative elements which represent Lebanon and its enduring beauty, creating a sense of longing, nostalgia, love and belonging to the land (see Figures 15 and 16). Furthermore, this imagery of the land and historical sites is used as a message for Lebanese unity— in the video *Nation of Light*, the lyrics "Lebanon, your South and your North long for unity, and your Beka' and your high mountains meet with Beirut" (author's translation)—this connection of the

Figure 15   Raouché.

Figure 16   Remnants of Roman artefacts in Lebanon.

South and North with the East and the West symbolizes community solidarity and ties of the people with the land while suggesting the unity of Lebanon and its people.

The images of (historical) stone structures produces a discourse of eternity—for example, in *Lebanon the Green*, the words "The letters of Lebanon are glaring fire and are engraved in *siwan* (a very hard) stone," with the image of Roman ruins built of stones, in the historical city of Baalbek. This represents the eternal link of the people with its soil, that they are engraved within the *siwan*, which can never be erased or washed away. Using the linkage of the engraving of the word Lebanon in stones with images of remnants of Roman ruins in historical cities is a historical linkage to Lebanon's unique civilization and past as well as symbolizes the "eternal" future of Lebanon and that its people and land will remain standing (as these strong historical stone foundations have over the centuries) in the face of any aggression or invasion.

Farming and Agriculture

Almost one-fourth of Lebanon's land is cultivable—the highest proportion in the Arab world. Agriculture in Lebanon is the third most important sector in the country after the tertiary and industrial sectors, and contributes nearly 7 percent to gross domestic product and employs around 15 percent of the active population.[20] Agriculture and farming, along with crops, are featured prominently in all four of the videos through repeated images of wheat, tobacco, and citrus fruits—the main crops of Lebanon that are a symbol of Lebanon and its bounty. These crops are also a sign of steadfastness—during the Israeli invasion in 1978 the crops most affected by the destruction are the ones from which Lebanon depends on its agricultural wealth—that is, specifically, wheat, tobacco, and citrus fruits (Collelo, 1997).[21] Even in the 2006 war with Israel, crops (along with infrastructure) were damaged severely; therefore, it is no coincidence that the images of Lebanon's famous crops are shown intact, flourishing, and bountiful, as though they are resisting any aggression which befalls them as Hezbollah does. Furthermore, the working lives of farmers digging in the land with old traditional tools such as the scythe, planting, and picking lemons and tobacco are consistently shown. As these videos were broadcast in the aftermath of the Israel-Lebanon War, this represents the return to their "everyday way of life," which suggests that regardless of any conflict, the people will live on, as will their way of life, while their crops will remain bountiful and unchanged. Furthermore, these natural elements are unique to Lebanon, serving to emphasize ways of life and practices which are part of their culture (Figures 17 to 19).

The Cedar Tree

The cedar, Lebanon's national emblem, is an important asset in the country's national heritage and cultural patrimony.[22] As Lebanese

Figure 17   Man and woman picking tobacco.

Figure 18   A farmer ploughing the land.

Figure 19   Woman planting crops.

historian Joseph Chami says, the Cedar can be classified as an archaeological monument, as the 400 Cedars of Becharreh are just as valuable historical remains as the ruins of the historical cities of Baalbek or Tyre.[23] Pierre Hubac, a historian, writes in his book on Carthage and its Phoenician antecedents, of the Cedar's religious significance and uses:

> The Cedar is precious, more than precious—it is sacred. In Egypt, the Cedar is the Zed tree, the tree that is a god, it is Osiris. It is also the incorruptible material that bestows immortality. It is the wood for religious objects. Later, the Cedar was to remain the religious wood par excellence, used in churches. For Islam, the Cedar is the sacred wood, the pure wood....[24]

The historian Lamartine gave the most beautiful description of it:

> The Cedars of Lebanon are the most famous natural monuments in the Universe. Religion, poetry and history have all celebrated them because of the reputation for magnificence and holiness that these prodigies of vegetation have enjoyed since the earliest antiquity...these ancient witnesses of past ages know history better than does history itself...[25]

In nearly all religions, the Cedar has a place apart, and is celebrated as an object of "veneration, a subject of meditation, comparison, and exaltation."[26]

To emphasize the Cedar's historicity, in the video *Lebanon the Green*, the lines "Glory, dignity, and the alphabets (*abjad*) are drawn in its soil" (author's translation) are connected to the images of the majestic cedars in the mountains. The use of the alphabet refers to the Phoenicians (who lived in present-day Lebanon), who are credited with inventing the world's first alphabet, and are among the first peoples (according to records) to use the Cedar's wood for construction, as well as exportation to the Pharaohs.[27] Therefore, the connection to the use of the alphabet by the Phoenicians links the past with the present, highlighting the cedar's "eternal" status as the symbol of the Lebanese nation. For example, in the video *Lebanon the Green*, there is an image of a large cedar tree followed by the lines of a song which say: "Lebanon the Green, Lebanon the Green, with our blood we will sacrifice for your soil" (author's translation). In terms of connecting the strength of the cedar to Lebanon and the fighters, in the video *My Homeland, We Guarded Your Borders* we see an image of mountains lined with cedar trees accompanied with the words "We stood firmly in line, in the hills and the valleys, and we raised our voices high" (author's translation). The song equates the firmness of the fighters with the firmness of their national tree, thus accentuating their rootedness to the land. Moreover, these images of fighters saluting the Lebanese flag (with the cedar tree at its center) are a sign of loyalty to Lebanon and its people, which is in contrast to earlier video clips which showed fighters saluting the Hezbollah flag (Figures 20 and 21).

Shaq'eq Al Numan

Shaq'eq Al Numan, or red windflowers, are a common type of flower that grows in Lebanon and the rest of the Levant. Images of these plants appear consistently throughout each of the videos. This is not only used for aesthetic purposes or to show the beauty of the flower, but to emphasize its long history in Arabic literature and its symbolic meaning when referring to the blood of martyrs. That is why, for example, in the video *My Homeland, We Guarded Your Borders,* the lines "My homeland, your people wished for your freedom, and they sang of your victory. Your people dyed your soil

Figure 20   Hezbollah fighter saluting the Lebanese flag.

Figure 21   Hezbollah fighters standing next to the Lebanese flag.

Figure 22   Image of a field of the Shaq'eq Al Numan.

with their blood—glory needs your men" (author's translation). When the word "blood" appears, the image of a field of red flowers (Figure 22) appears on the screen, and when the lines "glory needs your men" is sung, the image of a fighter holding the red flower appears (Figure 23).

This image is highly symbolic. This red flower has been used to symbolize the blood of martyrs, hence the image of a field of red flowers symbolizing the martyrs who have fallen in battle for the country, who are the people that dyed Lebanon's soil red with their blood. Moreover, the image of the fighter holding the red flower is symbolic—he is the red flower, and the red flower is him—in the

Figure 23   Resistance fighter holding a Shaq'eq Al Numan.

sense that this fighter is a potential martyr, willing to dye (*double entendre*) the soil with his blood for his country (which is revered as a glorious and selfless deed), and the flower is the representation of the martyr—hence the lines "glory needs your men." In the video *Lebanon was Victorious*, the first line of the video is narrated by a voice which says: "On land whose soil was written in blood, the invader was defeated and withdrew, the sword engraved in the stone 'Lebanon, due to its martyrs, was victorious'" (author's translation). Once again the word blood is correlated with the red flower.

The symbolism of the blood of the fighters in the soil with the red flowers on the land is a reference to selfless sacrifice in Arab history and literature, as these flowers received their name *Shaq'eq Al Numan* from the life of Munzer Al-Numan, the last Lakhmid (Arab-Christian) King of Al-Hirah (located in present-day Iraq), which was a significant pre-Islamic Arab city in the fifth and sixth centuries BC.[28] Legend narrates that Munzer Al-Numan loved the *Shaq'eq Al Numan*, and therefore ordered them to be planted around his castle (which was named Al-Khornaq) and demanded they be preserved.[29] The circumstances of his death serve to show the symbolic character of the flower; according to legend, the Sassanid Persian King Khosrau II demanded Munzer Al-Numan's daughter in marriage as part of his extensive harem, and when he refused his demands, Khosrau II had him crushed by elephants.[30] Since then, the flower has been named after Munzer Al-Numan, and the flower is associated with legendary folktale in the Arab world, which has been adapted in contemporary theatrical works such as the political play entitled *Shaq'eq Al Numan*.

The protagonist in this play (acted by Syrian actor Dureid Laham) regularly mentions the flower in his reference to the defiance and glory of martyrs who died for their land. Therefore, this flower symbolizes the sacred meaning of sacrifice and martyrdom, and thus holds an esteemed place in Lebanese (and Arab) cultural narratives which are embedded within the culture of resistance.

Cultural Tradition—Dabkeh

Dabkeh (translated from Arabic it literally means "stamping of the feet") is a popular Arab folk dance in Lebanon, Syria, Jordan and Palestine. Also performed in Iraq, Egypt and Saudi Arabia, it is a dance of people standing in line and is usually performed at weddings or joyous occasions. It is thus not surprising that this cultural expression of celebration is present in these videos, such

Figures 24 and 25   Men performing dabkeh in the streets

as *Lebanon was Victorious* and *My Homeland, We Guarded Your Borders,* in which the songs glorify the ability of the fighters to protect their land and people. In these two videos, there are repeated images of men celebrating and dancing *dabkeh* in the street (Figures 24 and 25). *Dabkeh* has several important meanings; it symbolizes an ancient cultural tradition, and at the same time is a public performance and therefore can be construed as a "sign of intimate present identity since it is linked to marriage parties, relations of solidarity, feasts and ritual.... [I]n this way, *dabkeh* is linked to various contexts of reinterpretation of music and dance, and expresses various levels of belonging."[31]

Dabkeh can provide a sense of belonging and identification with the land and the people; indeed, dance constitutes an intensive social arena where identity markers are displayed, a "cultural site"[32] where cultural "expressions of Lebanese (and Arab) identities"[33] are negotiated and performed.

Conclusion

> Being Hezbollah doesn't mean that you are a military woman or a military creature. Hezbollah, the "Party of God" is mentioned in the Qur'an. It's a way of thinking or acting. We are ordinary persons. —Farah Noor Eddine, Al Manar film editor[34]

Figure 26   Image of a man and woman embracing, superimposed on the Lebanese flag.

Al Manar's videos serve a purpose: they produce emotions, they reflect ideas, they give new forms of knowledge and they create meaning through the use of images and language. Indeed, these videos clearly support the argument that meaning is "produced whenever we express ourselves in, make use of, consume or appropriate cultural 'things'; that is, when we incorporate them in different ways into the everyday rituals and practices of daily life and in this way give them value significance, or when we weave narratives, stories—and fantasies—around them" (Hall, 1997: 3–4). This chapter has shown, through a detailed analysis, how these videos incorporate everyday ordinary rituals and practices, people, faces, and objects to produce a cultural language which represents Hezbollah's way of life as integrated within the wider

Figures 27 and 28   Fighter watching over the land and people.

community. This cultural language—embedded within and reliant on historical, religious, social and political meanings—is part of the larger discourse that projects Hezbollah's "culture of life" (in contrast to the "culture of death" portrayed by Western media) by illustrating its members' ways of life, where they come from and subsequently what and who they are protecting, in order to legitimize itself as the vanguard of Lebanese sovereignty.[35] This argument is portrayed in the finalized sequence of the cultural narrative: the images of Hezbollah resistance fighters watching over the land and the people (Figures 27 and 28).

This topic can be examined in much greater detail by exploring how Al Manar, as a cultural discourse, can challenge Western mainstream stereotypes and representations, not just of Hezbollah or the resistance movements in general, but of Arabs and Muslims worldwide. It can also pose questions about the relationship between Al-Manar's "videocracy" defined as "the power of the [moving] image over society"[36] and the changing media landscape of the Middle East, where there is an ongoing battle for the contestation of meaning in the "war of ideas" at a time of convulsive change and conflict.

Notes

1. *The Listening Post* (2008). "Hezbollah and the Media." Al Jazeera English. Available at: http://www.stormfront.org/forum/showthread. php?t=536676. Accessed June 24, 2009.

2. Schuh, T. (2006). "Israel Targets, Flattens Beirut TV Station HQ." *Counterpunch*. Available at: http://www.counterpunch.org/schuh 07192006.html. Accessed June 26, 2009.

3. Al Manar Website, (2009). *About Us*. Available at: http://www.almanar. com.lb/NewsSite/AboutUs.aspx?language=en. Accessed May 17, 2009.

4. Ibid.

5. Baylouny, A. (2006). *Al-Manar and Alhurra: Competing Satellite Stations and Ideologies*. George C. Marshall Center for Security Studies, pp. 8–9. Available at: http://www.marshallcenter.org/mcpublicweb/MCDocs/ files/College/F_Publications/occPapers/occ-paper_2-en.pdf. Accessed June 24, 2009.

6. Schuh, T. (2006). "Israel Targets, Flattens Beirut TV Station HQ". *Counterpunch*. Available at: http://www.counterpunch.org/schuh 07192006.html. Accessed June 26, 2009.

7. S. Hall (ed.) (1997). *Representation: Cultural Representations and Signifying Practices* (London: Sage Publications) p.8.

8. Ibid.
9. Cordesman, A.H., W.D. Sullivan, G. Sullivan (2007). "Lessons of the 2006 Israeli-Hezbollah War." Significant Issue Series, *Center for Strategic and International Studies*, 29(4) 22: Washington D.C.
10. Ibid., p.55, 56.
11. Al Manar (2009). *Harasna Hdudak Ya Blady.* YouTube. Available at: http://www.youtube.com/watch?v=1kH9y2g7n6E. Accessed June 12, 2009.
12. Al Manar (2009). *Libnan Al Akhdar Libnan.* YouTube. Available at: http://www.youtube.com/watch?v=2Ci05JuaSfM. Accessed June 12, 2009.
13. Al Manar, (2007). *Watan Al-Nour.* YouTube. Available at: http://www.youtube.com/watch?v=zEF-1i9BZRM. Accessed June 12, 2009.
14. Al Manar, (2008). *Libnan Bel Shuhada Intasar.* YouTube. Available at: http://www.youtube.com/watch?v=tji_qgoVWkI. Accessed June 12, 2009.
15. Doi, A.R., (2002). *Women in the Qur'an and the Sunna.* Witness-Pioneer. Available at: http://www.witness-pioneer.org/vil/Books/AD_wqs/index.htm. Accessed June 21, 2009.
16. Amin, R. (2007). *Everywoman: The Women of Hezbollah.* Al Jazeera English. Available at: http://www.youtube.com/watch?v=P2QaqseIGv8. Accessed June 21, 2009.
17. Ibid.
18. Discover Lebanon (2009). *Olive Oil: Where it All Began.* Available at: http://www.discoverlebanon.com/en/panoramic_views/history-olive-oil.php. Accessed June 12, 2009.
19. Ibid.
20. Ibid.
21 Collelo, T. (ed.) (1987). *Lebanon: A Country Study.* Washington, GPO for the Library of Congress. Available at: http://countrystudies.us/lebanon/71.htm. Accessed June 18, 2009.
22. Cedars of Lebanon, 2006. Cedars of Lebanon – A Cultural Asset. Available at: http://www.habeeb.com/cedar.of.lebanon/cedars.of.lebanon.a.cultural.asset.html. Accessed June 21, 2009.
23. Ibid.
24. Ibid.
25. Ibid.
26. Ibid.
27. Ibid.
28. Britannica Online. (2009). *Lakhmid Dynasty.* Available at: http://www.britannica.com/EBchecked/topic/328265/Lakhmid-dynasty#ref157806. Accessed June 13, 2009.
29. Ibid.

30. Ibid.

31. Van Aken, M. (2006). "Dancing Belonging: Contesting Dabkeh in the Jordan Valley, Jordan." *Journal of Ethnic and Migration Studies*, 32(2): 203–222, 206.

32. Olwig and Hastrup (1997), cited in Van Aken, M., 2006. "Dancing Belonging: Contesting Dabkeh in the Jordan Valley, Jordan." *Journal of Ethnic and Migration Studies*, 32(2), 203–222, 206.

33. Ibid, p. 204.

34. Schuh, T. (2006). "Israel Targets, Flattens Beirut TV Station HQ." *Counterpunch.* Available at: http://www.counterpunch.org/schuh 07192006.html. Accessed June 26, 2009.

35. *Saida Online Magazine* (2009). "Sheikh Qassem Says Hezbollah Ready for Any Israeli Attack." Available at: http://www.saidaonline.com/en/news.php?go=fullnews&newsid=9760 [June 13, 2009].

36. Jonasson, D. (2009). "Swedish Movie Raises Attention in Venice". *Stockholm News.* Available at: http://www.stockholmnews.com/print.aspx?NID= 3917. Accessed June 23, 2009.

References

Amin, R. (2007). *Everywoman: The Women of Hezbollah, Al Jazeera English.* Available at: http://www.youtube.com/watch?v=P2QaqseIGv8. Accessed June 21, 2009.

Al Arabiyah (2006). *Libnan Intasar.* YouTube. Available at: http://www.youtube.com/watch?v=B7OC0MU1ZGQ. Accessed June 12, 2009.

——— (2006). *Watan Al-Nour.* YouTube. Available at: http://www.youtube.com/watch?v=zEF-1i9BZRM. Accessed June 12, 2009.

——— (2007). *Interviews.* YouTube. Available at: http://www.youtube.com/watch?v=lbWqp0t8nGk. Accessed June 23, 2009.

——— (2009). *Harasna Hdudak Ya Blady.* YouTube. Available at: http://www.youtube.com/watch?v=1kH9y2g7n6E. Accessed June 12, 2009.

——— (2009). *Libnan Al Akhdar Libnan.* YouTube. Available at:_http://www.youtube.com/watch?v=2Ci05JuaSfM. Accessed June 12, 2009.

Barder, C., and D. Galasinksi (2002). *Cultural Studies and Discourse Analysis: A Dialogue on Language and Identity* (London: Sage Publications).

Bakhtin, M. ([1935] 1981). *The Dialogic Imagination* (Austin: University of Texas).

Baylouny, A. (2006). *Al-Manar and Alhurra: Competing Satellite Stations and Ideologies.* George C. Marshall Center for Security Studies. Available at: http://www.marshallcenter.org/mcpublicweb/MCDocs/files/College/F_Publications/occPapers/occ-paper_2-en.pdf. Accessed June 24, 2009.

Blanford, N. (2001). "Hezbollah Sharpens its Weapons in Propaganda War." *The Christian Science Monitor.* Available at: http://www.csmonitor.com/2001/1228/p6s2-wome.html. Accessed June 23, 2009.

Britannica Online (2009). *Lakhmid Dynasty.* Available at: http://www.britannica.com/EBchecked/topic/328265/Lakhmid-dynasty #ref157806. Accessed June 13, 2009.

Carbaugh, D. (2007). "Cultural Discourse Analysis: Communication Practices and Intercultural Encounters," *Journal of Intercultural Communication Research,* 36(3), 167–82.

Cedars of Lebanon (2006). *Cedars of Lebanon: A Cultural Asset.* Available at: http://www.habeeb.com/cedar.of.lebanon/cedars.of.lebanon.a.cultural.asset.html. Accessed June 21, 2009.

Collelo, T. (ed.) (1987). *Lebanon: A Country Study.* Washington, GPO for the Library of Congress. Available at: http://countrystudies.us/lebanon/71.htm. Accessed June 28, 2009.

Cordesman, A. H., W.D. Sullivan, and G. Sullivan (2007). "Lessons of the 2006 Israeli-Hezbollah War." Significant Issue Series-*Center for Strategic and International Studies,* 29(4), Washington D.C.

Doi, A. R. (2002). *Women in the Qur'an and the Sunna.* Witness-Pioneer. Available at: http://www.witness-pioneer.org/vil/Books/AD_wqs/index.htm. Accessed June 21, 2009.

Discover Lebanon (2009). *Olive Oil: Where it All Began.* Available at: http://www.discoverlebanon.com/en/panoramic_views/history-olive-oil.php. Accessed June 12, 2009.

Dubowitz, M. (2006). "Watching Al Manar: Violence in the Media". *National Review.* Available at: http://article.nationalreview.com/?q=ODQyZGE2Z TYxMDZiZjViMTliNDViZmIxYWZjYzllOGM=. Accessed June 18, 2009.

Dyer, R., (ed.) (1977). *Gays and Film* (London: British Film Institute).

El Mokadem, I. (2009). "Al Manar: A Light That Refuses to Go Out." Available at: http://www.almasryalyoum.com/en/news/al-manar-light-refuses-go-out. Accessed June 18, 2009.

European Union Election Observation Mission (2005). *West Bank and Gaza Presidential Elections: Final Report.* Available at: www.amin.org/eng/uncat/2005/mar/mar002.html. Accessed June 24, 2009.

Foucault, M. (1980). *Power/Knowledge: Selected Interviews and Other Writings 1972–1977,* (ed.) C. Gordon, (London: Harvester).

Free Press TV (2007). "Robert Fisk on False Representation of Hezbollah". YouTube. Available at: http://www.youtube.com/watch?v=QaCN9qZJNsw. Accessed June 23, 2009.

Gray, A., and J. McGuigan, (1993). *Studying Culture: An Introductory Reader.* (Hodder Arnold Publication, Oxford University Press).

Hall, S. (ed.) (1997). *Representation: Cultural Representations and Signifying Practices* (London: Sage Publications).

—— (2004). "Foucault: Power, Knowledge, and Discourse." In: M. Wetherhell, S. Taylor, S.J. Yates (eds), *Discourse Theory and Practice: A Reader* (London, Sage Publications), pp. 72–82.

Hines, R. (1988). "Financial Accounting: In Communicating Reality, We Construct Reality." *Accounting, Organizations and Society*, 13(3): 251–61.

Jonasson, D. (2009). "Swedish Movie Raise Attention in Venice". *Stockholm News*. Available at: http://www.stockholmnews.com/print.aspx?NID=3917. Accessed June 23, 2009.

Jorisch, A. (2004). "Al Manar: Hizbullah TV, 24/7". *Middle East Quarterly*, 11(1). Available at: http://www.meforum.org/583/al-manar-hizbullah-tv-24-7. Accessed June 26, 2009.

—— (2004). *Beacon of Hatred: Inside Hizballah's Al-Manar Television*. Washington DC: Washington Institute for Near East Policy.

The Listening Post, 2008, "Hezbollah and the Media," *Al Jazeera English*. Available at: http://www.stormfront.org/forum/showthread.php?t=536676. Accessed June 24, 2009.

MacNeill, M. (2009). "Conflict behind Women Wearing the Veil in Egypt: How Colonialism Turned the Veil into a Symbol of Resistance. Suite 101". Available at: http://middleeasternhistory.suite101.com/article.cfm/conflict_behind_women_wearing_the_veil_in_egypt#ixzz0QERmZjQA. Accessed June 30, 2009.

Al Manar Website (2009), *About Us*, Available at: http://www.almanar.com.lb/NewsSite/AboutUs.aspx?language=en. Accessed May 17, 2009.

Matar, D. (2008). "The Power of Conviction: Narsrallah's Rhetoric and Mediated Charisma in the Context of the 2006 July War," *Middle East Journal of Culture and Communication*, 1(1): 122–137.

Matar, D., F. Dakhlallah (2006). "What it Means to be Shiite in Lebanon: Al Manar and the Imagined Community of Resistance," *Westminster Paper in Communication and Culture*, 3(2): 22–40. Available at: http://www.wmin.ac.uk/mad/pdf/2%20-%20WhatItmeanstobelebanaon.pdf. Accessed April 21, 2009.

Maluf, R. (2006). "When in Doubt, Tune in to Your Favourite Station?" *MEB Journal*. Available at: http://www.mebjournal.com/component/option,com_magazine/func,show_article/id,204. Accessed April 30, 2009.

Saida Online Magazine (2009). "Sheikh Qassem Says Hezbollah Ready for Any Israeli Attack." Available at: http://www.saidaonline.com/en/news.php?go=fullnews&newsid=9760. Accessed June 13, 2009.

Schuh, T. (2006). "Israel Targets, Flattens Beirut TV Station HQ." *Counterpunch*. Available at: http://www.counterpunch.org/schuh07192006.html. Accessed June 26, 2009.

Sharabi, H. (2003). *Arab Satellite Television: The New Arab Revolution?* Palestine Center. Available at: http://www.thejerusalemfund.org/ht/display/ContentDetails/i/2396/displaytype/raw. Accessed June 24, 2009.

Van Aken, M. (2006). "Dancing Belonging: Contesting Dabkeh in the Jordan Valley, Jordan." *Journal of Ethnic and Migration Studies*, 32(2): 203–222.

Warikoo, N. (2005). "Censoring Al-Manar TV: Banned from US Television, Does Station Broadcast is Simply an Alternative Viewpoint or Dangerous Propaganda?" *The Detroit Free Press*. Available at http://www.justicejournalism.org/projects/warikoo_niraj/warikoo_032005.pdf.

Williams, R. (1977). *Marxism and Literature* (New York: Oxford University Press).

Ziadah, R. (2009). "Targeting the Arts, Destroying Culture." *Palestine News Network*. Available at: http://english.pnn.ps/index.php?option=com_content&task=view&id=5135. Accessed March.

8

THE BATTLE FOR VICTIMHOOD: ROLES AND IMPLICATIONS OF NARRATIVES OF SUFFERING IN THE ISRAELI-PALESTINIAN CONFLICT

Kirkland Newman Smulders

This chapter contends that Palestinian and Israeli narratives of their conflict are carefully constructed, mediated, and communicated by both sides to garner maximum support and sympathy from internal and external agents. As such, the long-running conflict is, during its quieter moments, more of a struggle over public opinion fought on the battlefields of national and international media, than one fought on the ground. Indeed, both sides need to convince outsiders of the legitimacy of their argument and position, and both use narratives of victimhood to do so. Understanding how these narratives are constructed and communicated by politicians and lay people, the role they play in the conflict, their effects on identity formation, and their implications for peace, this chapter argues, can help open new avenues for containing and resolving the conflict.

Narratives of Victimhood

Narratives of victimhood have been central to the foundation of modern Israel. Theodore Herzl, the father of modern Israel, drew on the history of Jewish persecution and victimhood in nineteenth-century Europe to legitimize the nationalistic project of the Jewish

State, while Israel's Declaration of Independence contends that "the Holocaust...in which millions of Jews in Europe were forced to slaughter again proved beyond doubt the compelling need to solve the problem of Jewish homelessness and dependence by the renewal of the Jewish state in the land of Israel, which would open wide the gates of the homeland to every Jew" (Waxman, 2006: 35). Such narratives of victimhood draw their strength from tragic events, starting with the Jewish Masada in the first century AD to the Pogroms in the nineteenth century and culminating in the Holocaust in the twentieth century. These historically significant narratives have been referenced time and again by Israeli politicians, such as former Prime Minister Golda Meir when she commented that Jews had a "Masada complex", a "pogrom complex", and a "Hitler complex," and former Prime Minister Menachem Begin who drew parallels between the Palestinians and the Nazis (Waxman, 2006: 49–56). These narratives of victimhood have also continued to feed the view that criticism of Israel's actions is evidence of enduring anti-Semitism, a sentiment which became more widespread after the Israeli victory of 1967 and the subsequent occupation of Palestinian territory, when Israel faced increased international criticism, particularly following UN Resolution 3379 (1975) which equated Zionism with racism, to which (late Prime Minister Yitzhak) Rabin responded: "The whole world is against us—when was it not so!" (Waxman, 2006: 53–54).

The dominant Jewish and Israeli narrative of persecution is often reinforced by another narrative; that of innocence, illustrated by the widespread belief that all Israel's wars with its Arab neighbors were "wars of no choice" (Bar-Tal, 2006; Waxman, 2006). For some, such as Phyllis Chesler, this narrative of innocence even extends to the 1982 Israeli invasion of Lebanon and the two Palestinian *intifadas* (Chesler, "New Anti-Semitism", in Finkelstein 2005: 34). Such attitudes are reproduced in the Western press, such as in *The New York Times*, which repeatedly portrays Israeli aggression as *self-defence*. For instance—an example among many—an article by Isabel Kershner on Israel's killing of seven Palestinians in Gaza in February 2008, emphasizes *Israeli retaliation* to *Palestinian aggression*, putting the blame for Palestinian victimhood squarely on their shoulders.[1]

The theme of innocence also pervades the discourse surrounding the peace process. According to many Israeli and Jewish narratives, the Palestinians are responsible for the breakdown in peace negotiations and do not want peace (Ellis, 2002; Bar-Tal, 2006).

Central to these narratives is the assumption that Jewish victimhood is unique, surpassing all other narratives of suffering, an assumption that is also highlighted in much press coverage of the conflict. Many news reports of the conflict gloss over high numbers of Palestinian victims, while going into detail on the often emotional rather than physical victimhood of the Israelis. One example is a *New York Times* article under the headline: "Rockets Hit Israel, Whose Strikes Kill Five Palestinians" (creating arguably deliberate confusion as to whether it was the Palestinians' own rockets which had killed five Palestinians).[2] The focus on Jewish suffering is accompanied by a belittlement or denial of Palestinian suffering. For instance, despite repeated condemnations of the Gaza siege in 2007/2008 by various international organizations (UNRWA, Oxfam, WHO) and by politicians, such as Benita Ferrero-Waldner of the European Commission, Israeli officials focused only on the rockets on Sderot. This collective position is mirrored in individual stories which reiterate the theme that Jewish victimhood is unique. Arnold Roth, whose daughter was killed by a suicide bomber, says in a conversation with the British Jewish academic Arthur Neslen:

> I'm repelled by the idea that we're two sides of the same coin or that we're doing to them what they're doing to us. We're protecting ourselves and they want us destroyed. *"You don't see any relation between Israel's behaviour in the West Bank and Gaza and the attacks in Israel?"* That position has some logic but as someone whose sons put on the uniform of the IDF, I know that it's bogus. The terror attacks and the hatred that motivates them were here long before there was a state of Israel. I'm not naive enough to say "poor desperate people". They're not poor and they're not desperate. (Neslen, 2006: 204)

Meanwhile, narratives of Palestinian victimhood are mainly based on accounts of daily hardship, tragedy and hopelessness, as well as the loss of freedom, rights and land. This comes across in statements such as: "We know we are Palestinians because we suffer so much" (Fatin I, Burj al-Barajna, in Khalili, 2007: 103). Or: "Every morning, when I leave my house and say good-by to my mother, I never know if I will see her again. (...) The Israelis massacred my family in my village. They took our land, our house, and now they want even the 22 percent of Palestine, the only thing we Palestinians have left. No, I cannot talk to these people" (Yasmine, survivor of the Deir Yassin Massacre, in Sultan 2006: 201). Similar narratives have surfaced again and again since the Palestinian *Nakba* (Catastrophe) in 1948 when close to 800,000 Palestinians were exiled from their lands by the Zionists (Pappé, 2006). Palestinian narratives of victimhood also draw on sentiments of abandonment by the foreign powers, which date back to the early days of the Zionist project, when the Palestinians felt betrayed by the British Balfour Declaration of 1917, then by the Americans who supported the 1947 UN partition plan, and then by the Arabs, especially Jordan and Egypt, who had territorial ambitions in Palestine. These sentiments continue to this day, exacerbated by the international community's, and the Arab world's, perceived unwillingness to enforce international law and basic human rights.

Irrespective of these narratives of victimhood, facts show the Palestinians have suffered the most in the conflict based on quantitative and qualitative data from Israeli and international humanitarian organizations. Fatalities among Palestinians are consistently higher than fatalities among Israelis. From 2000 to 2008, according to B'Tselem, the Israeli Human Rights organization, 6.6 times more Palestinians were killed than Israelis, and 7.7 times more Palestinian children were killed than Israeli children.[3] In Gaza, the Israeli blockade that started in June 2007 continues in violation of International Law, cutting off some 1.4 million Palestinians from food, basic and medical supplies, and causing extreme conditions of poverty, unemployment and hardship. According to Amnesty International and UNRWA, currently four out of five Gazans are dependent on humanitarian aid; the number of refugees living in abject poverty has tripled since the blockade began; and more than 60 percent of households are currently "food insecure."[4] In the West Bank, Israelis completely control the water supply and use 80 percent of the water from the Mountain Aquifer while Palestinians are restricted to 20 percent, despite the fact that the aquifer is the only source of water for Palestinians but one of several for Israel.

Palestinian daily water consumption is barely 70 liters per person, while Israeli water consumption is 300 liters per person. In some parts of the Occupied Territories, Palestinians survive on barely 20 liters per day (the minimum according to aid organizations), and 10 percent have no access to running water.[5]

Furthermore, the occupied West Bank is divided into six areas with little contact among them, and these areas are further subdivided into controlled enclaves separated by impassable roads and the Israeli Wall (or Separation Barrier). The Separation Barrier, judged illegal by the International Court of Justice in 2004, continues to be built east of 1967 borders, eating into private Palestinian lands, cutting Palestinian farmers from their land, students from their schools, and worshipers from their holy sites. Systematic house demolitions by the Israeli army in the West Bank and East Jerusalem reached record levels in 2011, displacing over a thousand Palestinians, half of whom are children.[6] In parallel, illegal settlements have continued to expand, increasing by 15,000 in 2011, and doubling in the past twelve years, to 350,000.[7] Settler violence against Palestinians increased by 160 percent from 2009, and over 10,000 olive trees were destroyed by settlers, further undermining Palestinian livelihoods.[8] Israeli jails hold between 4,300[9] and 11,000[10] Palestinian prisoners, including women, children, and members of the Palestinian government. B'Tselem and Amnesty International, as well as other human rights organizations, have documented routine beatings (including of minors) and the practice of torture by the Israelis. B'Tselem points out that many cases of abuse are not reported because they have become the norm, and because filing complaints is difficult, dangerous and time consuming, and usually complaints are dismissed by the occupation powers anyway.[11]

The Battle of Narratives

Since its independence in 1948, Israel has been particularly adept at advancing its narrative of victimhood, based on the historic persecution of Jews and then on terrorism experienced by Israelis. In the process, it has managed to get Britain and the USA, at different times, to support the creation of the State of Israel, and has continued to benefit from USA, and to an extent European, financial and moral support to advance its territorial and strategic interests (Said, 1988). Israel's ability to ensure the hegemony of its narrative of victimhood is partly due to the fact that as the more powerful party in the conflict, it has more resources to propagate its version of reality, particularly as historians "are forced to tell the story of the powerless (...) in the words of those who victimized them" (Khalidi, 1997: 117). The pervasiveness of this narrative is the result of carefully crafted political and media pressure. Edward Said explains the predominance of Israeli narratives of victimhood as follows: first, USA's and Britain's strong support of Israel was partly due to an Orientalist affinity with Jewish rather than Arab culture. Second, the Jewish narrative of the underdog overcoming immense odds, with its biblical connotations, was particularly appealing to Western culture. And finally, the Holocaust was a uniquely powerful narrative with which to garner support, and the Palestinians had no equivalent (Said and Hitchens, 1988: 6).

From a psychological perspective: "The victim stance is a powerful one. The victim is always morally right, neither responsible nor accountable, and entitled to sympathy."[12] From a public policy perspective, there are also benefits to being the victim: "The more heartbreakingly human rights and humanitarian organizations can portray suffering, the more they can appeal to their transnational publics for "sympathy, attention and money"" (Bob, Clifford "Merchants of Morality" Foreign Policy, March/April 2002: 36 in Khalili, 2007: 36), or what Daniel Bensaid has called capital victimaire" (Khalili, 2007: 35). Some critics have argued that Israel uses narratives of victimhood to mask violence against the Palestinians. Finkelstein notes, for example, that Israel's brutal repression of the second Palestinian *intifada* in 2000, coincided with a rise of "New Anti-Semitism" according to which, as Abraham Foxman (head of the Anti-Defamation League) suggested, "we [the Jews] currently face as great a threat to the safety and security of the Jewish people as the one we faced in the 1930s—if not a greater one" (Abraham Foxman, "Never Again? The Threat of the New Anti-Semitism," 2003: 4 in Finkelstein, 2005: 21). Indeed, narratives of suffering help to deflect external criticism of Israel's actions and the continued illegal occupation of Palestinian territory. "The consequences of the calculated hysteria of a new anti-Semitism haven't been just to immunize Israel from legitimate criticism. Its overarching purpose, like that of the 'war against terrorism,' has been to deflect criticism of an unprecedented assault on international law" (Finklestein, 2005: 45). The Israeli tendency to respond to criticism of its actions with knee-jerk claims of anti-Semitism and persecution is illustrated by Former Foreign Minister Tzipi Livni in her address to the Global Forum for Combating Anti-Semitism in Jerusalem on February 24, 2008: "The most recent development in anti-Semitism is the anti-Zionist or anti-Israel approach, which is classical anti-Semitism disguised as legitimate, political criticism of Israel."[13] While real anti-Semitism does of course exist, there is little doubt that many Israelis and Jews use it to shield against legitimate criticism of Israel—which paradoxically undermines merited accusations of anti-Semitism—in order to maintain external moral, financial and military support.

The Palestinians, too, use narratives of victimhood to achieve certain purposes. Given the daily hardships of occupation, these narratives help mobilize and motivate Palestinian resistance to the Occupation; garner external support; legitimize claims to Statehood; and deflect personal responsibility. Abu Husayn, a Palestinian refugee in the Burj al-Barajna camp in Lebanon, cited by Laleh Khalili, sees suffering as the basis of action. In asking him: "Do you want your children to know the story of your life [rather than the history of Palestine]?" his response was unequivocal, "Absolutely. I suffered a lot and they should know and they have to do something about it" (Khalili, 2007: 105–106). As in the case of Israel, narratives of victimhood are designed to garner both moral and financial support for the Palestinians, and to eschew responsibility for violence. This is illustrated for instance in the paintings of the Palestinian artist, Kamel Moghani, reproduced in postcards.

> In the art works of victimization, the Palestinian is devoid of responsibility for political disunity, violence and aggression. It is a utopian view of victimization, wherein the act is always cruelly premeditated, dramatic, extremely painful and attributable only to the "Other." Palestinians are collective victims of perpetrated acts, but they are never the perpetrators. The Israeli "Other" is depicted as the ultimate, evil oppressor of the Palestinians, and even of humanity as a whole. (Semmerling, 2004: 96–97)

Palestinian narratives of victimhood grant emphasis to Palestinian political and national claims to historic Palestine, just as Jewish narratives of victimhood had served to legitimize claims to a Jewish homeland. Given that Israelis and the rest of the world would happily forget Palestinian national aspirations if they could, a reminder of Palestinian suffering through narratives of victimhood helps to keep the discourse of Palestinian statehood on the table. Indeed, "Palestinian refugees (...) use the tragic language of suffering as an authorizing discourse which legitimates a stateless and 'powerless' public's persistent nationalist claims" (Khalili, 2007: 38).

Imagined Communities; Identities and Action

Broadly speaking, Palestinians and Israelis define themselves *in relation* to the narratives of victimhood they have created, suggesting that these discourses are crucial to the "imagined communities" that are central to both Palestinian and Israeli national identities. Narratives of victimhood, in particular, seem to galvanize a sense of collective identity and belonging, as common suffering tends to strengthen solidarity between victims. Israelis and Palestinians often seem entrenched in these narratives and identities, unwilling, and sometimes unable, to move beyond them. As Ellis points out, there is a certain reluctance to heal and to move beyond the cycle of suffering and violence: "the possibility of healing by ending the cycle of suffering and violence is itself jarring" (Ellis, 2002: 34).

A tangible consequence of Israeli and Palestinian narratives of victimhood is the development of alternative narratives—and actions—to *counter* these narratives: these include narratives of identity based on *struggle*, embodied in real life by the Israeli *Sabra* and the Palestinian *Fedayeen*, both of which have acquired mythical status. Both developed during the early days of their respective nationalist projects—the former in the early days of the State of Israel in the 1940s, the latter with the rise of Palestinian national resistance in the late 1960s and 1970s. While the narrative of victimhood is passive, the narrative of the resistance fighter is active, manifesting through acts of violence and resistance, which, in a vicious circle, contribute to perpetuating the conflict and therefore victimhood. Both sides' fighters respond with varying degrees of violence to perceived threats, or actualities of victimhood. In order to determine whether a fighter is actually a "resister", one must determine first whether to buy into their narrative of victimhood.

Early pioneers of the modern State of Israel made a conscious effort to create a new Israeli identity based on strength and power, distinct from the traditionally weak and persecuted European Jew. Israelis took great pride in this new identity, believing that it was essential to avoiding future victimhood. In the words of the early Zionist Vladimir Jabotinsky:

> Our starting point is to take the typical Yid [the derogatory Russian term for Jew] of today and to imagine his diametrical opposite ... because the Yid is ugly, sickly and lacks decorum, we shall endow the ideal image of the Hebrew with masculine beauty. The Yid is trodden upon and easily frightened and, therefore, the Hebrew ought to be proud and independent. The Yid is despised by all and, therefore, the Hebrew ought to charm all. The Yid has accepted submission and, therefore, the Hebrew ought to learn how to command. (Waxman, 2006: 25)

This narrative of the proud and powerful Hebrew as an antithesis to the weak and victimized Jew has remained a cornerstone of Israeli national identity. Within Israel, however, the two identities are often seen to confront each other, and there is a division between Israelis who see themselves as citizens of a strong country, and those who see themselves as still weak and persecuted—a division Waxman defines as between the "Israeli" and the "Jewish" identities (Waxman, 2006: 16).

Many Jews and Israelis feel they must choose between the identity of fighter and that of victim, and communicate these beliefs to the world in corresponding narratives. The fighter identity and narrative enables them to feel safe, powerful, and honorable, as opposed to ashamed, vulnerable and persecuted. While the Sabra is the embodiment of the strong, resilient Jew, the State of Israel is the embodiment of victory over victimhood. This understandable preference for the fighter narrative, however, has significant implications for Israeli policy and actions, explaining a high degree of belligerence.

There is also a darker side to the fighter narrative, usually espoused by the more right wing Israeli factions, which manifests a desire for vengeance for—rather than just protection from—Jewish and Israeli victimhood. This desire for vengeance seems either driven by excessive fear and anger towards perceived threats, or by the drunkenness conferred by power, or simply by a desire to rid the land of Palestinians standing in the way of Eretz Israel, the whole land of Israel. Amos Oz, the Israeli writer, detects "a 'reprisal' underside to the 'ideology' of survival. (...) According to this sentiment, the purpose of the State of Israel [was] not to save the Jews but to teach the non-Jews a lesson and vent our rage on them and particularly to show them how tough and warlike and cruel we too can be, and how much they ought to respect us for being as bad as they are if not more so" (Caplan, 1999: 71). Jeff Halper, the Israeli activist and academic, claims that this dehumanizing and vengeful attitude towards the Palestinians, which is the extreme version of the fighter identity, is enabled by Israelis' belief in their own victimhood: "[Israelis] see themselves as the victim, and if you're the victim, you're not responsible for anything you do. (...) If you combine three elements: the idea that we are right, with the notion that we're the victim, with our great military power, you have a lethal combination."[14]

Palestinian narratives of struggle follow a similar pattern. Given their acute sense of victimhood, Palestinians have developed an alter-ego: the powerful and honorable resistance fighter, the Fedayeen. The Palestinian discourse of resistance and national liberation matured during the 1970s, partly as a result of the defeat and occupation in 1967, but also as a result of "the coming of age of the first exiled generation, whose parents had experienced the *Nakba*, and who turned the narratives of grief and loss into narratives of resistance and struggle" (Sayigh, 1979 in Lindholm Schultz, 2003: 2, 124). The dichotomy between the identities of victim and fighter is illustrated by Kamel Moghani in his painting "West Bank." It features Lena Nabulsi, a Palestinian student killed in Nablus by an Israeli sniper.

> Lena symbolizes victimization, innocence abused, ruthless murder, and defeated Palestine. In counterpoint is the summarizing symbol of the *Fedayeen*, who is Palestine's guerrilla soldier, fighting from behind the lines to defeat the

perpetrator and willing to sacrifice himself to avenge such murders. (Semmerling, 2004: 80)

Israeli and Palestinian fighter/resistant narratives share similar goals: to restore a sense of honor and purpose to victims of persecution, loss and shame. Palestinians voice this sense of shame: "When we were in this country before the Palestinian revolution, we didn't dare say we were Palestinian, we were ashamed of ourselves;" (Christison, 2001: 190, in Lindholm Schultz, 2003: 125) and pride in the resistance: "Don't tell them only about our suffering. Tell them that we are strong; that we are still resisting" (Mahir Yamani, a former PFLP guerrilla, in Khalili, 2007: 90).

The narrative of martyrdom presents an interesting bridge between the identity of victim and that of fighter/resistant, given that "martyrdom" can be both victimhood *which is inflicted by the enemy,* and victimhood *which is actively chosen by the subject as an act of resistance.* Both are direct results of actual suffering and the narratives of suffering, but one is an extreme version of the victim identity (passive martyrdom—death at the hands of another) while the other is an extreme version of the fighter identity (self-chosen martyrdom as resistance). Self-chosen martyrdom is paradoxically seen as the only way to a meaningful life, as opposed to victimhood which robs daily life of meaning. Martyrdom is also seen as a way to restore honor in the face of shame, as shown by the Palestinian psychiatrist Eyad Sarraj, much like the Israeli Sabra identity served to restore the Jewish sense of pride after the shame of the Holocaust:

> Shame is the most painful emotion in Arab culture, producing the feeling that one is unworthy to live. The honourable Arab is the one who refuses to suffer shame and dies in dignity. The 35 years of Israeli military occupation of the West Bank and the Gaza Strip has served as a continuous reminder of Arab weakness. (...) Suddenly Palestinians felt that they were restoring their honour by fighting the aggressor, by not being helpless victims. (...) In every case of martyrdom, there is a personal story of tragedy and trauma.[15]

Narratives of Palestinian martyrdom have often been seen as evidence of pure evil or brainwashing of young people. Daniel Pipes, for example, claims that: Islamic Jihad, which along with Hamas trains the suicide killers, explains: "We do not take depressed people. If there were a one-in-a-thousand chance that a person was suicidal, we would not allow him to martyr himself. In order to be a martyr bomber, you have to want to live." The same strange logic applies for Hamas, which rejects anyone "who commits suicide because he hates the world."[16] Pipes calls this "strange logic;" however, the point is that suicide bombers choose to die not because they are depressed, but to protest against an enemy who has robbed their life of meaning. As the Palestinian writer Ghassan Kanafani wrote:

> Self-sacrifice, within the context of revolutionary action, is an expression of the very highest understanding of life, and of the struggle to make life worthy of a human being. The love of life for a person becomes a love for the life of his people's masses and his rejection that their life persists in being full of continuous misery, suffering and hardship. (Khalili, 2007: 20)

It is worth noting that similar narratives of martyrdom *as acts of resistance to victimhood* fuelled acts of terrorism committed by Jews during the British Mandate period in Palestine.

> Even those stories [in the national heroic literature] that end in suicidal acts related to a Samson-like heroism rather than to the staunch valour of the fighters on Masada; the suicides are deeds of action that result in a semblance of physical victory rather than acts of passive, albeit courageous, acceptance of fate. (Gertz, 2000: 43)

Another narrative resulting from Palestinian victimhood is that of "steadfastness" or *Sumud*, characterized by a stoical and patient attitude towards victimhood. As such it is a more peaceful alternative to the narrative of violent resistance, while restoring some dignity to the victim through their *attitude* rather than *actions*.

Implications of Narratives of Victimhood for Peace

Whether Israeli or Palestinian narratives of victimhood are based on genuine victimhood or are constructed for a purpose, they are central to policies and actions. Indeed, narratives of victimhood serve to legitimize violent and often pre-emptive acts against the enemy, and can lead to "ethnic cleansing and genocide" (Bar-Tal, 2006: 32), as well as terrorism, thereby perpetuating the cycle of violence and victimhood indefinitely. In order for healing, and eventually peace, Israelis and Palestinians need to move beyond entrenched narratives of victimhood to espouse new, common narratives, as advocated by Ilan Pappé through "joint historiographical reconstruction involving individuals from both sides who absolve themselves of their national and positional identities" (Rotberg, 2006: 13). This common narrative could be based on a historical sharing of the land, a common Semitic origin and cultural similarities, as well as on common suffering. However, given the current situation, this might seem utopian. As Bar-On and Adwan note, "bridging narratives will be impossible in the foreseeable future" (ibid.).

Indeed, for Israelis and Palestinians to be reconciled enough to develop a common narrative, several conditions must be met: first, each side must recognize the subjectivity and therefore the legitimacy of the other's narrative. Second, there is a need for each side to align subjective *narratives* with *facts*. Third, there needs to be international recognition of the legitimacy of both narratives, as well as an acknowledgement of the disparity between narratives and facts. Fourth, victimizing the other must stop before either side can move beyond its narratives. Fifth, the assumption, already made in most of this chapter, is that the onus must be on Israel as the more powerful party, to take the lead. Sixth, alternative voices for peace must be empowered.

Moving beyond deeply entrenched narratives and identities of victimhood and resistance is a painful and difficult process, given the over sixty years of conflict between the two sides. As Caplan says, it would take an "almost-impossible series of mental gymnastics (...) for most Israelis and Palestinians to imagine 'the other' as victim rather than aggressor" (Caplan, 1999: 78–79). Hence, the first step should be the less ambitious *recognition of the legitimacy* of the other's narrative, based on *recognition of its subjectivity*. This process starts by listening to the other's narrative, and accepting that while it may be very different from one's own, it is legitimate as it represents the personal experience of the other. It is especially important that each side recognize the other's narrative of suffering, as this can entail empathy, and a recognition of their humanity. Israelis must acknowledge the legitimacy of Palestinian narratives of suffering under a brutal and illegal Occupation, and the Palestinians must acknowledge the legitimacy of Israeli and Jewish narratives of historical suffering and trauma. Palestinians must understand that aggressive statements touch a raw nerve with a people who in the past were decimated in the most barbaric of ways (Waxman, 2006). By denying the validity of the other side's narratives of victimhood, Israelis and Palestinians are denying each others' suffering, and thus their humanity. Bar-Tal (2006: 37) underlines the importance of each side seeing its opponent not only as a perpetrator, but also as a victim, while Tessler (2006: 174) says: "Rather than demonizing one's historic adversaries and thus believing that they are driven by irrational or immoral principles, accepting their narrative makes them human." Dehumanizing the opponent enables untold violence against them, without guilt, thus perpetuating the conflict indefinitely.

Not only is there a need to recognize the *legitimacy* of the other side's narratives, but there is also a need for an alignment of narratives with facts. As discussed above, factual indicators of *present* victimhood weigh heavily towards Palestinian suffering. Furthermore, against the backdrop of Israeli narratives of victimhood, Israel has the world's fourth most powerful military complex and is the only nuclear power in the Middle East, with over 150 nuclear warheads, and is backed politically, militarily and financially by American superpower. Yet many Israelis and Jews speak and act in ways that project a sense of Israeli vulnerability and fear of their enemies' capacity to destroy them. This attitude, and the glaring disparity between Israeli narratives of victimhood and facts, is detrimental to peace. Whether this is driven by genuine fears of victimhood, or by the political goal of gaining more time to build facts-on-the-ground and thus making a Just Peace impossible, this insistence that Israelis have to be completely secure from *perceived and potential victimhood* before the Palestinian issue is addressed negates all hope of a solution to the conflict. An urgent realignment of narratives with facts is necessary, both within Israel but also in the international community.

Another obstacle to aligning narratives and facts is the negligible amount of contact between Israelis and Palestinians. Before the two *intifadas* of 1987 and 2000, there was some contact between the two populations, with approximately 180,000 Palestinians working in Israel, however movement between the two sides has been drastically reduced, a situation exacerbated by the Separation Wall. This lack of contact between the two sides is a considerable impediment to peace: each side lives in a vacuum, entrenched in its own narratives, unable and unwilling to contemplate "the other" except in the context of self-as-victim versus other-as-aggressor. Furthermore, apart from the few valiant and visionary Israelis and Palestinians working together for peace, much of the contact between the two sides is based on *negative* experiences. Palestinians experience Israelis as a humiliating occupying force through their daily contact with Israeli soldiers who control their lives, while Israeli experience of Palestinians is often limited to direct or mediatized violence and expressions of anger against an occupation which Israelis barely acknowledge, and experience mainly as occupying soldiers. This is exacerbated by a nationalistic Israeli media which further entrenches these narratives (Dor, 2004; Liebes, 1997).

It is my contention that until each side is able to see, and accept, the other's reality, they will never be able to move beyond each other's narratives. Palestinians must "see" Jewish paranoia and fear as stemming from a history of persecution and exacerbated by the effects of terrorism, while Israelis must "see" the daily persecution of Palestinians. It is also imperative that the international community recognize Israeli and Palestinian narratives of victimhood and the disparity between these narratives and facts. Israelis and Jews have benefited from substantial acknowledgement of their suffering, through public apologies and moral and financial support, and their narratives of victimhood have, mostly, been embraced by the West, in public discourse, history books, museums, etc. While there remain certain Holocaust deniers and despicable neo-Nazi groups, the uproar around these is testimony to their unacceptability, and indeed illegality, as Holocaust denial is forbidden by law in nine European countries and in Israel.[17] Meanwhile the Palestinian *Nakba* is denied by many in the Israeli mainstream, while in the West, Palestinian narratives of victimhood are accepted by many journalists, aid workers and politicians, but misunderstood by the mainstream (Philo and Berry, 2004), and barely reflected in foreign policy.

Alternative voices for peace in Israel draw their wisdom precisely from Jewish narratives of victimhood, but are able to transcend these to empathize with the suffering of the enemy, thereby turning *unique* suffering into an understanding of the lessons of *universal* suffering. For instance, despite losing one son to a suicide bomber, and another later to suicide, Roni Hirschenson is able to rise above his own suffering to see the legitimacy of his enemy's narrative of suffering: "I don't want even my enemy to share this pain. No human being deserves this. I don't want to take another life because I can't avenge all the people" (Nelsen, 2006: 196). Through this sense of *shared* victimhood, narratives of victimhood become unifying rather than dividing, as illustrated by Finkelstein: "I will suggest that in studying the Nazi Holocaust we can learn much not just about 'the Germans' or 'the Gentiles' but about all of us. Yet I think that to do so, to truly learn from the Nazi Holocaust, its physical dimension must be reduced and its moral dimension expanded" (Finkelstein, 2003: 8).

Conclusion

One of the most striking facts about the long-running conflict between Israel and the Palestinians is the similarity between Israeli and Palestinian narratives: both peoples have legitimate claims to victim status (though mainly at different times), and both have created collective identities and narratives around this status. Both have created alternative identities and narratives based on the perceived need to transcend victimhood through violence, and both sides realize the importance of justifying violence through narratives of victimhood, in order to maintain external support and claim moral immunity. Therefore, both parties have engaged in a battle to ensure that their narrative of victimhood gains the upper-hand in the national and international public spheres where ideas and policies are formed. Yet while the parallels between each side's *narratives* are striking, so are the disparities between each side's *factual* realities. Therein lies the power of the narrative: in its ability to affect perceptions of reality, and therefore, reality itself.

Facts tell us that the Palestinians are the greater victims of the conflict. And yet, international policies towards the Palestinians continue to espouse positions of "equivalence" between the two sides, condemning the weaker party for acts of resistance against the stronger party, on the basis that the stronger party is victimized by the weaker party's resistance. As this chapter has shown, this is partly due to the predominance of Israeli narratives of victimhood which, while often driven by genuine feelings of vulnerability, also enable Israel to justify its territorial ambitions and military actions. This seemingly intractable problem can only be addressed by a re-alignment of narratives with facts within Israel and the International Community. And Israelis and Palestinians must work in their respective societies and together to create a *realignment* of narratives with facts, a *legitimization* of the other side's narratives of victimhood, and a *transcendence* of these narratives through recognition of common suffering, without which there can be no progress towards peace. This requires both sides, but especially the Israelis as the more powerful party, to use narratives of suffering as instruments of rapprochement predicated on the recognition of *common victimhood,* rather than as excuses for the advancement of territorial and nationalist agendas.

Notes

1. Isabel Kershner, *The New York Times,* February 8, 2008 http://www.nytimes.com/2008/02/08/world/middleeast/08mideast.html?scp=69&sq=israel&st=cse.
2. http://www.nytimes.com/2008/01/18/world/middleeast/18mideast.html.
3. http://www.btselem.org/english/statistics/Casualties.asp.
4. http://www.amnesty.org/en/news-and-updates/suffocating-gaza-israeli-blockades-effects-palestinians-2010–06–01.
5. http://www.btselem.org/english/Water/Statistics.asp.
6. http://www.amnesty.org/en/news/record-number-palestinians-displaced-demolitions-quartet-continues-talk-2011-12-13.
7. http://www.guardian.co.uk/world/2012/jul/26/jewish-population-west-bank-up.
8. http://www.amnesty.org/en/news/record-number-palestinians-displaced-demolitions-quartet-continues-talk-2011-12-13.
9. http://www.btselem.org/statistics/detainees_and_prisoners.
10. http://www.adalah.org/newsletter/eng/apr08/5.pdf.
11. http://www.btselem.org/English/Beating_and_Abuse/Index.asp.
12. Dr. Ofer Zur, "Reflections on a Culture of Victims & How Psychotherapy Fuels the Victim Industry," http://www.zurinstitute.com/victimhood.html.

13. http://www.mfa.gov.il/MFA/Anti-Semitism+and+the+Holocaust/
    Documents+and+communiques/Address%20by%20FM%20
    Livni%20to%20the%20Global%20Forum%20for%20Combating%20
    Antisemitism%2024-Feb-2008.
14. Kathleen and Bill Christison, March 29, 2003, "Like Being Autistic
    with Power," *Counterpunch,* http://www.counterpunch.org/christison
    03292003.html.
15. "Why We Blow Ourselves Up," *Time Magazine,* April 8, 2002, http://
    www.time.com/time/magazine/article/0,9171,1002161–1,00.html.
16. Pipes, Daniel (2001), "Arafat's Suicide Factory," *New York Post,* http://
    www.aish.com/jewishissues/middleeast/Arafats_Suicide_Factory.asp
17. http://neo-neocon.blogspot.com/2006/02/we-didnt-start-fire-
    should-holocaust.html.

References

Bar-On, Dan and Sami Adwan (2006). "The Psychology of Better Dialogue Between Two Separate But Interdependent Narratives." In Robert Rotberg (ed.), *Israeli and Palestinian Narratives of Conflict History's Double Helix* (Bloomington & Indianapolis: Indiana University Press).

Bar-On, Mordechai (2006). "Conflicting Narratives or Narratives of a Conflict: Can the Zionist and Palestinian Narratives of the 1948 War Be Bridged?" In Robert Rotberg (ed.), *Israeli and Palestinian Narratives of Conflict History's Double Helix* (Bloomington & Indianapolis: Indiana University Press).

Bar-Tal, Daniel and Gavriel Salomon (2006). "Israeli-Jewish Narratives of the Israeli-Palestinian Conflict Evolution, Contents, Functions and Consequences." In Robert Rotberg (ed.), *Israeli and Palestinian Narratives of Conflict History's Double Helix* (Bloomington & Indianapolis: Indiana University Press).

Caplan, Neil (1999). "Victimhood and Identity: Psychological Obstacles to Israeli Reconciliation with the Palestinians." In Kamal Jacobson and David Abdel-Malek (eds), *Israeli and Palestinian Identities in History and Literature* (London: Macmillan Press).

Dor, Daniel (2004). *Intifada Hits the Headlines: How the Israeli Press Misreported the Outbreak of the Second Palestinian Uprising* (Bloomington & Indianapolis: Indiana University Press).

——— (2005). *The Suppression of Guilt: Israeli Media and the Reoccupation of the West Bank* (London: Pluto Press).

Ellis, Marc (2002). *Israel and Palestine Out of the Ashes: The Search for Jewish Identity in the Twenty-first Century* (London: Pluto Press).

Finkelstein, Norman (2003). *The Holocaust Industry: Reflections on the Exploitation of Jewish Suffering* (London: Verso).

———— (2005). *Beyond Chutzpah: On the Abuse of Anti-Semitism and the Abuse of History* (London: Verso).

Friel, Howard, and Richard Falk (2007). *Israel-Palestine On Record: How* The New York Times *Misreports Conflict in the Middle East* (London: Verso).

Gertz, Nurith (2000). *Myths in Israeli Culture: Captives of a Dream* (Portland, OR: Vallentine Mitchell).

Khalidi, Rashid (1997). *Palestinian Identity: The Construction of Modern National Consciousness* (New York: Columbia University Press).

———— (1988). "Palestinian Peasant Resistance to Zionism Before World War I." In Edward Said and Christopher Hitchens (eds), *Blaming the Victims: Spurious Scholarship and the Palestinian Question* (London: Verso).

Khalili, Laleh (2007). *Heroes and Martyrs Of Palestine: The Politics of National Commemoration* (Cambridge: Cambridge University Press).

Lindholm Schultz, Helena (2003). *The Palestinian Diaspora: Formation of Identities and Politics of Homeland* (London: Routledge).

Mearsheimer, John, and Stephen Walt (2007). *The Israel Lobby and US Foreign Policy* (London: Penguin).

Neslen, Arthur (2006). *Occupied Minds: A Journey Through the Israeli Psyche* (London: Pluto Press).

Philo, Greg, and Mike Berry (2004). *Bad News from Israel* (London: Pluto Press).

Pappé, Ilan (2006). *The Ethnic Cleansing of Palestine* (Oxford: Oneworld).

Rotberg, Robert (2006). "Building Legitimacy through Narrative." In Robert Rotberg (ed.), *Israeli and Palestinian Narratives of Conflict History's Double Helix* (Bloomington & Indianapolis: Indiana University Press).

Said, Edward and Christopher Hitchens (1988). *Blaming the Victims: Spurious Scholarship and the Palestinian Question* (London: Verso).

Semmerling, Tim (2004). *Israeli and Palestinian Postcards: Presentations of National Self* (Houston: University of Texas Press).

Sultan, Cathy (2006). *Israeli and Palestinian Voices: A Dialogue with Both Sides* (Woodburg, MN: Scarletta Press).

Tessler, Mark (2006). "Narratives and Myths about Arab Intransigence Toward Israel." In Robert Rotberg (ed.), *Israeli and Palestinian Narratives of Conflict History's Double Helix* (Bloomington & Indianapolis: Indiana University Press).

Waxman, Dov (2006). *The Pursuit of Peace and the Crisis of Israeli Identity: Defending/Defining the Nation* (London and New York: Palgrave Macmillan).

Weiner, Eugene (1986). "The Death Taint and Uncommon Vitality: The Case of the Ever-Dying Jewish People." In Etan Levine (ed.), *Voices from Israel: Understanding the Israeli Mind* (Rosemont Publishing and Printing Corporation; Cornwall Books).

9

THE "I LOVE. . ." PHENOMENON IN LEBANON: THE TRANSMUTATIONS OF DISCOURSE, ITS IMPACT ON CIVIL SOCIETY, THE MEDIA AND DEMOCRATIZATION

Carole Helou

Since 2005, political campaigns have increasingly become an intrinsic feature of political and public life in Lebanon, particularly during elections, commemoration of events, as well as during political upheavals, including assassinations of prominent political leaders. In November 2006, a few months after the July war with Israel, Lebanon saw a campaign with a different message than others they had been accustomed to during the 15-year civil war, carrying the words "I Love Life" (ILL) on billboards and other spaces throughout the country. Shortly after that, another campaign "I Love Life in Colours" (ILLC) appeared, only to be followed by a series of business-oriented marketing campaigns riding the "I love life" wave and several parodies by bloggers, all of which provide a new visual dimension to the battle over discourse and power in the divided country. With this in mind, this chapter aims to unpack the "I love" phenomena and contextualize how these various messages evolved, as well as examine their implications to the Lebanese political landscape. It begins by sketching the contours of the political domestic context before and during the campaigns before offering an analysis of the campaigns and discussing prospects for civil society, the media and the democratization processes in the country.[1]

The Political Context

On February 14, 2005, a massive blast in Beirut claimed the life of former Prime Minister Rafic Hariri, MP Bassil Fleyhan, and 22 other individuals. The assassination of Hariri led to the formation of the March 14 coalition by the Future Movement (Sunnis), the Progressive Socialist Party (Druze which left the coalition after 2009), the Phalanges and Lebanese Forces (Christians), the Free Patriotic Movement (Christians who left the coalition in 2005) and independent political personalities. The March 14 coalition staged a series of demonstrations in February and March 2005. Under domestic and international pressure, the Syrian military forces[2] left Lebanon on April 26, 2005. Elections were held in May 2005, following which a unity government was formed. However, the relative easing in political tension after the elections did not translate onto the security level, as a series of small blasts occurred in various Christian areas, while bigger blasts targeted politicians and journalists resulting in death or severe injuries. In April 2006, Michel Aoun, head of the Free Patriotic Movement (FPM) and a sizeable parliamentary bloc, signed a Memorandum of Understanding with Hezbollah's Secretary-General Hassan Nasrallah, thus steering his (Christian) followers further away from the March 14 coalition.

The memorandum was widely contested as it was seen as giving Christian legitimacy to a party (Hezbollah) which some considered at the time as a state within a state (Saghieh, 2006).[3] In July 2006, Israel launched a massive assault on Lebanon after Hezbollah captured two Israeli soldiers. The assault placed a heavy burden on an already exhausted Lebanese population in the economic, social and psychological arenas. In November 2006, the five Shi'i ministers who served in government resigned, leaving it crippled amid some arguments that the government was unconstitutional since it lacked adequate sectarian representation. At that time, the opposition comprised the Shi'i group Amal, Hezbollah, the FPM, the Marada (Christians mainly from north Lebanon) and other smaller pro-Syrian parties. On December 1, 2006, the opposition staged an open-ended sit-in at Riad Al Solh Square below the seat of the government in a bid to force it to resign. The sit-in was to last until May 2008, and tensions, especially among Shi'as and Sunnis, were palpable (Lellewyn, 2010). Space here does not allow for further intricate details of the complex internal Lebanese situation, but it was within this complex and highly charged political context that the "I Love..." campaigns were inscribed.

The "I Love..." Phenomenon: I Love Life (ILL)

The "I Love Life" campaign was launched on November 22, 2006 while the country was mourning a prominent leader of the March 14 group, Pierre Gemayel, who was assassinated the day before. Posters displaying these words were much simpler than other posters and billboards Lebanon had been accustomed to, as they only used a clear red background on the canvas with the message written in white. The posters were written in three languages, Arabic, English and French. The word "love" was replaced by a heart with two olive leaves. The red, white and green colors symbolized the "colours of the Lebanese flag,"[4] while the trilingual message aimed at the diverse Lebanese population, where French and/or English, along with Arabic, languages are taught at most schools. While seeking to avoid generalizations, clearly, a trilingual message was seen by the organizers of the campaign to be the best way to appeal to all in a language they speak, and also to reflect Lebanese pluralism. Each language is associated with several factions of society. Broadly speaking, the French language is usually associated with the Christians and the upper social classes, the business community speaks English and lower-income people speak Arabic. Hence the use of the three languages suggests that the audience is one that comprises all Lebanese, irrespective of their differences. The campaign was inspired by "I Love New York,"[5] whose momentum still sustains New York (ArabAd, 2007) with the hope that such a momentum will be created in Lebanon.

These three visual posters were followed by six others with the words: *baddna n'ich* (we want to live); *ba'i houn* (staying here), *endi saf* (I have a class to attend); *nezil 'al cheghel* (going to work); *rayeh eshar* (going to party) and *raje' min el safar* (I am coming back from abroad). These messages, all in colloquial Lebanese, were written in white against a red background with the smaller "I love life" appearing in Arabic at the bottom of each poster. The posters were "disseminated on billboards, television ads, mobile advertising and even the Christmas trees lining the streets of Beirut [...] then came the editorials in the newspapers and magazines, spreading the broader message [...] eight vans coloured in the 'I Love Life' livery drove around 12 locations [...] meanwhile students handed out stickers, badges, pens and balloons to emphasize the message of the campaign".

While a campaign coordinator referred to ILL as a "socio-political campaign with a political message," media scholars have long argued that political advertising should be viewed as a controlled message communicated through any channel designed to promote the political interest of parties, groups, governments or other organizations (Holz-Bacha and Kaid, 2006). Premised on this definition, and even if we contend with the coordinator that the message was brought out by a "group of people, without a single entity behind it,"[6] this campaign can be described as a form of political advertising because it intended to convey a particular political message. A campaign review in *ArabAd* proposes that ILL was "conceived by individuals from all walks of life—businesspeople, artists, journalists" (*ArabAd*, 2007) whose aim was to "put a firecracker under the seat of social lethargy" (ibid.), in itself an implicit political message. The campaign was not signed for. *ArabAd* pointed out that "no one knew where it came from or who was behind it," and when probed, the coordinator said that "they have asked not to be named" (ibid.). This quest for anonymity became problematic, bearing in mind that ILL falls within what McNair (2003) calls "constructed reality," which brings to mind Bennett and Entman's (2001) argument that anonymity impedes on citizens' abilities to engage in rational deliberation, a deliberation which is crucial to ensure any democratizing effect of political advertising.

Interest in who created the campaign soon shifted to who funded it. As the integrated campaign unfolded, it became obvious that the coordinators had a generous budget at their disposal. But no one knew where that came from. Published figures account for nearly two million dollars spent on Out of Home ads (OOH), TV, radio, newspapers and magazines (Shehabeddine, 2007), data that covers money spent on conventional advertising, but still falls short of the overall budget since it doesn't account for the various promotional items and below-the-line activities. One ILL coordinator only acknowledges that "there was a huge amount of money involved and contributions came from several entities." *ArabAd* states that "the campaign was funded by local businesses and private donations while the media offered its support with free airtime contributions."[7] However, many disagreed with that version. Journalist and writer Tim Llewellyn (2010) says partial funding came from the Americans, "ploughing in money through all sorts of democracy-pushing but essentially unreliable NGOs" while an article in *ArabAd* pointed at Saad Hariri as the financer. What is interesting is that barely a week after ILL was launched, an opposing campaign was unveiled, constituting a direct reply to ILL under the slogan "I Love Life in Colours" (ILLC).

"I Love Life in Colours" (ILLC)

The "I Love Life in Colours" was first seen as using the same logo and typography[8] as its predecessor, but closer scrutiny showed that there were slight differences. While the background was red and the writing in white, the texts were different. Some messages said "I love life in dignity," "I love life undictated," and the eponymous "I love life in colours." Other messages read "we want to live in Lebanon; safely." The ILLC messages were trilingual, as a direct rebuttal to ILL, but also because this was built on the same reasoning of speaking to each and everyone in his or her preferred language. The olive leaves topping the heart were removed and replaced by a rainbow drawn at the bottom left, bearing the signature of the Lebanese Opposition. The rainbow colors were not what you would usually expect as these were red, orange, yellow, green, blue and light green, the colors of the flags of several parties in the opposition. At that point, in Lebanon colors had become associated with political sides, inspired by the many "colour" revolutions which happened elsewhere, such as in Ukraine, for example. As Michael Young notes, these revolutions "had a powerful impact in showing how displeasure could be portrayed visually and how the media […] could be used to the advantage of those voicing the displeasure. This combination of imagery and political slogans forming a cornerstone of political strategies was new in Lebanon" (Young, 2010). In addition, the colors of the rainbow seemed to refer to the predominant colors used by the country's opposition parties: yellow for Hezbollah, orange for FPM, green for Amal and light green for Marada (pro-Syrian Christian party whose stronghold is in the north of the country).

Clearly, ILLC set itself outright as a political campaign. It was an overt political response to what was perceived as a covert political message through ILL. Sami Saab, creator of the ILLC concept, says that "the Lebanese opposition as a structured entity was born with this campaign signed by the Lebanese Opposition with a conceptual logo, the rainbow, reflecting the diversity of Lebanese groups and parties."[9] The several parties and groups behind ILLC chose to self-style themselves as Lebanese Opposition, allowing the intended audience to recognize who was behind the message. However, Saab contends that though he "totally agreed with the ILL concept, the problem was that the message was incomplete. [...] The second problem was the timing after the 2006 war, so the indirect message was that the opposition hates life and loves war". The aim of ILLC was to "to agree with this general message but with a complete and national version [...], the idea was to adopt the ILL concept because I love life too, but I love life in dignity".[10]

Several businesses built on these campaigns with similarly designed layouts using the red and white background, as well as a similar typography and slogans tailored to specific products. Everywhere on the streets, there were posters and adverts such as "I love carpets," "I love life in diamonds," while there were some promoting restaurants, frozen food, and even an institute for higher education. The blogosphere from all political sides took keen interest in the "I love..." trend and various other versions were created, a lot more than can be accounted for in this space.

Implications of the Campaigns on the Lebanese Media Scene

The transformations of the initial "I love life" motto, its mutations form the "socio-political" ILL to the openly political ILLC, and then to an eye-catching marketing initiative for businesses and finally to a means of protesting against both political sides while exposing inequalities is an interesting phenomenon in the history of modern Lebanese advertising. Nothing similar had taken place before and the response was something that even the initial ILL creators could not have expected.

While there is an assumption that media provides a key rallying point for national identity and identification with the nation, "the relationship [...] is perhaps seen most clearly in times of political crisis and change" (Oates, 2008: 65). In the context of the continuing struggle over power and discourse, if not influence, in Lebanon, it is not surprising that various forms of communication were enlisted as tools in the ongoing battles between March 14 and the Lebanese Opposition over the control of the Lebanese political scene. Saab considers that "without political communication, the political scene is boring and the party dead [...] the political party is like any other brand, it needs awareness and has to communicate"[11]. The ILL campaign coordinator argues that while there is a need to communicate, "[...] advertising per se isn't a harbinger of results unless followed by grassroots activities"[12]. Sarah Oates separately argues that "it is important to consider not only the usage of various types of media, but the amount of trust and attention paid to different media outlets" (Oates, 2008: 65).

Broadly speaking, Lebanese media are considered to have played a major role in the uprising of early 2005 or what was known as the Cedar Revolution (Khatib, 2007)[13] highlighting the centrality of mediation to the Lebanese political process. Specifically, both campaigns made use of various outlets although ILL was more integrated with a focus on OOH (50 percent of the budget) and ILLC was almost solely reliant on OOH. To try and understand the choice of media, one must keep in mind the Lebanese context in which every major political party owns or is closely affiliated to one or more media outlets spreading across television (Noetzold, 2008), press and radio. These outlets cater mainly to diverse party followers and to a lesser extent to the wider public, leading to criticism of the media's role in society, and to critiques by media scholars, such as Marwan Kraidy who has argued that "the convergence of political power and media ownership at the expense of civil society constitutes a threat to democracy in Lebanon" (Kraidy, 1998: 387–

400). However, in contrast to concerns around the convergence between power and media, Lila Abu-Lughod notes that: "state television and those who produce for it can try to reflect certain social transformations [...] yet they cannot control the experiences people seek outside of television-watching or the everyday social worlds in which people live their lives" (Abu-Lughod, 2002: 115–133). In Lebanon, convergence does not only refer to state-owned media as it is more inclusive, involving several media outlets and forms and the myriad political parties, all offering competing narratives. Thus, advertising space provides one public and visual medium where these competing narratives can encroach on a domain supposedly outside of their control—the domain of the "everyday social worlds" and one that might constitute an even bigger threat to democratization processes.

Encroaching on everyday social worlds in the Lebanese setting takes place mainly through OOH for various reasons. First, this is one of the few mediums not to be associated with political parties. OOH is dominated by independent businesses free of any direct political affiliation. Second, among unaffiliated media OOH is the only sector capable of boasting national coverage as opposed to other consumer magazines or dailies which are limited in coverage. Radios could provide national coverage, but the legislation requires a special license to broadcast content of political nature (Kraidy, 1998). Stations that have such licenses are affiliated, therefore leaving the remaining radios to be entertainment based only. It is no surprise then that OOH was extensively used in ILL and ILLC, to the degree that "no billboard [...] was left unused."[14] Another important factor stems from the nature of OOH as it reaches, or aims to reach, a larger population, and not only a particular party's followers.[15] Significantly, OOH turned out to be a "fair" battle ground for various voices and discourses. Driven by profits, especially since the political events of 2005 and 2006 had left them struggling, the OOH sector was willing to provide for both ILL and ILLC. Having already booked locations for ILL, they gave the remaining to ILLC, sometimes with the two campaigns ending up on different sides of the same panel.

The campaigns had a massive influence on the Lebanese advertising scene. Most local publications ran articles on the intricacies of the two campaigns and their repercussions. Independently from the Audio-Visual Law of 1994, "the advertising industry favoured a code of ethics"[16] to regulate business. Prior to 2006, there had been no reported attack advertising or even comparative advertising campaigns. ILLC was a *coup de maitre;* it wasn't directly attacking but it wasn't copying either. The differences between the ads were enough so that people could spot them, while the similarities were enough to allow ILLC to build on ILL. The opinions within the industry diverged, with some highly enthusiast about the advent of attack advertising.

Political Intricacies

Both campaigns were highly influential on the political scene, none the least since ILL managed to alienate part of the population, which at first glance appears surprising given the generic nature of the message. ILLC was also the first time when the Lebanese Opposition branded itself as such and engaged in a concerted and concrete counter-communication campaign that was highly visible to all the Lebanese public. However, it transpired that ILLC was mainly driven by the Lebanese party Hezbollah which is widely accepted as the main driving force behind the Opposition and all of its activities (Llewyn, 2010).

From its inception, and to this date the coordinators of ILL argue that "it was not a March 14th campaign,"[17] despite observers warning "there was a risk that the political connotations would overwhelm it" (Abdo Kahi, 2007: 52) and that "if the campaign is identified with a political group it will lose significance and be seen merely as a first-rate marketing campaign with a good slogan" (Karam quoted in *ArabAd*, 2007: 52). Saab believes that ILL was a "March 14 coalition campaign sponsored and supported by several countries,"[18] an opinion shared by others.[19] It is clear that the intentions of the campaign coordinators were to be dissociated from the March 14 coalition, but ILL failed at remaining independent, in view of the local media coverage. The Coordinator argued that ILL wasn't linked to March 14 since the visual bore connotations to the Lebanese flag and to a previous campaign "Independence 05".[20] However, these connotations turned out to be specifically what caused the public to believe that March 14 was behind it. Red and white are indeed the color of the Lebanese flag, but they are also the colors of the Cedar Revolution of February 2005, during which politicians wore red and white scarves around their necks at every demonstration (Young, 2010). The olive leaves were the link to, and reminder of "Independence 05" and this perhaps was the biggest pitfall.

Michael Young argues that "much of the branding for the *Independence Intifada* had been prepared before Hariri's assassination, the intention being to launch the campaign during the summer 2005 parliamentary elections [...] the Independence 05 brand (was) to be unveiled at demonstrations during the elections period [...] but it was Hariri's assassination that prematurely kicked off the branding campaign" (Young, 2010: 38). This insight rips off ILL's claim to autonomy. If ILL is linked to Independence 05, and the latter was to be used by the nucleus of what developed into March 14, it becomes nearly impossible to dissociate ILL from March 14. It is widely recognized that "corporate and political elites, while needing to communicate with larger publics, spend a significant amount of time targeting rival elites at all levels" (Davis, 2007: 60). If ILL was aimed at the "silent majority," ILLC was aimed at the general public, but also at elites within civil and political society, with which the Lebanese Opposition felt it was in competition. When ILLC appeared, ILL coordinators were admittedly "angry...but after a couple of days we were happy because we wanted to open a debate, a space for dialogue and exchanging ideas" (ibid.). However, one couldn't credit ILL with opening the debate. The slogans brought a breath of fresh air through the sheer positivism they imbued, but they merely affirmed facts applicable to many people in many locations, and the initial buzz around ILL was more curiosity geared towards its origins rather than anything else. It was only after ILLC was launched that the debate was ignited and people started probing both campaigns' slogans.

In his analysis of Lebanese society, Young argues there is little doubt that it remained fractured politically since 2005, which was further accentuated through the campaigns with diverse groups pitched against each other. Furthermore, he adds that while some parties, like March 14, seemed to want to revive Lebanon's pre-civil war cosmopolitanism, "Hezbollah was the antithesis of such an aspiration, a party that was autocratic and seemed to love death, when the essential Lebanese trait was to love life" (Young, 2010: 133). Premised on the above, it emerges that the main point of contention around ILL was the initial message, "I love life" and later, "we want to live". Saab pins this down: "someone is claiming that he loves life, which means in his opinion that there is someone who hates it, and of course here the hidden message is to attack the image of Hezbollah [...] the indirect message was that the Opposition hates life and loves war."[21] Seen from the perspective of a population that glorifies martyrdom, a simple slogan as "I love life" could be highly divisive.

How divisive such a slogan could be, particularly in an already divided society, is worth questioning further in relation to the power of words. As Judith Butler observes: "We ascribe an agency to language, a power to injure, and position ourselves as the objects of its injurious trajectory..." (Butler, 1997: 1). She proposes that if addressing the subject means interpellating the subject, then "the offensive call runs the risk of inaugurating a subject in speech who comes to use language to counter the offensive call" (ibid.: 2). Mikhail Bakhtin (1986) argues that utterances, or discourses, do not happen in isolation from other utterances, a point that Butler takes further to suggest that the contexts of speech acts need to also be thought through to assess the injuries caused by speech, which can lead to "a loss of context. [...] Indeed, it may be that what is unanticipated about the injurious speech act is what constitutes its injury, the sense of putting its addressee out of control" while "exposing at the moment of such a shattering, [...] precisely the volatility of one's 'place' within the community of speakers" (Butler, 1997: 3–4).

It might be possible to suggest that a claim such as "I love life" can have the effect of making people feel out of control, or out of place, because it does provoke questions about their own place or positioning in these discourses. However, the implications of the "I love life" claim might be about existence, in a country where conflict and violence are structured into people's everyday existence. Indeed, as Judith Butler argues "we [...] are, as a community, subjected to violence, exposed to its possibility, if not its realization. This means that each of us is constituted politically in part by virtue of the social vulnerability of our bodies. [...] Loss and vulnerability seem to follow from our being socially constituted bodies, attached to others, at risk of losing those attachments, exposed to others, at risk of violence by virtue of that exposure" (Butler, 2004: 20). This vulnerability, however, becomes highly exacerbated under "certain social and political conditions, especially those in which violence is a way of life and [where] the means to secure self-defence are limited" (ibid.: 28–29).

Conclusion

The normative arguments having been laid down, the real aims of the ILL campaign are hard to pin down because of the secrecy around it. In Lebanon, and the Arab world in general, more is expected from media and media performance than anywhere else, with continuing questions raised about whether the media can or will "articulate the voices of society" (Hafez, 2008: 1). These questions have been considered by several media scholars, drawing on the concept of the new Arab public sphere, which Hafez contends "has opened up over the past decade might be intertwined with the modernization of political values and attitudes and the whole fabric of Arab political culture" (ibid.: 4). Though the public sphere originated in the works of Jurgen Habermas, what is interesting to examine is how the concept evolved throughout the years and how it evolved in diverse societies other than the Western democracies within which it was formulated. In her rethinking of the public sphere, Nancy Fraser proposes that in stratified societies "whose basic institutional framework generates unequal social groups in structural relations of subordination and dominance [...] arrangements that accommodate contestation among a plurality of competing publics better promote the ideal of participatory democracy than does a single overarching public" (Fraser, 2007: 497).

A plurality of competing publics, this chapter notes, is a far more useful approach to assess socio-politics in Lebanon than the overly acclaimed new Arab public sphere (see Lynch, 2006) even though the mere presence of competing publics doesn't necessarily lead to an expansion of contestations, and the beginning of democracy. In the Lebanese stratified social setting, there are several competing publics and narratives, reflected in the country's diverse media. Having said that, one must keep in mind that, the availability of a diversified media scene is not inherently democratic and the Lebanese media is highly polarized across political lines, as a result of convergence between politics and media ownership. Consequently, the media falls short of providing an adequate and equally accommodating platform to the various existing publics. In his study of the expanding Arab media spaces, Marc Lynch concludes that "the most promising research avenue lies with media effects theories that emphasize framing and agenda setting" and "that there is relatively thin support for region wide claims about mass media effects on political attitudes and behaviours" (Lynch, 2008: 18). Lynch makes a distinction between attitudes and behavior with regards to the political effects of Arab media, recognizing that "part of the problem is conceptual: defining the political attitudes or behaviours of interest, and their relationship to political outcomes" and differentiates between "attitude(s), to be measured in opinion surveys and public discourse, whose manifestation doesn't necessarily lead to any particular political effects" and "democratization a political process whose manifestation can be seen in political behaviour—elections, protests, parliamentary manoeuvring—that is not reducible to attitudes" (ibid.: 22). In light of the above, it might prove more constructive if political campaigns were geared towards democratization rather than aiming at influencing attitudes. That could favor the emergence of "subaltern counter-publics [...] parallel discursive arenas where members of subordinated social groups invent and circulate counter-discourses to formulate oppositional interpretations of their identities, interests and needs" (Fraser, 2007: 497).

Lynch (2008: 29) notes, "the impact of media on democratization can best be described as shaping the political opportunity structures, transforming the strategies and repertoires of political activists" while Hafez (2008: 8) argues that "winning the media contest is not enough for the transformation of political systems—new Arab media have to be followed by new political and social movements." From this perspective, it would be fair to believe that television shaped the internal and foreign political opportunity structures in early 2005. However, what emerged from that media event was far from a social movement. The nearly 1 million people who took to the streets on March 14, 2005, were a mix of politically active groups and independent individuals who felt they had an opportunity to assert their demands, and that mix could have formed the nucleus of a new social movement. Instead they were hastily pulled into an umbrella coalition which soon lost its impetus thanks to its leaders' political maneuvering. Most media outlets were as compliant and enthusiast in justifying these maneuvres as they were in calling for unity earlier on.

In Lebanon's post-independence history, there is a battle around what constitutes truth, which, as Foucault has articulated, is "the ensemble of rules according to which the true and the false are separated and specific effects of power attached to the true. [...] It's not a matter of battle *on behalf of the truth* but of a battle about *the status of the truth* and the economic and political role it plays" (Rabinow, 1977/2003: 317).[22] In Foucault's conception, truth is a thing of things of this world, and in this world each society has its own general politics and political economy of truth. The political economy of truth is characterized by five traits:

> it is centred on the form of scientific discourse and the institutions that produce it; it is subject to constant economic and political incitement [...]; it is the object, under diverse forms, of immense diffusion and consumption [...]; it is produced and transmitted under the control, dominant if not exclusive, of a few great political and economic apparatuses [...], finally, it is the issue of a whole political debate and social confrontation. (ibid.)

The battle around truth is a contemporary feature of the Lebanese political and social scene with competing narratives staking their claims on diverse traditional media, but also in OOH ads and organized events. While, as Foucault argues, there is a need for "detaching the power of truth from the forms of hegemony, social, economic and cultural within which it operates at the present time" while avoiding the chimera of attempting to free truth from every system of power since truth is already power (ibid.), it is unclear what role Arab media, specifically the Lebanese media, could play in the attempt to 'detach' the truth and provide activists with a platform for action. So far great hopes have been pinned on the Lebanese media, mainly since these media operate in an environment which is considered free when compared to other Arab countries.[23] However, working in a relatively free environment cannot guarantee a free media, as the Lebanese alignment of political clout and media corroborates. Indeed, one must bear in mind that establishing the correlation among politics, society and the media is still very hard, and that our assessment of it depends on our vantage points. The Lebanese media appears to be very powerful in terms of reaching the population and raising awareness, as we have seen in the case of ILL and ILLC, but it remains weak in terms of representing a pluralist society and rather serves the interest of the political elite. The hope is that as political awareness grows, and as democracy becomes more desirable (for some) and attainable (for others), conventional and new media will be able to enhance integration rather than polarization.

Notes

1. The empirical evidence supporting this essay was gathered in Lebanon through material collection of some of the visuals employed, press reviews and coverage of the campaigns; and interviews with one coordinator of ILL and the creator of the concept of ILLC. The translations in this chapter are the author's own.

2. Syrian forces had been in Lebanon since 1976, and their presence became "official" after the Ta'if Accord.

3. Hazem Saghieh, "Aoun-Hezbollah: The Opposites Unveiled..." (author's translation). *Al-Hayat*, (September 3, 2006). Available at http://www.daralhayat.com/archivearticle/102454. Accessed January 20, 2011.

4. ILL Campaign Coordinator, *Discussion Around I Love Life*. Interview on June 16, 2010.

5. Ibid.

6. ILL Campaign Coordinator.

7. *ArabAd*, "Talk of the Town: The I Love Life Story".

8. Tarek Chemali, "I Love Life: Intricacies of Lebanese Politics." in *ArabAd*. [Listed SOURCE]

9. Sami Saab, Regional Creative Director at Publicis-Graphics Beirut (at the time of the events) and creator of ILLC concept, *Discussion around I Love Life in Colours and Political Communication in Lebanon*, personal communication on July 5, 2010.

10. Sami Saab, personal communication.

11. Sami Saab, personal communication.

12. ILL Coordinator.
13. Lina Khatib, (2007) "Television and Public Action in the Beirut Spring" in Naomi Sakr, *Arab Media and Political Renewal: Community, Legitimacy and Public Life,* (London: I.B.Tauris), ch. 3.
14. Chemali, "I Love Life: Intricacies of Lebanese Politics."
15. ILL Coordinator.
16. Jean Claude Boulos quoted in Marwan Kraidy, (2000) "Television and Civic Discourse in Postwar Lebanon" in Leo A. Gher & Hussein Y. Amin (eds), *Civic Discourse and Digital Age Communications in the Middle East.* (Stamford, CT: Ablex Publishing), ch. 1, p. 10.
17. ILL coordinator.
18. Saab, personal communication on July 5, 2010.
19. See *La Revue du Liban*: "Government vs. Opposition: Two Lebanons Battle It Off Again" or *L'Hebdo Magazine*: "The Majority Loves Life...The Opposition Too" or even *Le Commerce du Levant*: "Out of Home dverting panels were in 2006 the battlefield of the Majority and the Opposition through the campaign and counter-campaign of I Love Life".
20. ILL Coordinator.
21. Saab, personal communication on July 5, 2010.
22. Michel Foucault, (2003) 'Truth and Power' in Paul Rabinow and Nikolas Rose (eds), *The Essential Foucault: Selections from Essential Works of Foucault, 1954–1984,* (New York; London: [1977] 2003), pp 300–317, 317. Emphases added.
23. www.rsf.org

References

Abu-Lughod Lila, (2002). "Egyptian Melodrama-Technology of the Modern Subject?" In Faye D. Ginsburg et al. (eds), *Media Worlds: Anthropology on New Terrain* (Berkeley, CA: University of California Press), pp. 115–133.
Althusser, Louis ([1971] 2001), *Lenin and Philosophy and Other Essays,* trans. B. Brewster (New York: Monthly Review Press).
ArabAd, (2007). "Talk of the Town: The I Love Life Story," 17(1): 39–54.
Bakhtin, Mikhael ([1970–1971] 1986), *Speech Genres and Other Late Essays,* trans. V.W. McGee (Austin: University of Texas Press).
Boulos, Jean Claude quoted in Marwan Kraidy (2000). "Television and Civic Discourse in Postwar Lebanon" in Leo A. Gher and Hussein Y. Amin (eds), *Civic Discourse and Digital Age Communications in the Middle East* (Stamford, CT: Ablex Publications).
Butler, Judith (1997). *Excitable Speech: A Politics of the Performative* (New York, London: Routledge).
———— (2004). *Precarious Life: The Powers of Mourning and Violence* (London: Verso).

Chemali, Tarek (2001). "I Love life: Intricacies of Lebanese Politics," *ArabAd*, 17(2): p. 170

Davis, Aaron (2007). *The Mediation of Power: A Critical Introduction* (London: Routledge).

Entman, Robert M. and W. Lance Bennet (2001). "Communication in the Future of Democracy: A Conclusion" in W.L. Bennett and R. M. Entman (eds), *Mediated Politics: Communication in the Future of Democracy* (Cambridge: Cambridge University Press).

Foucault, Michel ([1977] 2003). "Truth and Power" in Paul Rabinow and Nikolas Rose (eds), *The Essential Foucault: Selections from Essential Works of Foucault, 1954–1984* (New York, London: New Press).

Fraser, Nancy (2007). "Rethinking the Public Sphere: A Contribution to the Critique of Actually Existing Democracy" in Simon During (ed.), *The Cultural Studies Reader* (3rd edn, London: Routledge).

Habermas, Jurgen (1974). "The Public Sphere," *New German Critique*, 1(3): 49–55.

Hafez, Kai (ed.) (2008). *Arab Media: Power and Weakness*, (London: Continuum).

Holtz-Bacha, Christina and Linda Lee Kaid (2006). "Political Advertising in International Comparison" in L. L. Kaid and C. Holtz-Bacha (eds), *The Sage Handbook of Political Advertising* (Thousand Oaks, CA: Sage Publications), ch. 1.

Hutchinson, John (2005). *Nations as Zones of Conflict* (London: Sage Publications).

ILL Campaign Coordinator, *Discussion around I Love Life*. Interview on June 16, 2010.

Kahi, Abdo (2007), Interview "How Do You Feel about I Love Life?" *ArabAd*, 17(1): 52.

Karam, Elie (2007). Interview "How Do You Feel about I Love Life?" *ArabAd*, 17(1): 52.

Khatib, Lina (2007). "Television and Public Action in the Beirut Spring" in Naomi Sakr (ed.) *Arab Media and Political Renewal: Community, Legitimacy and Public Life* (London: I.B.Tauris).

Kraidy Marwan (1998). "Broadcasting Regulation and Civil Society in Postwar Lebanon," *Journal of Broadcasting and Electronic Media*, 42(3): 387–400.

Llewellyn Tim, (2010). *Spirit of the Phoenix: Beirut and the Story of Lebanon* (London: I.B.Tauris).

Lynch, Marc (2006). *Voices of the New Arab Public: Iraq, Al-Jazeera, and Middle East Politics Today* (New York: Columbia University Press).

———— (2008). "Political Opportunity Structures: Effects of Arab Media" in Kai Hafez (ed.) *Arab Media: Power and Weakness* (London: Continuum).

Maasri, Zeina (2009). *Off the Wall: Political Posters of the Lebanese Civil War* (London: I.B.Tauris).

McNair, Brian (2003). *An Introduction to Political Communication*; 3rd edn, (London, New York: Routledge).

Notzold, Katharina (2008). "The Political Elite's Dominance over the Visual Space: A Qualitative and Quantitative Content Study of Lebanese Television" in Kai Hafez (ed.), *Arab Media: Power and Weakness* (London: Continuum).

Oates, Sarah (2008). *Introduction to Media and Politics* (London: Sage Publications).

Saghieh, Hazem (2006). "Aoun-Hezbollah: The Opposites Unveiled..." (author's translation). *Al-Hayat*. Available at http://www.daralhayat. com/archivearticle/102454. Accessed January 20, 2011.

Sami, Saab (Regional Creative Director at Publicis-Graphics Beirut at the time of the events and creator of ILLC concept), *Discussion around I Love Life in Colours and Political Communication in Lebanon*, personal communication on July 5, 2010.

Shehabeddine, Hanad (2007). "The War of Billboards Escalates" *ArabAd*, 17(2): 124–27.

Young, Michael (2010). *The Ghosts of Martyrs' Square: An Eyewitness Account of Lebanon's Life Struggle* (New York: Simon & Schuster).

III

MEMORIES AND NARRATION

10

MAKING SENSE OF WAR NEWS AMONG ADOLESCENTS IN LEBANON: THE POLITICS OF SOLIDARITY AND PARTISANSHIP

HELENA NASSIF[1]

Growing up in a war-torn country, I carry the heavy baggage of the war images I had watched on news broadcasts every night. One image struck me fifteen years after the Lebanese civil war was over. I was at home alone on February 14, 2005, when I received a phone call from a friend checking if I was still alive and told me to switch on the television.[2] The screen opened on an image I knew very well: burning cars and dead bodies on the ground, but one detail was new and almost surreal: a man on fire opened the door of a car and walked out. It was not that image alone that drove me hysterical that day, but the rush of similar images from my childhood and the memory of Lara. I knew Lara from the poems her father wrote after she died in a car bomb in Beirut.[3] She was still in school and she was the only child of my parents' friends. Although I have never experienced a car bomb in person, the TV images were personal; it is this personal experience of televized images of war that drove me to study how adolescents in Lebanon make sense of daily war images.

The experience of adolescents who were born during the peaceful years between 1993 and 1995 is different than mine. These teens are not expected to remember the 1996 Israeli offensive on Lebanon called the "Operation Grapes of Wrath," but most probably remember the assassination of Prime Minister Rafic Hariri in a car bomb in 2005 and the many car explosions and assassinations that continued to take place until the Israeli major war on Lebanon during July 2006. War images (including images of atrocities) are shown without reservation on Lebanese television where real violence on the news doesn't only come from inside Lebanon, as wars in Palestine and Iraq are priority news. The Lebanese adolescents of today, born after the end of the civil war, continue to live with news of war with various degrees of proximity as they live in a conflict-ridden region. This chapter, based on a study undertaken for academic research, aims to answer the question of how adolescents in Lebanon make sense of war news in their region. The historical context for the research is a critical phase in the history of Lebanon where international, regional and local events that preceded and followed the assassination of Hariri in 2005 caused an escalation in political conflict that still persists during 2012.

Internal Conflicts and the War on Lebanon

The Hariri assassination divided Lebanon into two conflicting political camps; the first (later to be named the March 14 Alliance) accused Syria of the assassination and the second (later to be called the March 8 Alliance) pointed an accusing finger at the USA and Israel.[4] Many factors contributed to the escalation of the situation, leading to the growth of distinct March 8 and March 14 political loyalties. For the purpose here, it is also important to emphasize the role of the media in a highly mediated conflict. Lebanese media outlets belong to various political factions and political elites use their respective mouthpieces, as their TV stations are often called, to communicate their positions to their followers. Lebanese citizens become hooked to TV stations of their preferred political parties in search of additional information.

The political explanations for the severe divide are multi-fold. The 2003 Iraq War and the Syrian role in post-occupation Iraq changed the status quo between the USA and Syria, resulting in the UN Council Resolution 1559 (Fisk, 2005). The resolution demanded that all foreign troops—a reference to Syria—withdraw from Lebanon and called for the disarmament of all Lebanese militia, meaning Hezbollah (United Nations Security Council, 2004). Hezbollah refused to be named a "militia" and insisted on keeping the name of "national resistant movement," thereby keeping itself out of the resolution. The resolution nevertheless initiated internal political tensions among Lebanese groups that held different internal and external political agendas.

Hariri was a major player in the Lebanese political scene with strong regional and international ties mainly to the French president at the time, Jacques Chirac, and the Saudi monarchy. Hariri's alleged role in the passing of the resolution created tensions with the Syrian president, which meant that his assassination was interpreted by his followers and allies as to have been "made in Syria." The USA and France also accused Syria, calling for its troops to withdraw from Lebanon.[5] Syria denied any responsibility, but withdrew all its troops due to international pressure and Lebanese public protests known as the "Cedar Revolution" or "Independence Uprising." The Lebanese official position after the Hariri assassination remained supportive of Hezbollah as a national resistance (CNN, 2005).

The 2006 war on Lebanon took the internal divisions to new levels.[6] The March 14 leaders were accused by the opposition to have tolerated the attack by Israel in the hope the hostilities would lead to the disarming of Hezbollah. Hezbollah survived the invasion and the March 8 alliance requested a bigger share in the government. The government refused and the opposition initiated an open sit-in on December 1, 2006 asking the government to resign. The situation was not resolved until the opposition organized a coup-like control of the capital during May 2008.[7] The armed dominance on the ground forced the government to participate in talks in Qatar. The talks resulted in the elections of the Lebanese president and a new government of "national unity."

On December 27, 2008, Israel launched a military attack on Gaza. At that time, I was in Lebanon planning my fieldwork. The offensive continued for 23 days, during which more than 1000 Palestinians and 13 Israelis were killed.[8] The images of atrocities on Lebanese and pan-Arab television stations were extremely disturbing and the question of "how do adolescents in Lebanon make sense of war news" became both pressing and more sensitive!

Children as News Audiences

In the large body of literature that exists on media violence and children, the majority of research focuses on fictional representations of violence and minority investigates children as audiences of factual war news.[9] Research on children as audiences that aims to assess emotional reactions to war images is mainly set in Europe/US contexts far from war zones. This literature on mediated violence and children has been critically scrutinized. The first criticism warns scholars studying violence and its "effects" on children from falling into the role of the "self-appointed 'experts' of the so-called 'moral majority'" (Tulloch 2000, 84). It deconstructs the value systems of researchers who identify media violence as a problem and approach children as a "vulnerable" group without questioning the wider cultural context that the literature on the "effects" of media violence serves (Weaver and Carter, 2006). Weaver and Carter also called for "de-westernizing media violence" research and examining "factual media violence formats and audiences" (ibid.: 14), which coincides with calls for "third-generation" audience theory in media studies which shifts the ground away from the "'effects' of television's 'bad' content on passive and susceptible audiences" and beyond the trend of resisting audience (Tulloch, 2000: 83). This chapter takes these critiques into account while it aims to research children as audiences of "real" war news in the context of the Lebanon.

Research on children and the news and that specifically emphasizes emotional responses to traumatic news, as Carter and Davies (2005) note, can be divided into two trends; the first emerges from developmental psychology and uses mainly quantitative methods to identify the emotional and psychological harm caused to children across age and gender, while the second is influenced by critical theory and seeks to understand how children respond emotionally and intellectually to frightening news (ibid.: 226). Although the two approaches differ significantly in their adopted theoretical constructions of childhood, it is important to break free from limitations set by any one approach and to adopt Alasuutari's "third-generation" research that proposed not to confine research to the "effects" or "no effects" positions.

Researchers in the developmental psychology trend shed light on the importance of developmental differences in understand- ing the emotional consequences of nationally-significant wars fought in distant countries on children watching television (Cantor et al., 1993). However, certain studies show contradictory results along various variables. For example, developmental difference is challenged by a study that does not confirm age as a variable that affects emotional responses to frightening news (Carter and Davies, 2005). Similarly, different studies do not agree on the relation between children's emotional reactions and gender for while certain studies confirm no relation (Van der Voort et al., 1993, Carter and Davies 2005), one study proves that "girls ... report a greater number of fears and more intense fear responses than boys" (Cantor et al., 1993, 335). A third study provides an explanation to how gendered differences appear in the way children talk about war, for boys do not want to admit anxiety while girls are "taught to worry" (Morrison and MacGregor, 1993: 360). Carter and Davies criticize research that regards children as "largely unable to understand what is being reported in the news" and "emotionally ill-equipped to cope with it" as well as puts emphasis on "children's negative emotional responses to frightening news" and "depoliticizes the events to which children are reacting" (2005: 227).

These criticisms emphasize some of the limitations of a number of studies, but do not negate other important conclusions. One conclusion highlights television as a major source of news for children especially during wars (Wober and Young, 1993). Another establishes a relation between children's emotional responses to war news, exhibiting ideological positions towards war and patriotic identifications with their countries (Van der Voort et al., 1993). A third study introduces parents and not the news as the main factors influencing the children's responses to war (Morrison and MacGregor, 1993).

The second approach identified by Carter and Davies (2005) is the critical theory adopted by David Buckingham in his chapter "Facing Facts: The Emotional Politics of News" (1996). Buckingham puts "effects" in italics or between inverted commas because he understands "effects" as possibly related to emotional responses that "might lead to certain kinds of behaviour" in which the "connections between them are likely to be complex and diverse" (ibid., 280). He regards the emotional "effects" as "negative" and "positive" responses and argues that "the consequences of such emotional responses cannot easily be categorized as either 'positive' or 'negative'" (ibid., 281). He differentiates between the feelings induced by television material and the range of coping strategies developed by children. Buckingham highlights that coping strategies become problematic when applied to non-fictional material: "There may be very little that children can do in order to come to terms with their 'negative' responses to non-fictional material, precisely because they are so powerless to intervene in issues that concern them" (2006: 282). Buckingham identifies limitations to children's agency but he doesn't adopt victimhood as a theoretical construction of childhood.

Buckingham's work on news as genre provides a good reference for replication in the context of children watching war news in war-affected regions. His work is critical, comprehensive, allows for the implementation of exploratory work in an under researched area in Lebanon and tends to go beyond the "effects" or "no effects" positions.[10] Working with adolescents is extremely problematic and I took all measures to respect ethical practices specific to working with children.[11] Prompts were used during focus groups in order to explore the emotional responses of a group of adolescents to real violence on television by listening and learning from them talk on news of war taking place in geographically proximate locations. The analysis was based on the results of an initial questionnaire and the focus groups conducted with teens aged between 12 and 14 years.[12]

These results presented below are "tentative" generalizations that are valid in terms of the unrepresentative sample and can prove to be valuable for further quantitative or qualitative research on the topic. They tell the story of 13 children I met during February 2009 in a middle-class private school in Beirut. The importance of these results rest not in their representativeness or generalizability, but in the insights they provide about the adolescents' complex relation with television, real-life experiences, politics and identity presentation. The analysis of the children's narratives was grouped under three sub-themes; children talking about news as genre, emotional responses to war news and opinions on regulating war images.[13]

Children Talking About the News

Data generated from the population of 73 seventh grade students between 12 and 14 years, suggest that children do watch the news, as reported by 65.7 percent of them. Yet, the results don't indicate whether it is attentive viewing or not. Children might watch the news because they are simply in the room where the news is being followed by their parents. Buckingham explains, based on Barwise and Ehrenber (1988) and Morley (1986), that children and others who have less power in the household, have less control of the television set (1996: 179). Radi,[14] one of the children in the mixed group, said he watched the news even when he did not intend to because "the family is sitting and dad is watching the news so I log onto the internet and we watch the news." Many children, like Radi, said they watched the news while doing something else, mainly browsing the internet. Knowing that more than half of the children said they watched the news, I looked into whether their viewership changed during wartime.

Results show an increase, from 65.7 percent to 91.8 percent, in the number of students watching the news during the war on Gaza. Of those who watched the news, those who specify that they watched all the news and looked for more information increased from 4.1 percent during "peace" times to 16.4 percent during the assaults on Gaza.

The results of the focus group sample support that of the population for news viewing increased for majority of children in the sample. Only one girl, Halima, indicated that her viewing decreased. In the focus group session, Halima revealed that she was avoiding the news because it was making her cry. Mona who mentioned she was avoiding the Gaza war coverage still wrote that she remembered the sounds of crying mothers who have lost their children. Preliminary results from Lebanon support those of Wober and Young (1993) that children tend to watch more news during wars.

The fact that the teens did watch the news more often during wartime does not mean that they "liked" it. Only one child in the selected population nominated news as his favorite program while majority of focus group participants described news as "boring". Rejection of political news was explained to be a result of the continuous conflict between Lebanese political factions. Raed mentioned that he spent majority of his time using the net because television news made him feel bored because "each time it is the same story; they fight then reconcile." The others agreed and Mona added that the political elites "don't do anything for us."

This conversation showed that the children were cynical about the political elites from both the government and the opposition. However, the same children changed their mind later in the focus group session, showing complete support to the March 14 Alliance. The children's earlier expressions of cynicism can be explained by adopting the notion of "cynical chic" from Eliasoph (1990) and Gamson (1992). Buckingham, however, differentiates between cynicism and apathy and specifies that the children's "expressions of cynicism serve as a valuable and indeed pleasurable – way of rationalizing ... [their] own sense of powerlessness, and even of claiming a degree of superiority and control" (1999: 176). Carter supports this claim that children find the news boring because "they feel they are not being taken seriously and that their opinions and ideas don't count for anything" (Carter, 2004: 69). One of the boys said that the news is boring but when there is something interesting like war he watches. None of the adolescents in Lebanon expressed any pleasure associated with watching war news and images.

The children's motivation for watching the news was defined primarily in terms of seeking information. To explain possible reasons for differences between children watching or avoiding war news is not within the scope of this research. However, an interesting observation suggests that few children tried to avoid graphic images of war, but kept an interest in knowing "what is happening" by asking their parents for updates. They defined their motivation for watching factual material in terms of seeking information. The boys highlighted their interest in information on general security and safety. Karim explained that the news of importance to them is the one that reveals "what killing is taking place" and Joubran added that he is interested "if there is danger or something" and not interested in "what this or that person says."

The discussion among the boys highlights the children's attitude towards political news; they are interested in it and cynical about its main players. War news is not treated with the same cynicism as political news. This observation leads me to re-question the "cynical chic" explanation in the context of war news. Children do not show interest in war news because of a regained sense of power.

Carter reveals that British kids identify news about war and conflict "as being of vital importance to them" (2004: 77). It is important to further investigate what factors make news about wars and conflict interesting for children taking into consideration the problematic of defining P/politics.

Emotional Responses to War News

The absence of pleasure associated with watching news raises questions about emotional responses to war news. Here, I move to discussing the children's narratives after viewing the prompts. It is important to keep in mind that discussing emotional responses must be understood in social terms "as discursive performances, in which children attempt to take on particular social roles, and hence to lay claim to a particular identity" (Buckingham, 1996: 197). That is, it is necessary not to mistake "rationalistic expressions" of emotions as ways to assess emotions (Hage, 2009: 63). The children's narratives are complex manifestations of emotional, cognitive and social expressions.

The children, after viewing the prompts, described images of atrocities that were more graphic than those included in the clips: the image of a child whose brain was blown open or whose "heart was outside his body." They referred to wars they have personally experienced and were comfortable sharing their stories that were tolerated and respected by their mates. The memories of war overlapped with other fear filled real incidents and fiction films about war. In all three focus groups, they mentioned the practical joke stink bomb planted in the school by older high school students during the same academic year. The little explosion was remembered with enthusiasm as an event that contains the ingredients of war.

The adolescents differentiated between war as an internal conflict they all disapproved of and war with Israel, which opened a discussion on whether it is important to be victorious against it. The refusal of "killing" in the boys group didn't lead to a total refusal of war. After screening the prompt on the war on Gaza, Karim exclaimed:

> Miss[15] I want to say something, now these people who are dying who are not guilty of the war, not related to Hamas or others, they can, since these people are dying, why don't all

the Palestinians carry guns and fight Israel, since they are
anyways dying without weapons ...

The boys in different parts of the dialogue voiced their criticism of
Israeli military action, but their disagreement with the occupation
didn't necessarily lead them to demonize the Israeli people. Karim
emphasized that "not everyone in Israel accepts what is happening,
the war." Yehya, for his part, specified that "not all Israeli are against
Lebanon" and Mazen differentiated between Israel "not being good"
and the Jews "having lived in Lebanon before Israel existed."

A similar dialogue took place among the girls when Lamia
rejected war as futile, then later expressed her dilemma on how to
reject injustice without fighting back. Mary who adopted the identity
of the rebel, was convinced by Lamia that Israeli non-combatants
are not directly responsible. Similarly, a dialogue between Fares and
Mazen continued back and forth until Fares accepted the morality
of shelling the Israeli army and Mazen acknowledged the need to
safeguard Israeli non-combatants.

The children adopted two positions on the war with Israel. The
first position totally rejected war and believed it led nowhere, while
the second saw value in fighting Israel to end injustice. The children
in Lebanon rejected war because it kills, but when it came to Israel
the discussion grew more complex. The many children that agreed
that "they are like us" as individuals still did not accept their deeds
as a state or army.

This refusal led the children to express empathy for the victims
that were mainly the children and adults of Gaza and Lebanon.
Raed, in talking about the war on Gaza, said he felt he was in their
place and that when they were hurting, he was also hurting. The
word "haram" which translates as ill-gotten, taboo or illegal was
used to describe what was happening to the victims. Their death
and suffering was perceived as an act of injustice. The children
analyzed both wars and agreed that the war on Gaza was more
dreadful. I anticipated the problem of translation and every time
the children mentioned "haram," I asked them to explain it. None
of the explanations included the pity dimension. "Haram" meant for
them mainly injustice or unfairness and their emotional responses
served to what I call the politics of solidarity.

The findings from Beirut show that Lebanese and Palestinian children and civilian adults were viewed as innocent victims, but concern was mostly about children victims. The discussion in both the boys and girls groups referred to non-combatants in Israel as victims. Later in the discussion I asked them what differentiates children from adults. They explained that they are the same, but adults have lived their lives while children have yet to live theirs, adding in way of explanation that adults can escape while children are helpless. Mazen specified that "all people who are not related to the war are innocent."

The girls gave the same value to the lives of men, women and children. They declared children as special because of their emotional appeal on the screen. Mary explained that people are most affected by the image of a child. Halima also clarified that children suffer when they lose their parents. These remarks are meaningful because they show that the girls are sensitive to the sufferings of war for the victims are not necessarily the dead alone but those whose lives are altered by war.

The adolescents in Lebanon mentioned both positive and negative emotional responses to war news. They talked about feelings of guilt, sadness, happiness, anger, pride and excitement. These answers were prompted by my questions; however, the adolescents didn't talk about fear in relation to the images but to war. Buckingham identifies the emotions of pity, physical disgust, luck and gladness as evoked in relation to news about places far away from home. He adds that these emotional responses are assumed based on a perceived distance from "the objects of pity" (1996, 184). The Lebanese children did not feel physical disgust towards the war victims in Lebanon or Palestine although they felt privileged in comparison. The fact that the Lebanese children felt lucky or glad is associated with a high degree of empathy.

Another conversation among Mary, Halima, Lamia and Diala is a good example of their sense of privilege, which allows them to reflect on what they have and how they behave in comparison to their subjects of identification. The guilt that some of the girls talked about was not expressed with a sense of distance from the victims. Clothes, shopping, being fashionable and cool are important discursive topics for girls their age and the images of war made these priorities seem trivial. All these expressions are specific to the girls' results, for only Joubran among the boys mentioned briefly that in Gaza, innocent people are dying while they (in Lebanon) were living the best life. The boys did not dwell much on their feelings of guilt and those who highlighted the issue of guilt and consumption were mostly girls.

The boys delved into political analysis and talked about the emotions of sadness/happiness and proposed actions for "help." As children, they knew their limitations: to donate money, send food and prayers. Karim compared himself to the dying children and said he felt happy he was still alive and that he and his friends had survived the war on Lebanon. He stated that he was ready to fight but his parents would not allow it. Karim, Mazen and Mary who expressed that they were willing to fight were not among those who avoided war news, but wrote that they watched the news and looked for more. Mary and Karim identified with the Palestinians; Mazen preferred to die in his own country. None of the children showed any clear political alignment with the opposition or the government and there was no observable difference among adolescents from different political loyalties concerning their identification with the Palestinians. The differentiation Hage (2009) makes between "identification with" and "identification through" helps explain the range of compassion expressed for the victims. While all children said they identified with the Palestinian victims, only two children identified through Palestine or did not "allow for any separation" (ibid.: 71). More adolescents showed identification through Lebanon.

The discussion among the girls below reveals no positive but negative emotional responses to war images:

> *Lamia*: The first day they hit Gaza, I was watching, I saw images that blow the mind, I went to sleep a bit, I kept on imagining, whenever I close my eyes, I see the scenes.
> *Halima*: Me too.
> ...
> *Mary*: I wish I could take an anaesthetic to sleep directly.
> *Lamia*: Yes, I said I don't deserve this, why do I deserve it while they don't? I kept on thinking all night until it was time for school, and then I couldn't concentrate on studying.

Lamia moved on to talk about how her mom helped her relax by assuring her that a solution would be found. She was able to sleep the following nights. Halima dreamt of the images for two nights. Although both girls had trouble sleeping at the start of the war, they dealt with the war images very differently. Halima tried to avoid the war news while Lamia kept watching. All girls openly revealed that they cried; however, Mary cried because her parents prevented her from watching the news. Guilt, privilege and tears were prominent concurrent expressions in the girls' narratives. They also talked about fear comfortably when asked and said the July war on Lebanon caused them more fear than the war on Gaza.

The children said the war scared them and they were afraid of their parents' reactions to it. During the war on Lebanon, not all children had 24-hour access to electricity to watch the news. Another interesting result around fear is the way boys talked about it with ambivalence. In one conversation the boys tried to construct their gender role as the fearless protectors. When asked if they were afraid of Israel, Mazen, Fares and Karim said they were not afraid, while Joubran added "but, it is better that they remain away; we want to live." The internal dynamics among the boys led to the dominance of a collective masculine gender identity. This tension didn't take place in the mixed group for the boys in the presence of girls were more comfortable to talk about fear and tears. However, I cannot generalize this observation because the mixed group happened to include friends who most probably didn't have to assert themselves towards each other or whose power relations were already established.

The results of the girls-only focus group raised an issue that I had missed taking into consideration. I knew from the beginning that my research did not include parents and that future research must fill this gap. What I failed to notice was that the Lebanese parents of today's children of 12 to 14 are themselves the generation of youth who lived the civil war. The research question no longer only relates to children who live in war-torn areas, but to children of parents who have survived wars. Any future research must take into consideration the war experiences of parents as an important factor affecting the emotional responses of children to war news.

Trusting Images: Suspecting Texts

To investigate the emotional politics of war news is to look also into the children's perceptions on what to be broadcasted on television and for what purposes and to understand their views on the power and interpretation of images and text. Children in all three focus groups challenged the credibility of the news on Lebanese stations. The criticism stemmed from their knowledge of the sectarian and political affiliation of each television station. This knowledge did not prevent few children from showing trust in a preferred television station according to their parents' loyalties and did not translate into a critical understanding of news in general. The boys showed trust in foreign newspapers and news sites. They specified CNN and *The New York Times* as reliable sources of information. They explained that these institutions have no internal interest to support one side; they just cover "what is happening"!

The contradictions expressed by these children are multi-fold; they trusted the images, but suspected the text, had faith in the media in general as represented by "foreign" media, but distrusted the Lebanese media and the coverage of war. The boys were skeptical of the media that "hides" the numbers of dead soldiers.[16] Mary mentioned the lesson in civic education on news writing and how journalists should check the reliability of the information and not include their opinion. The little media literacy the children learn helped to reinforce the myth of the news process as "objective."

Even when the adolescents did not doubt the authenticity of visual images and perceived news as a genre to be reflective of "reality" and images as proof of "credibility," they had different opinions about their use and effectiveness. Halima and Lamia stated that they were not "affected" by old images or edited images of past wars and that images of "live" coverage are the most "attractive."

There is little evidence to support Halima and Lamia's claim, but the girls' explanation of the political function of images links seeing, to feeling, to action. Lamia said she felt disempowered to act, but later deduced that the images are meant to "affect" those who have the power to act. Mary specified that those are for example the president of the country. Lamia mentioned that the images are able to "affect even those without a good heart but not Israel." She regarded Israel to be beyond comprehension and mentioned more than three times that she seeks to understand "how they think."

Similarly to the girls, boys thought children should see war images in order to learn about war and as a result become less fearful. They also referred to Israel as the source of trouble. Fares mentioned that he has seen more graphic images than the ones edited in the prompts. Karim specified to have seen an image of a person "whose heart was out" and Mazen "whose head was cut." Joubran disclosed that he hides away from these images while Fares suggested that "it is better to see, to feel with the people of Gaza."

The boys made a link between seeing the images and developing a negative attitude towards Israel. The children identified Israel as an "aggressor" and rationalized the legitimacy of resistance. Mary, Lamia, Karim and Mazen adopted the imagined positions of victims and not perpetrators. The paradox is that the news did not help the children to understand the conflict or the war's political purposes, and violence seemed futile and inescapable. Only one boy suggested an explanation for the war: it was because Tzipi Livni, former acting prime minister, wanted to win the elections.

All the children suggested that parents must "manage" the images and that the images of wars with Israel should be screened. The news images, according to the children, gave information, induced emotions, developed attitudes and led to action. They thought highly of the images that allow people to feel with the victims and as a result become encouraged to help.

Buckingham argues that the "need to 'face up to the facts' and to learn about things that are 'important to know', outweighs the potential danger of being upset or disturbed" (1996: 204). He talks about the dilemma of regulating children's viewing as the balance between these two. Children in Lebanon emphasized their right to know and expressed their concern for younger kids. The boys agreed that children ten years of age are aware enough to be allowed to see the images. The girls did not agree on who should be protected from war images, but interestingly one of them suggested considering the elderly as part of the vulnerable group.

This awareness of the role of graphic images to "teach courage," "lead to negative attitudes towards Israel" and "instigate political action" is one example of the politicization of the children in

Lebanon. Their politicization is also clear in their call to distinguish between regulating war news covering wars with Israel and news on internal clashes. Karim emphasized the necessity of not causing incitement by "hiding" certain images of the internal conflict. All the boys agreed to refuse the use of provocative material during internal violent strife. The choice of what should or should not be broadcasted, for the adolescents in Lebanon, is political and reflective of a politicized awareness that is interested in politics when it relates to survival.

Conclusion

How do adolescents in Lebanon make sense of news about wars in their region? To answer the question, I first looked at whether children watched the news and their perceptions of the genre, then we talked about their emotional responses to war images and finally I investigated their perceptions on regulation. The children I interviewed in Beirut said they watched the news and that their viewing time increased during the war on Gaza. They watched the news because they wanted to know what was happening. They described the atrocities they saw on television and on the internet and told personal accounts from wars they have experienced. They refused killing by principle and identified with the victims of war. They rejected the internal violent conflict and debated the necessity to fight Israel back. They were all against the Israeli military assaults but showed empathy with Israeli non-combatants and regarded the principal victims of war to be children and older civilian adults in both Lebanon and Palestine.

The expression of emotional responses to war news varied among same-age teens. They mentioned feelings of guilt, sadness, happiness, anger and pride in relation to the news and fear in relation to war itself. Discussions about emotional responses were highly gendered and suggested action on the micro and macro political levels. Children's coping strategies were short from making them feel comfortable. Based on these preliminary findings, I suggest that future research considers investigating the complexity of anger and humiliation as discursive emotional responses, and not only focus on fear as a negative emotion associated with war news. I also recommend that research on emotional responses to war news in war-torn regions links between studies of media coverage of war news and children audience research while taking into consideration the war experiences of parents as an important factor relating to the emotional responses of their children and plan to work with children as a group and in their family context.

Parents were identified by the students as the regulators of war news content; nevertheless, all children refused the regulation of images except for those younger than themselves. Their justifications for deregulation were highly political. They expressed their belief in the power of the image, though their trust in images and news in general did not apply to Lebanese television stations. However, the children who declared the existence of bias in Lebanese TV stations repeated slogans communicated by these sources. News coverage in Lebanon is not concerned with whether children are interested in politics and which politics. What renders the news coverage more problematic is the continuous threat of internal violent conflict. This research provides conflicting evidence to the abilities of children to discern the news content, which makes it essential to provide young people with critical understanding of the television as a medium and subsequently equip them with the knowledge to participate in the media culture. This is crucial to Lebanon where the media systems are commercial and globalized and the region is in a constant turmoil. Trying to answer one research question led to another question: how could young people be supported to exercise their rights to conforming, non-conforming and expressing their voice?

Notes

1. This chapter is based on the dissertation research under the same title submitted to the Erasmus Mundus MA in Journalism and Media within Globalization, Department of Media and Communication, University of Wales, Swansea. In writing this chapter, I offer my thanks to Charles Critcher, Tarek Sabry, Joumana Seikaly, Sami Hermes, Jad Abi Khalil and Tamer El Said for their insightful critique, encouragement and friendship, as well as to the students who participated in the focus groups, responded to the questionnaire and shared their opinions, emotions, experiences, energy, wit and sense of humor. I also want to mention the management of the Beirut Baptist School for believing in the importance of research and facilitating access.

2. February 14, 2005, marks the date former Lebanese Prime Minister Rafic Hariri was assassinated along with 22 others in a huge explosion. Hariri's assassination was followed by a series of events that took Lebanon to the verge of an internal war. His assassination also led to the establishment of the UN Special Tribunal for Lebanon. For more information see Special Tribunal for Lebanon (2009) Mandate and Jurisdiction. [Online] Available from: http://www.stl-tsl.org/section/AbouttheSTL. Accessed May 21, 2009.

3. An excerpt from the poetry book by Matar (1990): "I will start from the first sound: from the scream/ Oh God what have you done/ why are you deformed inside me after you were complete?/ And I become silent./ I wish I never asked./ Slowly slowly don't wake her up/ and don't take the pen from her hand and guard her sleep.../ Light the candles of her exile and leave. it is her time to sleep/ leave me alone by her bedroom door/ let me recreate the details of her laugh/ her dance/ her hair/ her voice/ maybe I become Jesus and shout 'Come Back'..." For more information see G. Matar, (1990) [*Playing Music on Lara's Grave*]. Beirut: Fikr for Research and Publishing.

4. The March 14 and March 8 Alliances include a number of political parties and political figures out of which the most prominent are; the Future Movement, the Progressive Socialist Party and the Lebanese Forces (March 14) and Hezbollah and the Free Patriotic Movement (March 8). For more information see BBC (2009) Country Profile: Lebanon. [Online] Available from: http://news.bbc.co.uk/2/hi/middle_east/country_profiles/791071.stm. Accessed May 21, 2009.

5. The Syrian army entered Lebanon in 1976, one year after the start of the civil war, at the request of Lebanese Maronite Christian political leaders. For more information see R. Fisk (2001), *Pity the Nation*, 3rd edition. (Oxford: Oxford University Press). First published (1990).

6. The 2006 war on Lebanon took place between July 12 and August 14. Israel alleges that it raided Lebanon after Lebanese Hezbollah captured two soldiers. According to Amnesty International, Israel attacked Lebanon from land, sea and air killing more than 1,000 Lebanese civilians while Hezbollah launched thousand of rockets towards Israel killing around 40 civilians. The Lebanese death toll included an estimated one third of children fatalities. For more information see Amnesty International (2006) *Lebanon: Deliberate Destruction or "Collateral Damage"? Attacks on Civilian Infrastructure.* [Online] Available from: http://www.amnesty.org/en/library/info/MDE18/007/2006. Accessed May 21, 2009.

7. The clashes killed at least 71 people during the first two weeks and another 40 in sporadic clashes after the Doha agreement was signed, according to Human Rights Watch. For more information see Human Rights Watch (2009). *Lebanon: A Year Later, No Accountability for Killings.* [Online] Available from: http://www.hrw.org/en/news/2009/05/07/ lebanon-year-later-no-accountability-killings. Accessed May 21, 2009.

8. For more information on the war, see Al Jazeera (2009) *War on Gaza.* [Online] Available from: http://english.aljazeera.net/focus/war_on_ gaza/. Accessed May 21, 2009.

9. I use the four terms "teens," "adolescents," "children" and "kids" interchangeably throughout the study. Members of the age group 12–14 are regarded as early adolescents and defined as children according to Article 1 of the United Nations Convention on the Rights of the Child. See United Nations (1989) Convention on the Rights of the Child. [Online] Available from: http://www.unhchr.ch/html/ menu3/b/k2crc.htm. Accessed May 21, 2009.

10. The study by Karam (2007) confirms that youth in the Arab world are "highly marginalized and, although everybody talks about them and wants to give them advice, no one appears willing or able to give them a voice" (p. 83). For more information see I. Karam (2007). "Satellite Television: A Breathing Space for Arab Youth?" in N. Sakr (ed.), *Arab Media and Political Renewal* (London: I.B.Tauris).

11. Based on Graue and Walsh (1998) and Green and Hart (1999), I took choices that would guarantee that adolescents were aware and empowered not only to accept but also to refuse to participate in the research at every point in time. Another important ethical consideration was whether to use war images as prompts during focus groups. In the preparation phase I had planned to use the 2006 war on Lebanon and images from wars in the region. The war on Gaza, still very recent, could not be ignored. I edited two short clips and decided to leave it to the children in focus groups to permit the screening of the prompts. I was sensitive to the potential harm of the images, but the prompts would not have served their purpose if I had ignored all graphic images of death and selected only sanitized images of destruction. I made the choice to include in each clip one or two images of injured individuals and to rule out images of dead children. The length of images with dead or injured was shortened as much as possible. The clips were constructed without any emotional build up or use of music. The length of the first clip on the 2008 war on Gaza was 1 minute and 32 seconds. The second clip on the 2006 war on Lebanon was 1 minute and 20 seconds. Theoretical knowledge about the ethics

of working with children is different from its practical application. During the focus groups, I became aware of my inclination to retain an amount of power and learnt to accept that I will remain an outsider to the children's world.

12. Questionnaires were filled with all of class seven students (a total of 73), out of which 13 teens were selected randomly to participate in three focus groups. Material originally in Arabic was translated into English by the author.

13. The focus group participants were all between 12–14 years old.

14. The names of all children mentioned have been modified to safeguard confidentiality.

15. Green and Hart explain that in school settings, researchers "were clearly situated as 'honorary teachers' (being in some cases addressed as 'Miss')" (1999, 29). I am aware of the institutional meanings and implications of conducting focus groups in a school venue. To reduce the class setting limitations, I conducted the focus groups in the library at round tables. The students were still aware of their presence in the school environment but were comfortable talking to each other interactively. I have no way of knowing if this interaction would have been further facilitated had this focus group been conducted outside of the school environment; however, I am satisfied with the children's participation and internal group dynamics.

16. Israel put a ban on foreign journalists entering Gaza; for more information see McGreal (2009).

References

Al Jazeera (2009). "War on Gaza." [Online] Available from: http://english. aljazeera.net/focus/war_on_gaza/. Accessed May 21, 2009.

Amnesty International (2006). *Lebanon: Deliberate Destruction or "Collateral Damage"? Israeli Attacks on Civilian Infrastructure*. [Online] Available from: http://www.amnesty.org/en/library/info/MDE18/007/2006. Accessed May 21, 2009.

BBC (2009). Country Profile: Lebanon. [Online] Available from: http:// news.bbc.co.uk/2/hi/middle_east/country_profiles/791071.stm. Accessed May 21, 2009.

Buckingham, David (1996). *Moving Images: Understanding Children's Emotional Responses to Television* (Manchester: Manchester University Press).

——— (1999). "Young People, Politics and New Media: Beyond Political Socialization," *Oxford Review of Education*, 25(1–2): 171–84.

———(2000) *The Making of Citizens: Young People, News and Politics* (London: Routledge).

———(2006). "Children Viewing Violence," in C.K. Weaver and C. Carter (eds), *Critical Readings: Violence and the Media* (Berkshire: Open University Press).

Cantor, Joanne, Marie-Louise Mares and Mary Beth Oliver (1993). "Parent's and Children's Emotional Reactions to TV Coverage of the Gulf War," in Bradley S. Greenberg and Walter Gantz (eds), *Desert Storm and the Mass Media* (Hampton: Cresskill).

Carter, Cynthia (2004). "Scary News: Children's Responses to News of War, *Mediactive*, 3: 67–84.

Carter, Cynthia and Marie Messenger Davies (2005). "A Fresh Peach is Easier to Bruise," in Allan, Stuart (ed) *Journalism: Critical Issues.* (Berkshire: Open University Press).

CNN (2005). "Hezbollah Disarmament Unclear." [Online] Available from: http://edition.cnn.com/2005/WORLD/meast/05/06/lebanon.report/index.html. Accessed April 28, 2009.

Fisk, Robert (2001). *Pity the Nation* 3rd edn., (Oxford: Oxford University Press). First published (1990).

———. (2005). "US Rebuffs Assad Offer to Pull out of Lebanon". *The Independent.* Sunday, March 6, 2005. [Online] Available from: http://www.independent.co.uk/opinion/commentators/fisk/us-rebuffs-assad-offer-to-pull-out-of-lebanon-527374.html. Accessed May 21, 2009.

Graue, M. Elizabeth and Daniel J. Walsh (1998). *Studying Children in Context: Theories, Methods and Ethics* (London: Sage Publications).

Green, Judith and Laura Hart (1999). "The Impact of Context on Data," in Rosaline S. Barbour and Jenny Kitzinger (eds), *Developing Focus Group Research: Politics, Theory and Practice* (London: Sage Publications).

Hage, Ghassan (2009). "Hating Israel in the Field: On Ethnography and Political Emotions." *Anthropological Theory*, 9(1): 59–79.

Human Rights Watch (2009). *Lebanon: A Year Later, No Accountability for Killings.* [Online] Available from: http://www.hrw.org/en/news/2009/05/07/lebanon-year-later-no-accountability-killings. Accessed May 21, 2009.

Karam, Imad (2007). "Satellite Television: A Breathing Space for Arab Youth?" in Naomi Sakr (ed.), *Arab Media and Political Renewal.* (London: I.B.Tauris).

Khatib, Lina (2007). "Television and Public Action in the Beirut Spring," in Naomi Sakr (ed.), *Arab Media and Political Renewal.* (London: I.B.Tauris).

Matar, G. (1990). *Playing Music on Lara's Grave* (Beirut: Fikr for Research and Publishing).

McGreal, Chris (2009). "Ban on Foreign Journalists Skews Coverage of Conflict." *Guardian*, Saturday January 10. [Online] Available from:

http://www.guardian.co.uk/world/2009/jan/10/gaza-israel-reporters-foreign-journalists. Accessed May 21, 2009.

Morrison, David and Brent MacGregor (1993). "Anxiety, War, and Children: The Role of Television," in Bradley S. Greenberg and Walter Gantz (eds), *Desert Storm and the Mass Media* (Hampton: Cresskill).

Special Tribunal for Lebanon (2009). *Mandate and Jurisdiction.* [Online] Available from: http://www.stl-tsl.org/section/AbouttheSTL. Accessed May 21, 2009.

Tulloch, John (2000). *Watching Television Audiences: Cultural Theories and Methods* (London: Arnold).

United Nations (1989). Convention on the Rights of the Child. [Online] Available from: http://www.unhchr.ch/html/menu3/b/k2crc.htm. Accessed May 21, 2009.

United Nations Security Council (2004). *Resolution 1559 (2004).* [Online] Available from: http://daccessdds.un.org/doc/UNDOC/GEN/N04/498/92/PDF/N0449892.pdf?OpenElement. Accessed April 28, 2009.

Van der Voort, Tom H.A., J. E. Van Lil, and Marcel W. Vooijs (1993), "Parent and Child Emotional Involvement in the Netherlands," in Bradley S. Greenberg and Walter Gantz (eds), *Desert Storm and the Mass Media* (Hampton: Cresskill).

Weaver, C. Kay and Cynthia Carter (eds) (2006). *Critical Readings: Violence and the Media* (Berkshire: Open University Press).

Wober, Mallory, and Brian M. Young, (1993). "British Children's Knowledge of, Emotional Reactions to, and Ways of Making Sense of the War," in Bradley S. Greenberg and Walter Gantz (eds), *Desert Storm and the Mass Media* (Hampton: Cresskill).

11

NARRATING THE *NAKBA*: PALESTINIAN FILMMAKERS REVISIT 1948[1]

N A D I A   Y A Q U B

In 1972 a group of Palestinian and Arab filmmakers and came together to discuss the current state of Palestinian cinema and how they might work to shape its future (Hurani, 1972). Many of those present, such as Qays Zubaydi, Qasim Hawal, and Mustafa Abu Ali, went on to play major roles in the creation of Palestinian films and the establishment of the Palestinian film archive in Beirut, a repository for more than 100 films as well as film footage by or about Palestinians. The symposium covered a wide range of important topics, including the role of cinema in the Palestinian revolution; the state of contemporary Arab cinema and the role Palestinian cinema could play in reshaping it; the necessary characteristics of a politically engaged cinema; the types of films Palestinians should make; and what audiences they should serve. Participants hotly debated the question of whether non-Palestinians could make "Palestinian" films and the different aesthetics separating foreign and indigenous filmmaking as well as commercial and political cinema. They raised practical issues, such as the need for funding and distribution networks and the creation of formal institutions to facilitate the production of films. Strikingly absent from the discussion was any call for films about the *Nakba*, the violent events of 1947–1949 that led to the expulsion of more than 700,000 Palestinians from their homes. True, the Nakba was the subject of some of the earliest post-1948 Palestinian prose literature, including Samira Azzam's short story "Bread of Sacrifice," and a number of Kanafani's novellas and short stories. Abu-Lughod and Sa'id are correct, then, when they say that Palestinians have been telling the story of their own dispossession, but that the world has chosen not to hear (9–11). However, the only early Palestinian treatment of the Nakba is Qasim Hawal's 1981 release of *Returning to Haifa* (*A'id ila hayfa*), a film based on Kanafani's 1969 novella of the same name. Although Hawal is Iraqi rather than Palestinian, the film has often been called the first Palestinian fictional feature film because it was entirely funded by the Palestine Liberation Organization.[2]

It has now been more than 60 years since the 1948 war. Most Palestinians writing or making films today have had no direct experience with either pre-1948 Palestine or the war that divided it, and their access to those who have had such experience is rapidly disappearing. Most importantly, the dream of undoing history, of restoring Palestine as it once was has receded as events on the ground have forced a rethinking of what it means to be Palestinian in a world in which the possibility of a Palestinian state is increasingly called into question. Three Palestinian resistance movements (that emerged in Lebanon before 1982 as well as the two *intifadas* in the West Bank and Gaza Strip, in 1987 and 2000, respectively) and two quasi-states (that of the Palestine Liberation Organization in Lebanon and of the Palestine National Authority in Ramallah) have failed, leaving Palestinians both within the borders of historic Palestine and in exile more vulnerable to violence than ever.

Not surprisingly, the despair of political impasse has been the subject of a number of Palestinian films, particularly in the years immediately following the outbreak of the Al-Aqsa *intifada*. Elia Suleiman's *Divine Intervention* (*Yadun ilahiyya*, 2002), though full of biting humor, ends with a warning: a pressure cooker rattling over a high kitchen flame. Political despair is particularly evident in films from 2005 such as Rashid Masharawi's *Waiting* (*Intizar*) and Hany Abu Assad's *Paradise Now* (*Al Jannah al-An*), both of which reflect the utter loss of hope that followed the Al-Aqsa Intifada (uprising) that broke out in 2000. What is surprising is that in the second half of the 2000s there began to appear Palestinian films that look beyond the current political impasse for narratives of agency and a peoplehood dependent less on political possibilities for the future than on an ethical way of being in the present, however unacceptable present conditions may be. Najwa Najjar's *Pomegranates and Myrrh* (*Al-Murr wa-al-rumman*, 2008) and Masharawi's *Laila's Birthday* (*'Id milad layla*, 2008), for instance, both focus on the ways Palestinians living under occupation continue to engage in everyday practices of social, economic, and family life despite the obstacles thrown in their way.

A particularly provocative and important part of what one might call the "post-despair" Palestinian filmmaking of the 2000s has been a number of works that return thematically (if not always historically) to the Nakba to reconsider its meaning for Palestinians today. These contemplative films—Annemarie Jacir's *Salt of This Sea* (*Milh hadha al-bahr*, 2008), Elia Suleiman's *The Time That Remains* (*Al-Zaman al-baqi*, 2009) and Michel Khleifi's *Zindeeq* (2009)— though very different from each other, all situate their characters in circumstances and narratives that address not just the oppression that Palestinians face today, but also the historical trajectory of those circumstances and the ways in which the past can be engaged productively in the interest of living ethical and dignified lives in the present. Through a close reading of the films I will demonstrate how these filmmakers refuse to be defined by the defeat of 1948 while insisting on a Palestinian right to remember it.

Salt of This Sea

In *Salt of This Sea,* director Annemarie Jacir signals in the first minutes of her film that she will be playing with narrative conventions. Viewers are introduced to the film's main character, Soraya, through an intimate and detailed documentation of her security screening as she enters the country. Nearly five minutes are devoted to her interrogation and search by Israeli uniformed personnel at Ben Gurion airport. This extraordinarily long scene does almost nothing to move the plot forward; what viewers learn about Soraya and the circumstances of her travel to Israel/Palestine could have been conveyed in a few well-chosen lines of dialogue. Rather, Jacir wants viewers to understand viscerally what Soraya is going through, to get under the skin, so to speak, of the power play inherent in the repeated questioning, the minute search of body and luggage, and the sexual innuendoes of one of the guards. Thus, the film's opening also signals that plot will play a relatively minor role in the film, and viewers' temporal expectations will be constantly challenged.

The unusual pacing suggested by the film's first minutes resurfaces throughout *Salt of This Sea*. Periodically the plot slows down or stops altogether as Jacir focuses on her characters' interaction with their environment. The film begins two generic plot lines—that of the romance and the road movie—but in each case the expected story line is either truncated or elided. In Ramallah Soraya meets Emad, a young waiter who is waiting for a visa to emigrate to Canada to attend university. Soraya and Emad are kindred spirits, and clearly attracted to each other, but the film does not chronicle the development of their relationship. There are no misunderstandings to overcome as the characters get to know each other, no first kiss. Soraya, in loose fitting pants and polo or T-shirts is never sexualized. When conditions in Ramallah turn sour (Soraya loses her apartment and fails to convince the British Bank of Palestine to release her grandfather's frozen assets; economic sanctions against the Palestinian Authority mean that neither she nor Emad will be paid for their restaurant work; and Emad is denied his visa) they decide, along with Emad's fun-loving friend Marwan, to rob the British bank and escape to the west, to Israel where they will see Soraya's family home in Jaffa and visit the ruins of Dawayima, the village of Emad's forebears. The heist is successful, and as a result, the characters spend the second half of the film on the move, visiting Jerusalem, Jaffa and the sea, Dawayima and finally Haifa where they are picked up by the Israeli police. However, contrary to viewers' generic expectations, Soraya and her companions are not chased by the authorities, and when they are finally arrested, it is on residency violations (Emad has no identification or permit to enter Israel and Soraya has overstayed her visa) rather than for bank robbery. As a road movie, *Salt* is also unusual in that its protagonists have almost no meaningful interactions with people, although interactions with environments are depicted in detail.

In fact, this last substitution of places for people is telling, for in each plot line there is a displacement such that Palestine, as the unobtainable object of desire, stalls or perverts the expected trajectory of the narrative. The displacement is most evident in the love story between Soraya and Emad. The characters enjoy an easy intimacy, but even in their closest moments their physical contact is more affectionate than passionate. They nuzzle rather than kiss, and Soraya is as likely to touch or hug Marwan as Emad. Emad and Soraya share a bed in Dawayima, and speak shyly of homemaking and children, but not of love or of each other. Passion is reserved instead for their encounters with the land which they crave but cannot possess. On a hilltop overlooking the old city of Jerusalem, the three characters pause to look at the view. Although the Dome of the Rock is visible in the distance, the focus in this scene is on the aimless antics of the three protagonists as they play with the peels from the oranges they have picked from gardens in formerly Palestinian areas of West Jerusalem.

One can imagine another filmmaker showcasing Jerusalem's iconic skyline, as is done lovingly by Hany Abu Assad in *Rana's Wedding* (*Al-Quds fi yawm akhar*, 2002), and satirically by Rashid Masharawi in *Maqlubah* (2000) and Elia Suleiman in *Divine Intervention*. However, Jacir is less interested in the contested symbolism inherent in images of the city than she is in communicating to viewers the physical sensations of her characters as they gaze on that scene. For much of the scene the camera is focused tightly on the characters heads such that most of the view is blocked out, but we can see the play of the wind in their hair. Emad brings an orange peel to his nose and breathes deeply. There is almost no dialogue in the scene, just the sound of the wind drowning out their scattered and barely audible comments. Similarly, when the three arrive at the beach, the forward momentum of the plot stops as the characters play in the water. There is horseplay typical of the beach—running, splashing noisily in the waves, pretending to drown. Marwan lies at the water's edge as waves lap over him. Soraya recites some dramatic lines, raising her hands into the air to catch the breeze. At one point Emad holds an empty water bottle to his ear, listening to the sound of the wind whistling past its neck. For more than a minute the camera circles around him as with eyes closed, and slowly turning he concentrates on the sound and feel of the wind. Just as sensual is Soraya's interaction with the Palestinian architecture she encounters.

She is constantly touching walls, whether in the gardens of Jerusalem, the narrow streets of her grandfather's neighborhood in Jaffa, or the ruins of Dawayima. At one point she even attempts to taste Dawayima, bringing to her lips the hand that she has just run along an old stone wall. Again the pace of the film slows down (for four minutes Soraya and Emad explore Dawayima) as Jacir focuses not on the place of these buildings in the story line, but rather on her characters' yearning for connection with them.

This lingering on the ways in which characters engage all their senses in absorbing their landscape feels like an extension of the landscape work that Michel Khleifi undertook in his early films, especially *Fertile Memory* (*Al-dhakirah al-khasibah*, 1980) and *Wedding in Galilee* (*'Urs al-jalil*, 1987). As the first Palestinian filmmaker to shoot on location in Palestine, Khleifi felt a tremendous responsibility to show his Palestinian audiences images of the homeland from which they had been exiled, to offer them concrete images of the place that played such an outsized role in their sense of self and community. Jacir uses the visual and sonic medium of film to communicate to her audiences not just images of Palestine, but what the place *feels* like. By stopping the story line periodically to focus on her characters' bodily engagement with their environment, she forces audience members to consider that engagement, to conjure up their own physical memories of touching stones, smelling orange peel, and feeling sand, waves, and wind and then to find a relationship between those memories and the characters' experiences.

There is, however, another crucial difference between Jacir's approach and that of early Khleifi. Khleifi's 1980s landscapes are optimistic offerings, not just in their beauty and expansiveness but in their mere existence. There is a Palestine in Khleifi's films, even if it is under Israeli control. As Gertz and Khleifi have already observed, without minimizing the effects of occupation and land confiscation, Khleifi is able to present his viewers with intact landscapes. Without delving into the politics of national control, occupation, and liberation, he suggests the possibility of redress merely by depicting what is there to be filmed. In contrast, *Salt of This Sea* has an elegiac quality. Jacir depicts the traces of a Palestine that has been irrevocably lost. Early in the film Soraya and Emad take a short drive through the hills near Ramallah. Soon,

Emad stops the car and tells Soraya "This is It. My limit. I am not allowed to go further than this." As he speaks the camera pans across the landscape, hills studded with Palestinian villages and Israeli settlements (it is too hazy to tell the difference) stretching to the horizon. This is the vast landscape, the Palestine, that is beyond Emad's reach. Viewers are not shown the roadblock that presumably defines the limits of Emad's mobility, a fact that renders his frustration all the more pressing; there is no object that can act as the focus of anger and protest, just the object of desire always in view and never attainable. This Palestine, which becomes the focal point of Soraya and Emad's quest, is what binds them to each other. In other words, their mutual attraction is based less on a desire for each other's bodies than in a shared desire for this forbidden land.

The characters' road trip is essentially a journey to find this lost Palestine. They are not interested in discovering what this place has become, which means that their interactions with Israelis almost always register as little shocks that jolt them from their fantasy of returning to the homeland. On the beach the impassive stares of other bathers and in the hotel room the mistaken intrusion of an Israeli chamber maid into the room where Emad, Marwan, and Soraya are engaged in childish horseplay have a sobering effect on the characters, as if to remind them of the existence of a society and infrastructure that they had imagined away. Their physical and reverent (in Dawayima at one point Soraya kneels silently in the ruins of a stone house, apparently engaged in prayer or meditation) engagement with each remnant of Palestine they find arises from their status as seekers, almost as archeologists. But remnants are all they can hope to find. Even their encounters with other Palestinians—a gas station attendant who, it turns out, is originally from Dawayima and knows Emad's father; an undocumented restaurant employee from Ramallah—are brief and superficial, fragments of a society that once existed rather than evidence of, say, an underground Palestinian community. The real places— the houses of West Jerusalem and Jaffa, Dawayima, and even the beach—have been appropriated for other people and purposes. Soraya, Emad and Marwan can only visit them. They can see them, and, as a result of their transgression, experience them for a time with their other senses, but they are never allowed to inhabit them.

At one point they are literally reduced to searching for fragments from the past. When Irit, the young Israeli woman who now lives in Soraya's grandfather's house, tells Soraya that she does not know what became of the furniture that was in the house in 1948, Soraya and Emad search through an antique market where artifacts from pre-Nakba Arab homes are for sale, and then through the heap of rubble on Jaffa's where the remains of destroyed Palestinian homes have been dumped, futilely seeking something, anything that will bring them closer to the Palestine of the past.

The thwarting of the generic expectations of the road movie and romance is not a flaw in the film, but rather a structural expression of the film's political perspective. Genre films create and fulfill expectations not just in relation to plot lines, but concerning their characters' interactions with society. Generically speaking, road movies are about the tension between conformity and individuality. They involve situations in which protagonists' needs or desires separate them from society, either because of a fundamental flaw in the construction of society itself (e.g., economic inequities, racism or other forms of intolerance, etc.), or in the character who over the course of the film must learn to conform to certain societal expectations. Romances are narratives of social reproduction. In romantic comedies, the problems that stand in the way of that reproduction are almost always resolved, whereas in dramas they often are not. Both genres, however, depend on the existence of a coherent (if flawed) society against which the individual story can play out.

The premise of *Salt of This Sea*, however, is that there is no Palestine with which Emad and Soraya's story can be in tension, and it is this lack that lies at the heart of Soraya and Emad's dilemmas. Having nothing to begin with—Soraya appears to have no family or close friends mooring her in Brooklyn, and Emad's visa denial confirms for him that he has no future—and no functioning society to belong to, they are driven to seek a world that no longer exists. In fact, Jacir emphasizes this lack in the details she provides about the society Soraya finds in Ramallah: a governing authority with no right to issue her a Palestinian identity and economically dependent on funds from the outside, cronyism, and a social structure marked by clear class divisions. In a different type of movie Jacir could have addressed these problems; Najwa Najjar's *Pomegranates and*

Myrrh (2008), Hany Abu Assad's *Paradise Now* (2005), and Rashid Masharawi's *Laila's Birthday* (2008) are all examples of films whose narratives engage these (or similar) social issues through plot lines that feel complete because they fulfill viewers' expectations with regard to pacing and narrative resolution. But for Jacir, Ramallah and the Palestinian Authority are not Palestine. Rather they are the manifestations of a structural flaw in a world order that allowed the Nakba to happen and that refuses to offer redress for that wrong. Thus, it is as wronged *global* citizens that Emad and Soraya act, not just as wronged Palestinians. Paradoxically, it is through her stunted road trip that Soraya is able to complete her personal journey towards a full understanding of the global nature of her problem.

Early on in *Salt of This Sea* the protagonist, Soraya, says "They wouldn't give me the right of return so I decided to take it for myself." A Palestinian American, the daughter of refugees from the port city of Jaffa who grew up in a refugee camp in Lebanon, Soraya has traveled to Ramallah where she plans to live. Thus she bears within herself almost all the major permutations of Palestinian lived experience: refugeehood, exile, and occupation. While the issue is not explicitly articulated in the film, Soraya's first attempt at a personal return is partial. Initially she tries to settle in Ramallah, the seat of the Palestinian authority, rather than Jaffa where her family is from originally, renting an apartment, taking a job as a server in a local restaurant, and applying for a Palestinian residency permit. Initially, her only claim for redress consists in her request that the British Bank of Palestine allow her to withdraw her grandfather's assets that were frozen in 1948. Her actions suggest a degree of acceptance of the political status quo, or at the very least no immediate desire to agitate against it. It is only after this attempt fails that she embarks on a full return, traveling to Jaffa to claim her grandfather's home.

As Soraya is deported from Israel at the end of the film she is once again questioned by uniformed personnel, just as she was upon entering the country at the start of the film. This time, however, she answers the guard's questions quite differently:

> Where are you from?
> I'm from here.
> Here where?

Palestine
How long have you been here?
I've been here all my life. I was born here.
It says here that you were born in the USA. Where *were* you born?
Jaffa, on Nuzhah Street.
Jaffa? Do you have another passport?
Just Palestinian.
Show it to me.
You have it in your hand.

Soraya is not mocking her interrogator. Rather, she is announcing her rejection of a global system of states and borders that separates people from each other and from places, and distinguishing her identity as a Palestinian from that system. Engaging with the Nakba and the irredeemable loss of Palestine has taught her that to be Palestinian is not to carry a national identity, but a way of being in the world.

The Time That Remains

In their recent films treating the Nakba Palestinians have, for the most part, eschewed traditional narrative structures and the retelling of historically significant events for unconventional narrative techniques and personal stories rooted in domestic spaces and historically inconsequential acts. Elia Suleiman's films have been an important part of this development. In his first two features, *Chronicle of a Disappearance* (*Sijill ikhtifa'*, 1996) and *Divine Intervention* he focuses on what appears to be a loosely structured series of small events—domestic scenes and neighborhood quarrels in Nazareth. The larger world of politics is always ironically represented, either through mockery or fantasy. In *Chronicle Two* Europeans in the American Colony Hotel speak pompously and nonsensically about the history of the Arab-Israeli conflict. A young Palestinian woman uses a found walkie-talkie to entangle the police force of Jerusalem in a wild chase through city streets. Police searching the protagonist's home do not see him even when he positions himself in front of them. In *Divine Intervention* a Palestinian woman fells an Israeli guard tower with her gaze. The protagonist, ES, blows up a tank with a peach pit. At a traffic light, he and an Israeli settler in the car next to him engage in a musical contest on their car stereos. Not only is politics in these films rendered ridiculous, but its role in people's lives is diminished through its juxtaposition with the repetitive everyday: ES's attempts to work on his film, his father's fishing expeditions, and quarrelsome encounters between neighbors in Nazareth.

Suleiman's third film, *The Time That Remains*, differs from the first two in that it narrates some 60 years in the history of Nazareth, the character Elia, and his family, beginning before Elia was born with the 1948 war itself, and including incidents from the early 1970s when Elia is a young child, his teenage years in the 1980s, and his return to Nazareth as a mature adult more or less in the present. Although *The Time That Remains* is more clearly chronological than Suleiman's earlier films and is epic in the sweep of history that is covered, Suleiman retains his signature technique of narrating through vignettes and repetition. Most of the film consists of short episodes, often humorous, that are complete in and of themselves either as jokes or wry observations. The relationship between individual vignettes is implied rather than explicit, and achieved through juxtaposition and repetition. For little Elia, for example, there is a strong association between politics, school, and his Aunt Olga's cooking. Twice Elia is scolded by the school principal for talking politics at school. The repeated scene is a complete anecdote in and of itself. The sight of an older man in suit and tie asking the small child in short pants "Who told you that America was imperialist?" suggests the precocity of the child, the hypocrisy of the educational system, and the impotence of the principal as an authority figure to control the mind of his charges.

However, in each case this scene is made to communicate even greater social and political complexity through its juxtaposition to another; both times the scolding is followed by a scene in which his aunt Olga, a teacher at the school, gives him a plate of *mujaddarah* (a dish of lentils, rice, and onions) to take home to his family. The *mujaddarah* is fraught with meaning; presented as an offering of love, this dish laden with tradition (not only is it historically eaten weekly by Palestinian families in the area, but it is mythically known as the pot of porridge for which the biblical Esau sold his birthright to his brother Jacob) also contains a subtle message of communal belonging and control. Elia dutifully carries the mujaddarah home where, with his mother's full knowledge and approval, he promptly discards it. In each case the scolding and mujaddarah are accompanied by fraught politics. The first follows immediately after his school choir wins a national contest by singing patriotic Israeli songs. In the second it follows news of the death of Egyptian president Gamal Abdel Nasser. The juxtaposition suggests the association in the child's mind between the mujaddarah and the scolding, both of which stand outside the close relations that bind Elia and his parents and differentiate them from the politically compromised community that surrounds them.

Elia both as a child and a teenager identifies completely with his parents. In scene after scene he is depicted sitting with them in the living room, drinking tea or eating in the kitchen. His posture and gestures mimic those of his parents. In one instance, when the police come to the house to arrest his father, Fuad, for suspected activities against the state (they mistake a pan of cracked wheat for gunpowder), Elia's mother tells him to go to his room, but he silently refuses. Instead he resolutely takes a seat on the couch between his parents, adopting a posture of solidarity with his family and in defiance of the uniformed men searching the house. Other characters from the childhood sections of the film are treated with ironic distance. Although both Fuad and teenage Elia have their close circle of friends, viewers never get to know them as characters. The two characters that are portrayed with some detail, Aunt Olga and the family's suicidal neighbor, are comic figures. Olga, obsessed with television and sexually repressed, is, through her work as a teacher, a stooge of the State; the neighbor, alcoholic and sexually obsessed, is a news junky and conspiracy theorist. The image of the family that emerges from the middle two sections of the film is of a tight circle of three who, by virtue of their perfect understanding and agreement with each other, survive in a world of political minefields and absurdity. Hence the ritual shared by mother and son of discarding the gift of *mujaddarah*.

The scolding/*mujaddarah* scene gains much of its significance from the fact that it appears twice in the film. Indeed, repetition, in conjunction with juxtaposition, is crucial to the structure of all of Suleiman's films, infusing superficially mundane scenes with significance. In *The Time That Remains,* Fuad is shown night fishing with friends three times. In each case they are interrupted by an Israeli patrol who asks them what they are doing and where they are from. Fishing, we know from other scenes in the film, is one of Fuad's greatest pleasures. The repetition of the scene, almost, but not exactly the same each time, underscores the importance of fishing as a praxis, one of the habits that constitutes Fuad's identity. As such it conveys not only his love for this hobby, but also the importance of his social circle (he always fishes with the same companions) and the constant intrusion of the apparatus of State security in the lives of Palestinian men. The second iteration of the scene occurs immediately after one in which Fuad is recuperating in the hospital after heroically saving the life of a young Israeli soldier. The latter scene ends with a nurse tenderly asking the soldier "Is everything all right?" The film immediately cuts to Fuad and his friends fishing. Police shine a search light at them, causing them to turn around and squint anxiously at the officers. "Is everything all right?" one of the policeman asks. The juxtaposition of these utterings of the same phrase, one by a female nurse, the other by an armed man in uniform, communicates everything about the socio-political position of Palestinian citizens of Israel.

While most repetitions in the film suggest the learning through praxis of individuals, there are a few scenes that subtly suggest the way in which repetitions across time—across generations, even—can haunt. One such repetitive action is the recurrence of uniformed men appearing at the door of the home. In the first occurrence, before Elia's birth, Zionist fighters arrest, detain, and torture Fuad for his resistance work. Uniformed men, this time the Israeli police, arrest Fuad again during Elia's early childhood. The third time a uniformed man comes to the door, it is to warn a teenage Elia that he must leave the country or face arrest. When a uniformed man rings the family doorbell immediately after Elia's return home as an adult, it is no wonder, then, that he recoils, hesitating before opening the door to face whatever encounter with security personnel must surely be in store for him (As it turns out, the uniformed man works as a domestic for his mother, and is merely delivering a plate of tabbuleh salad). In that recoiling is the knowledge internalized bodily by Elia as a result of repetitions that stretch from the Nakba to the present day, spanning not only Elia's personal experiences with the law, but also those he witnessed as a child, as well as those narrated in the tales of the Nakba passed on to him by his father.

Though the historical sweep of *The Time That Remains* is vast, Suleiman's technique in the sections of the film that narrate the various stages of Elia's life are essentially the same as those of his earlier feature films. The *Nakba* scenes, on the other hand, are treated quite differently. These scenes are based not on Suleiman's personal memory, but rather on the stories told to him by his father. As a result, events are presented chronologically, as history, without the repetition of scenes that Suleiman uses extensively to convey the repetitive practices of everyday life. While there are a few comical scenes—the lost Iraqi soldier from the Arab Liberation Army who marches past Fuad and his friends as they lounge at a Nazareth café, the mayor of Nazareth signing the surrender of the city to the Zionist forces, and the Zionist soldier who is so short he needs to stand on a stone in order to tie a blindfold around Fouad's eyes— most of this section of the film is serious. By keeping his camera at a distance from his characters and evoking from his actors a Bresson-like choreographed manner of moving, Suleiman avoids manipulating his viewers emotionally. Each incident is imbued not with the intimacy of the Elia anecdotes, but with the distance of second-hand narration. However, because Elia is absent from these scenes, they lack the ironic gaze within the frame that is a hallmark of Suleiman's style. The city of Nazareth has a different aesthetic as well. The modern architecture of the Suleiman apartment (the same apartment and camera angles appears in all three historical periods of Elia's life, as well as in the Nazareth scenes from Suleiman's earlier films) and little Elia's school do not exist. Instead we see a city of timeless stone structures whose living spaces are marked by elegant arches, lush garden courtyards, and rich, early twentieth century wooden furniture. These visual distinctions mark the temporal distinction of the Nakba period; it is historical in the sense of preceding personal memory.

Savvy viewers will understand that the major events of the Nakba portion—the surrender of Nazareth, the behavior of the Zionists, the fleeing of Nazareth residents, and the arrest of Fuad—color all later sections of the film, although direct connections are, for the most part, implied rather than spelled out. However, traces of the

Nakba-era practices leak into later sections of the film, or remind viewers of contemporary practices. The announcement of curfew in Nakba-era Nazareth is echoed in the curfew announcement in contemporary Ramallah. The Layla Murad song that Zionist soldiers play on a looted gramophone in 1948 emerges again from a cassette that Fuad inserts into his car stereo in the final scene before his death. The postures of a field full of blindfolded Palestinians who are made to kneel silently in an olive grove are reminiscent of those of detained Palestinians in decades of news photographs from the Israeli occupation.

Nonetheless, the overall effect is of a history walled off from the present, one vivid in terms of the effect it has on the lives of its survivors and their descendents, but one that has already acquired some of the fixed qualities of legend. Suleiman plays with this idea in the film's opening. The film begins with a scene in which an adult Elia has arrived from abroad and is taking a taxi, presumably to his family home in Nazareth. As the car heads down the highway it is suddenly hit by an apocalyptic storm. The driver loses power and radio contact with his dispatcher. The scene ends with the driver asking himself in bewilderment "Where am I?" By preceding the 1948 portion of the film with this scene from the present of the filmmaking, Suleiman suggests an other-worldliness about the past. It bears within itself the inscrutability of unknowable places and dimensions. One may trace vestiges of the past in the present through the repetitions that seem to pay no attention to the calendar—loudspeaker announcements of military curfew, an instinct to recoil when there is an unexpected knocking on the door at night—but one can never *know* the world that existed before one's conscious memory.

The Time That Remains ends with Suleiman sitting on a bench outside a hospital where his mother has just passed away, watching passersby. They include medical personnel wheeling gurneys; hospital visitors, many of whom describe their cases to friends and family via their cellphones; a trio of young punks who sit menacingly on the bench facing Elia; and a handcuffed acquaintance of theirs who is led past Elia by a policeman. The vignettes include many of Suleiman's signature tropes; the twin figures, in this case two men with identical head and body bandages; the serious treatment of absurdities (a doctor sending a man to the emergency room to cure him of a joke); the deadpan narration of fantastically violent altercations as a result of minor offenses; and of course, the flouting of authority (in this case, the handcuffed punk drags his arresting officer wherever he wants to go, rather than the other way around). Elia observes these actors, each completely absorbed in her or his own present, his or her own narrative, each oblivious not only to each other, but also to Elia who, like us, watches them. His blank stare embodies for viewers the family history we have just seen, but one realizes, as the notes of the Bee Gee's song "Staying Alive" begin and the credits role that, cruelly perhaps, life goes on, with or without Elia, his parents, or the Nakba.

Zindeeq

What distinguishes film from most other forms of visual art is its use of the temporal juxtaposition of images. Visually, meaning is created not just from the images themselves, but also from the ways in which images are sequenced and their duration. In *Zindeeq*, Khleifi pushes this feature of filmmaking to its limits, using juxtaposition not so much to narrate a story, but to create a psychological profile that suggests the ways in which the personal, the communal, and the political; the past (both as remembered and as narrated) and the present; desires, responsibilities, and imagination intersect in an emerging sense of self.

Zindeeq covers one long, nightmarish night in the life of M., a Palestinian filmmaker who has returned from abroad to make a documentary about the Nakba. While filming in Ramallah, he finds out that in his hometown of Nazareth, his nephew has killed a man and thus initiated a family feud. He returns to Nazareth, a city he hardly knows anymore due to his long residency abroad, in an attempt to help. There he spends a surrealistic and nightmarish night involving a failed attempt to find lodging for the night, several brushes with violence, and a rich variety of personal encounters. His experiences that night are interspersed with memories, especially of his mother, and images of Rasha, the young assistant on his documentary film project who has refused to sleep with him, as well as footage that he has shot for the documentary about the Nakba that he is in the process of shooting.

As a character, M. is haunted by his past. His work as a filmmaker is driven by a question that his mother has always refused to answer, "Why did you stay?" It is ironic and not accidental that Khleifi's Palestinian protagonist would be obsessed with this question and not its more stereotypical obverse "Why did you leave?" It is as if by not becoming a refugee M. feels alienated not only because of his exilic condition and the loss of his ancestral homeland in 1948, but also by his alienation from the Palestinian condition of refugee-hood, an irony heightened by the fact that M. has chosen the life of an exile for himself. The final effect of centering this character around the question of "why did you stay?" however, is to underscore not the differences that separate M. from other Palestinians, but rather the similarities, for it suggests that Palestinians who remained in their homes during the Nakba were traumatized by that event just as those who left and were prevented from returning were.

M.'s haunting by this question drives his work, a documentary on 1948 which he describes to his sister as "very important," so important, in fact that it prevents him from engaging in the social rituals that bind family and community. (At his uncle's funeral, for instance, he refuses to stay for dinner with his bereaved cousins.) He is making this documentary not just to educate his European audience about Palestinian history, but also in an attempt to find in the stories of the refugees he interviews the answer his deceased mother never gave him. However, it is also clear that he is not finding what he wants in his interviews for that project. As he films an elderly woman describing her experiences in 1948 (the interview, though incorporated into the fictional film is documentary, not fictional) his young assistant Rasha questions his project. "It's the same story. What more is there to say?" Rasha is much younger than M., a point she drives home when she tells him that her mother was born after 1948 and so has no experiences about the Nakba to hide from her offspring.

M.'s haunting by the past and failure to find answers to questions about 1948 also inform his decision to return to Nazareth. Although he claims to be motivated by a desire to help his family in their current crisis, it is clear to everyone (and certainly to M. himself) that there is little if anything he can do; he no longer understands the web of relations that are affected by his nephew's actions, and is generally regarded as an outsider when he arrives. He is both repelled by and drawn to the city of his birth, on the one hand refusing to remain there long enough to fulfill his social duties surrounding his uncle's funeral, and on the other hand insisting on traveling there (against the urgings of both Rasha and his sister) when his nephew kills a man. He speaks with distain of the violent nature of Nazarene society, and yet is constantly drawn to its violence, seeking to capture it in his camera lens.

Khleifi illustrates this haunting by intercutting the chronological narrative of M.'s nightmarish night in Nazareth with his memories, fantasies, and the footage he has shot for his documentary. Memories and film images of Rasha working with him on the film give way to fantasies of seeing her in bed and in his own neighborhood of Nazareth. These images are interspersed with both the interviews M. has conducted for his film, and older footage. There are rural scenes of agricultural practices, singing, and children's games, as well as images of violence and destruction of the first *intifada*. Further complicating the temporal dimension of the film is the fact that the older footage consists of clips from Khleifi's own films from 1980 through the 1990s. As a result they act as allusions, bringing those films and their contexts into *Zindeeq*.

Several truths emerge from this kaleidoscope of images. The stark contrasts between past and present suggest how much history has happened since 1948, how distant those events are even though their effects are very much a part of the Palestinian present. The rural Palestine of olive groves, sheep and traditional practices has given way to cities, highways, and thuggish behavior. The *intifada* has been replaced by the Israeli Separation Barrier. Children's games give way to child beggars whose organs are sold on the black market. Further separating a past characterized by wholeness and nurturing from the dystopian present are the multiple mini-Nakbas that also appear in M.s memory and film footage—house demolitions, *intifada* violence, etc. There is no undoing that history, no returning to the time before the Nakba, only, as M. himself realizes as he burns papers and photographs in his abandoned family home, desperate acts of purification, of hoping and working for the future.

However, this last point only becomes clear to M. himself towards the end of the film. Before that, his attachment to the past is made manifest in his relationship with his camera, the storehouse of images stretching back to 1980 (the time period of Khleifi's first Palestinian film, *Fertile Memory*) and interviews referencing a more distant past. M.'s camera is a source of comfort and intimacy. Twice he settles himself down in the seat of his car to gaze at images he has stored there. Later, as he lies down to sleep/dream in his family home, he cradles the camera in his arms like a lover. Not only does he mediate relationships through the camera, but his desire to create images often interferes with his ability to sustain meaningful human contact. I have already mentioned how M. leaves Nazareth early, excusing himself with his need to get back to Ramallah and his "very important" film project. Despite M.'s obsession with the past, he lives in what filmmaker Azza El-Hassan (2002) has termed "newstime," that is, a temporality marked by violent events. He is repeatedly distracted from a personal interaction (gazing at an image of Rasha on his camera screen, kissing Yael's daughter on her doorstep; drinking coffee with an old acquaintance in a Nazareth restaurant) by the sound of events—car doors slamming, sirens, gunshots, etc.—and is driven to capture such events on film. In the most explicit illustration of this problem, M. receives a phone call from his sister just as he is about to take up the camera to shoot images of a violent confrontation that has erupted around him. He brusquely cuts her off, refusing to hear what she has to say because of his desire to shoot pictures. M. is thus complicit in the creation of the association between Palestinians and violence in the global imaginary that El-Hassan critiques. It is significant, then, that at the end of the film M. sets his camera on the shore while watching Rasha as she walks, Jesus-like, on the surface of the water at the sea of Galilee.

The problem, though, is not in the qualities inherent within the camera itself but rather in the way M. uses it. While M. spends most of the film thwarting intimacy by inserting the camera between himself and others and attempting, futilely, to revive the past through the images he has shot, it is through the camera that he eventually learns to leave the past in the past and to build a relationship with the two boys from Gaza he finds squatting in his family home. As a filmmaker, M. sees the world through the camera's lens. The healing visions (fantastic images and conversations) of

Rasha and his mother are imagined to arise from the camera itself, either as footage he has shot or as an interview, much like those he has conducted with refugee survivors of 1948, of his mother in his family home. This message of the neutrality of the technology itself is most clearly stated in the conversation M. has with Ghassan, one of the Gazan boys, as he explains the telephoto powers of the lens. "We make films, not war," he tells the child, after they discuss the technical capabilities of the Israeli military's field glasses.

Zindeeq has two very different but complementary endings: one that, though inconclusive, ends the chronological narrative that structures the film, and the other a miracle that stands outside chronological events. In the very last scene of the film M. watches from the shore as Rasha appears clad in a flowing white dress and veil, walking on the surface of the Sea of Galilee. As she stops and beckons to him, he walks along the shore, gazing at her through his video camera. Finally, he lays down his instrument and looks out over the water with his bare eyes as her image fades away into the air. Throughout the film M. has had difficulties in his relationships with women. He is devoted to his all-giving mother, but eager to indulge his unruly sexual desires regardless of how they affect old friendships (e.g., with Yael whose daughter he seduces despite Yael's reservations) or working relationships (e.g., with Rasha who does not want a sexual liaison to negatively affect her work on his film). His final fantasy of Rasha walking on the Sea of Galilee suggests his movement beyond the Madonna/whore complex his behavior has thus far exemplified, but his continued inability to conceive of women outside the realm of the mythic; he is on his way, but has not yet reached an end to mythology. For M., Rasha, a working woman who offers him friendship and forgiveness, can now walk on water, but can she be fully human?

In the immediately preceding scene, M. rushes out of the café where he is having coffee with an old acquaintance to take photographs during an altercation, presumably between police and undocumented Palestinians. Suddenly, in the midst of the violence he sees Ghassan and his Gazan companion, the boy whose kidney has been stolen from h im. M. stops shooting photos, picks up the boys in his car and drives away. Like his mother before him in 1948, in the context of violence and confusion he makes a simple choice to save the children. Through this act viewers can understand that he has internalized his mother's wisdom when she tells him "All wars are the same.... What are people's chief concern in war time? That their children should remain alive. To live. That is the story. I am still worried about you." One could ask oneself what M. will do with the boys. Will he take them with him to Europe, to Ramallah, or back to Gaza?—but the answer is not nearly as important as his decision to save them, to care about the future more than the past, and about someone else's real needs more than one's own desires. That, finally, is M's lesson of the Nakba.

Conclusion: Mourning the Nakba

Although the cineastes who met in 1972 to discuss the future of Palestinian cinema did not think of making films about the Nakba, two important Palestinian novels from this period did address the meaning of that cataclysmic event at that time. Ghassan Kanafani's *Returning to Haifa* ('*A'id ila hayfa*, 1969) tells the story of a couple who return to their home in Haifa after the opening of the Mandelbaum Gate in Jerusalem in the immediate aftermath of the 1967 war. Emile Habibi's *The Secret Life of Saeed, the Pessoptimist* (*Al-waqa'i' al-ghariba fi ikhtifa' sa'id al-nahs al-mutasha'il*, 1974) is the tragic-comic tale of a Palestinian who survives in Israel by becoming a collaborator. Both novels address the Nakba from the perspective of the coming revolution. "What is the nation?" Sa'id, the protagonist, asks in *Returning to Haifa* "What does the *fida'i* fight for?" Kanafani himself asks in an interview following the publication of the novella. Not, he concludes, the collection of rapidly fading memories of a place, but rather an idea of justice and humanitarianism and an identity based in a polity such that Palestinians can interact with those around them as equals (Sammarah 1970, 7). In other words, for Kanafani the Nakba was an affliction from which Palestinians needed to cure themselves if they were to find agency in the shaping of their own future. Habibi's novel also exhorts his readers to relinquish a reified notion of the past "Do you really know how the beginning was, uncle?" the second Yuaad asks Saeed. "The beginning was not merely sweet memories of pines over Mount Carmel, or orange groves, or the songs of Jaffa sailors. And did they really sing anyway?" (154). Saeed, the collaborator disappears, first as he is carried off by his "brother" from outer space, and secondly from the records of the mental institution to which the narrator's search for Saeed leads. However Yuaad, the refugee, continues to return and confront the Israeli soldiers who deport her. At one point Saeed asks her "You're so young for so much wisdom, Yuaad; wherever did you acquire it?" Yuaad answers "From my long life that is still before me." Habibi, like Kanafani, sees a resolution to the Nakba in the possibility for change to arise from the agonistic politics of the future.

The "post-despair" Palestinian films of the late 2000s, like the novels of Kanafani and Habibi, call on Palestinians to alter their relationship with their own history—not to forget it or its implications for activism in the present, but to refuse to be defined by the defeat of 1948 or by the failed nationalist politics that are being practiced today in the name of Palestinians. In interviews about his film *Zindeeq* Michel Khleifi has spoken of "mourning" the Nakba, that is, of coming to terms, in a Freudian sense, with the loss of 1948 so as to move out of a debilitating state of melancholy. A number of scholars writing about Palestinian cinema have framed their analyses in a similar fashion (for example, Bersheeth, Gertz and Khleifi). While Ginsberg is correct in pointing out the depoliticizing effect of wholesale analyses of Palestinian cinema that are framed by trauma theory (317), it is also true that much like Kanafani and Habibi did through there literary works in the late 1960s and early 70s, filmmakers today are working towards a new Palestinian subjectivity. This time it is of necessity constituted in large part outside a politics of national liberation, but still committed to the notion of Palestinian agency.

Notes

1. The author thanks the American Council of Learned Societies, the Social Science Research Council, the National Endowment for the Humanities, and the University Research Council of the University of North Carolina at Chapel Hill for their support of this project.
2. Most Palestinian films made in exile before 1982 were lost with the disappearance of the Palestinian Film Archive during the 1982 Israeli invasion of Lebanon. However, descriptions of the films are available in Qays al-Zubaydi's annotated filmography, *Filastin fi al-sinima*.

References

Abu-Lughod, Lila and Ahmad Sa'id (2007). "Introduction." In Ahmad Sa'id and Lila Abu-Lughod (eds), *Nakba: Palestine, 1948, and the Claims of Memory* (New York: Columbia University Press), pp. 1–26.

Bresheeth, Haim (2007). "The Continuity of Trauma and Struggle: Recent Cinematic Representations of the Nakba" In Ahmad Sa'id and Lila Abu-Lughod (eds), *Nakba: Palestine, 1948, and the Claims of Memory* (New York: Columbia University Press), pp. 161–87.

Gertz, Nurith and George Khleifi (2008). *Palestinian Cinema: Landscape, Trauma, and Memory* (Bloomington and Indianapolis: Indiana University Press).

Ginsberg, Terri (2009), "Review of Palestinian Cinema: *Landscape, Trauma, and Memory* by Nurith Gertz and George Khleifi." *Middle East Journal of Culture and Communication*, 2: 315–25.

Habibi, Emile (2002), *The Secret Life of Saeed the Pessoptimist*, trans. Salma Khadra Jayyusi and Trevor LeGassick (New York: Interlink).

El-Hassan, Azza (2002), "Art and War." In Gerfried Stocker and Christine Schöpf (eds), *Unplugged: Art as the Scene of Global Conflicts = Kunst als Schauplatz globaler Konflikte*, (Ostfildern: Hatje Kanz), pp. 280–84.

Hurani, Hani (1972). "al-sinima wa-al-qadiyah al-filastiniyah: Nadwah adaraha wa harraraha: Hani Hurani. *Shu'un Filastiniyah*, 10: 199–228.

Kanafani, Ghassan (2000). "Return to Haifa." In *Palestine's Children: Returning to Haifa and Other Stories*, trans. Barbara Harlow and Karen Riley, (Boulder, CO: Lynne Rienner).

Sammarah, Samih (1970). "Ghassan Kanafani: mawaqif fi al-siyasah wa-al-adab wa-al-idiyulujiyat," *Al-Siyasah*, Kuwait, May 21.

Al-Zubaydi, Qays (2006). *Filastin fi al-sinima* (Beirut: Mu'assasat al-dirasat al-filastiniyah), p 99.

1 2

BEARING WITNESS TO
AL NAKBA IN A TIME OF DENIAL

TEODORA TODOROVA[1]

For decades the Israeli state narrative has dominated the story and history of the Israeli-Palestinian conflict. This narrative tells the story of Israel and its people as an endless chronicle of conflicts, a list of battles won and lost. It is "the story" of what happened to the Jewish people and what makes Israel "the nation" it is. This version of history has generally not been concerned with the others, the "non-Jews" who lived beside and among the Jewish people, namely the Palestinians. That is not to say that history was oblivious to their presence, it did note them in passing, but without a clear reference to who they were. Traditional Israeli history books will inform you that in 1948 Israel fought and won its War of Independence, and that the Jewish nation established a state in "a land without people for a people without land." However, in recent years Israeli state narratives have been subject to serious challenges and revisions.

Israel's so-called "new historians" have challenged linear and exclusionary historical account of pre-1948 Palestine as an uninhabited land, settled by the exiled Jewish people who established a state despite unrelenting opposition from its neighbors, and made the barren desert bloom. Benny Morris (1987; 2004) and Ilan Pappé's (2004; 2006) work in relation to the events surrounding the State's establishment have resulted in angry debates and social polarization within Jewish Israeli society. In their differing ways, Morris and Pappé have helped to dislodge the Zionist myth that

Israel prior to Jewish settlement was "a land without people for a people without land." According to their revisionist accounts, the Palestinian people did exist and lived in Palestine prior to their displacement in the war of Israel's founding. And moreover, that the new Israeli state played an active role in the displacement of the indigenous inhabitants and the continuing Palestinian refugee problem. These new historical accounts have contributed to growing attempts in the present to re-articulate the history of the Israeli-Palestinian conflict and the people of Israel-Palestine.

This chapter examines the proliferation in the past decade of Israeli and Palestinian collective, individual and historical narratives concerned with the events which took place in post-Mandate Palestine and/or the newly established State of Israel between 1947 and 49. It begins with the story of the public resurgence of the suppressed narrative of the Palestinian *Nakba* (Catastrophe) after decades of silence marked by a pronounced lack of officially-sanctioned narratives. The chapter continues with the story of how the Palestinian people have collectively held onto the memory of their dispossession and how that memory has more recently been utilized politically in order to articulate the Palestinian refugees' right of return. This account is fused with a theoretical analysis of the work of the Israeli NGO *Zochrot* (Remembering) which seeks to reintegrate the narrative of the Nakba in the Jewish Israeli collective consciousness by making pre-1948 Palestine and its people visible in the Israeli socio-cultural and political landscape. The chapter concludes that the work of critical historians such as Ilan Pappé, alongside progressive civil society institutions such as *Zochrot*, is creating a much needed "safe space" within Israeli society where acknowledgement and witnessing can begin to take place without fear of persecution or retribution.

Bearing Witness versus Denial

In *Remnants of Auschwitz* (1999) Agamben defines the *witness* as, on the one hand, a third party observer who is called upon to testify in a court of law, and on the other, the witness (victim) "who has experienced an event from beginning to end and can therefore bear witness to it" (ibid.: 17). In relation to the latter, Agamben argues that an ethics of witnessing is incompatible with a legal conceptualization of the witness because a separation of ethics and law becomes impossible given that, according to him, the necessary related concept of *responsibility* is already contaminated by law. Bearing witness thus becomes "a confrontation with the infinity of responsibility," thereby constituting witnessing as an impossibility (ibid.: 20–34).

However, Catherine Mills (2003) criticizes Agamben's legalistic account of witnessing for leaving out the role of the one to whom the testimony is being addressed, thereby ignoring the question of historical responsibility and its relationship to remembering and/or bearing witness (ibid.). She argues that by privileging the Latin origin of "responsibility" in the root word "spondeo" (to sponsor or guarantee), Agamben wilfully neglects its origin in the verb "responso" (to reply or respond to another). Paul Ricoeur (1999: 9) talks of the "duty to remember," which relates to our deep concern for the past *and* to our future orientation, noting that the ethical responsibility "to respond" to the testimony (account) of another is embodied in the duty to keep alive "the memory of suffering over and against the general tendency of history to celebrate the victors" (ibid.: 10). Here Paul Ricoeur emphasizes the role of the critical historian which is to reinforce the "truth-claim" of memory against falsifiability *and* to revise or refute dominant history:

> In admitting what was originally excluded from the archive the historian initiates *a critique of power* [my emphasis]. He gives expression to the voices of those who have been abused, the victims of intentional exclusion. The historian opposes the manipulation of narratives by *telling the story differently* [my emphasis] and by providing a space for the confrontation between opposing testimonies. (ibid.: 16)

In short, the responsibility to bear witness requires the conscious utilization of narratives which tell the dominant version of historical events "otherwise," or in other words "the duty to do justice, through memories, to an other than the self" (Ricoeur, 2004: 89). Conversely, the alternative response to the memories of the abused and/or oppressed is *denial* or the "need to be innocent of a troubling recognition" (Cohen, 2001: 25). "Denial is always partial; some information is always registered ...[the paradox of] knowing and not knowing" (ibid.: 22).

From Silence to Bearing Witness

In "Remembering Al-Nakba in a Time of Amnesia" (2008), to which the title of this chapter alludes, Ahmad Sa'di attributes the prolonged Palestinian "silence" about the Nakba, which he stresses is not the same as "amnesia" or wilful forgetting (see Ricoeur, 1999), in reference to the Palestinian collective experience of post-traumatic shock as a result of the unprecedented scale of dispossession and displacement of between 750,000 and 900,000[2] civilian Palestinians in 1947–1949. This collective silence has been characterized by the absence of publicly received testimony regarding the forced mass exodus and was further exasperated by the Palestinian refugees' expectation that the disastrous events which assailed them would be a temporary arrangement. The passage of time, the international failure to implement the refugees' rights, and the arrival of the second major displacement and dispossession of the Palestinian people following Israel's victory in the 1967 Six Day War and the ensuing military occupation of the Palestinian territories of the Gaza Strip and West Bank have proven the prospect of return futile.

The Palestinian silence in relation to the *Nakba* is also related to the political and ideological dominance of the Israeli state narrative that has perpetuated the longstanding and, until very recently, formally unchallenged characterization of 1948 as a "triumphant" war of independence during which the "Arab" population of Palestine took "voluntary flight" (see Peled-Elhanan, 2010; Pappé, 2006). These two conflicting narratives of the same event, one triumphant and one catastrophic, have been vastly unequal in terms of global public legitimacy, the former being the accepted and dominant version of 1948, while the latter has been historically absent from international debates on the Israeli-Palestinian conflict and the plight of the Palestinian refugees. The subject of the *Nakba* remains a contentious area within institutional discourses on the conflict because those who lay claim to having been its victims are a powerless and stateless people, while the overwhelming responsibility lies with one of the world's most influential nation-states.

Since the UN decision to partition Palestine in 1947[3] and the resulting Nakba the vast majority of Palestinians have been relegated to statelessness and exile. One and a half million Palestinians continue to reside in refugee camps in Lebanon, Syria,

Jordan, the Gaza Strip and West Bank.[4] The 3.5 million residents of the Occupied Territories have been subject to Israel's military rule since the 1967 occupation, and the remaining 1.5 million[5] Palestinians are second class citizens in a Jewish State which refers to them as the "Arab minority" and considers them a "demographic threat" (Alon and Benn, 2003). The Palestinians, in their millions, have for many decades spoken about the tragedy which assailed them in 1948, albeit their stories and testimonies have until recently been largely ignored within institutional discourses on the Israeli-Palestinian conflict.

The hegemonic narrative of the State of Israel has not only acted to omit Israeli perpetration of the Nakba but has been coupled with the active denial of the very existence of the Palestinian people as a national collectivity. This political strategy dates back to early Zionist representations of pre-Jewish settlement Palestine as "a land without people for a people without land." This claim was most explicitly articulated by the Israeli Prime Minister Golda Meir, who infamously declared in a newspaper interview: "There were no such thing as Palestinians," proceeding to publicly deny the catastrophic events of 1947–49 by adding: "It was not as though there was a Palestinian people in Palestine ... and we came and threw them out and took their country ... They didn't exist."[6] Such acts of public denial of the very existence of the Palestinian people have been possible because, as Edward Said (1984: 34) writes:

> Facts do not at all speak for themselves, but require a socially acceptable narrative to absorb, sustain and circulate them. Such a narrative has to have a beginning and an end: in the Palestinian case, a homeland for the resolution of its exile since 1948. But as Hayden White has noted in a seminal article, "narrative in general, from the folk tale to the novel, from annals to the fully realized 'history', has to do with the topics of law, legality, legitimacy, or, more generally *authority*".

The combination of the silence of an expelled, grief-stricken and distressed population on the one hand and the void in the memory and landscape of the perpetrating collectivity on the other is somewhat understandable in the context of what took place in Palestine in 1947–1949. However, as Sa'di (2008) laments and Pappé (2006) condemns, it is far harder to understand the response of the international community at the time and even more so subsequently. The passage of time appears to have entrenched not only perpetrator denial but the amnesia of the international bystanders. Despite the existence of numerous UN resolutions, among them UN Resolution 194 (1949) which calls for the implementation of the Palestinian refugees' right of return to their former homes, and the later UN Resolution 242 (1967) which calls for the establishment of an independent Palestinian state in the West Bank and Gaza Strip, there has been a mesmerizing absence in academic literature on the subject of the story of the Palestinian dispossession.

The international academic neglect of what happened to the Palestinian people in 1948 is particularly prominent in the fields working with collective memory and post-conflict studies. Perhaps understandably, scholars in the field of collective memory who deal with issues of victimhood and perpetration are reluctant and uncomfortable with applying theory, which has been largely developed in the wake of the Jewish Shoah,[7] to an event perpetrated by a section of the Jewish collectivity against another Semitic people in the period immediately succeeding the European Holocaust. Another perfectly plausible explanation is presented by the argument that the Shoah is a unique and unprecedented event of mass devastation in the history of human existence and is therefore not comparable to other smaller (and arguably less significant) events of collective suffering (for the claim of the Shoah's "uniqueness" see Wiesel, 1985: v. iii., 162, 1; also, to a lesser extent, Kearney, 2002: 69).

However, a case could be made that the above argument is almost irrelevant given that no comparison between the Shoah and *Nakba* is required considering that while each historic event is unique in its specificity, there are enough other cases of national dispossession and inter-communal violence with which moral analogies, if not strict comparisons, can be drawn. To name a few analogous cases, South African Apartheid, ethnic cleansing in Bosnia and the troubles in Northern Ireland are to greater or lesser extent comparable cases given that they constitute contemporary points of departure for theorizing ethical responsibility for the suffering of others. Furthermore, in *Multidirectional Memory: Remembering the Holocaust in the Age of Decolonisation* (2009), Michael Rothberg makes a compelling case against "the framework that understands collective memory as *competitive* memory—a zero-sum struggle over scarce resources" (ibid.: 3). Rothberg proposes that memory is

> *multidirectional*: as subject to ongoing negotiation, cross referencing, and borrowing; as productive and not privative (ibid.: 3).... Not strictly separable from either history or representation, memory captures simultaneously the individual, embodied, and lived side *and* the collective, social and constructed side of our relation to the past (ibid.: 4).... A model of multidirectional memory allows for the perception of the power differentials that tend to cluster around memory competition within a larger spiral of memory discourse in which even hostile invocations of memory can provide vehicles for further, countervailing commemorative acts. (2009: 11–12)

Yet, despite the pre-existence of credible Palestinian scholarship documenting the history and geography of pre-1948 Palestine, such as the influential works of Walid Khalidi (1959, 1992), the narrative of the *Nakba* began to gain widespread legitimacy within Western and Israeli academic and political discourse only with the arrival of Israel's revisionist historians. The newly declassified Israeli Defence Forces' archives from the 1948 war, featured in Morris's book, *The Birth of the Palestinian Refugee Problem* (1987), and the revisited edition in 2004, revealed that the over 800,000 Palestinians who "left" Palestine during the period were in fact subjected to an organized campaign of ethnic cleansing, including forced expulsions, a number of recorded massacres, and numerous cases of rape carried out by the pre-state Jewish forces against the civilian Palestinian population.

Staggeringly, Morris's consecutive reflections on the very revelations he helped to bring to public knowledge have been strikingly amoral. According to Morris, his opinion reflecting the contemporary Israeli consensus, "In certain conditions, expulsion is not a war crime. I don't think that the expulsions of 1948 were war crimes. You can't make an omelette without breaking eggs.... There are circumstances in history that justify ethnic cleansing" (interview with Shavit, *Ha'aretz*, 2004). For Ilan Pappé, on the contrary, the dispossession of the Palestinians in 1948 by Israel represents a crime against humanity which has "been erased almost totally from the global public memory"

> ...This, the most formative event in the modern history of the land of Palestine, has since been systematically denied, and is still today not recognised as an historical fact, let alone acknowledged as a crime that needs to be confronted politically as well as morally. (Pappé, 2006: xiii)

The Ethnic Cleansing of Palestine (2006) represented one of the first scholarly attempts to bear witness to the *Nakba* outside of the Palestinian collectivity. To bear witness is to act as a bridge between remembrance and forgetting, between memory and oblivion, between the living and those whose lives have been rendered meaningless. Bearing witness is about speaking truth to power, making manifest buried lies and concealed crimes and making an ethical and political demand for justice. Moreover, as Paul Ricoeur (2004) asserts, the role of a critical historian is not only to revise and update the history of a given community, in this case the Israeli collectivity, but to correct, criticize and even refute taken-for-granted historical narratives (ibid.: 500). Given that Pappé is a Jewish Israeli, his ethical stance represented an almost unprecedented and exemplary undertaking. For his moral courage and outspoken demand for justice on behalf of the Palestinian victims, he paid a high price in the aftermath of the publication of his book which resulted in his being subjected to slander, death threats and, ultimately, his self-imposed exile.

Pappé (2006) defined the event of 1947–1949 as an organized campaign of *ethnic cleansing* by the pre-state Jewish armed forces against the indigenous civilian population of Palestine. Further, he documented the ways in which the concealment of the *Nakba* was achieved and continues to be maintained by the careful ideological and political orchestration and machinations of the Zionist leadership and institutions of the State of Israel. Among the acts of what Pappé terms Nakba *memoricide* (ibid.: 225), which began in the immediacy of the ensuing state-building and power consolidating project in the aftermath of 1948, he lists the wholesale destruction, dynamiting, bulldozing, and erasing of 500 depopulated Palestinian villages in order to prevent the return of their expelled inhabitants. Other acts of *memoricide* include the declaration of depopulated and confiscated Palestinian lands as Israeli State property, giving newly expropriated localities "ancient" Hebrew names, and handing the land over to the Israeli Land Authority for the establishment of Jewish settlements. Palestinian land was also turned over to The Jewish National Fund (JNF) for "archaeological" and "reforestation" programmes (ibid.: 232).

> The archaeological zeal to reproduce the map of "Ancient" Israel was in essence none other than a systematic, scholarly, political and military attempt to de-Arabise the terrain—its names and geography, but above all its history (ibid.: 226)...the erasure of the history of one people in order to write the history of another people's over it. (Pappé, 2006: 231)

Bearing Witness in a Time of Denial

The success of Israel's concerted effort to erase the memory of Palestinian life before 1948 is precisely what the narrative of the *Nakba* seeks to combat. The politicization and public mobilization of the narrative of the *Nakba* began in earnest during the 1990s, as an increasing number of Palestinian scholars noted the pronounced absence of officially chronicled *Nakba* survivor testimonies. Similarly to scholars in Europe and North America during the 1990s who were driven to make record of and preserve Holocaust survivor testimonies for dissemination to future generations, Palestinian academics feared that with the passage of time the generation which lived through the *Nakba* would be lost forever before the possibility to document and make public their memories. The most recent of these key contributions is Dina Matar's *What It Means to be Palestinian* (2011), a monograph which recounts the Palestinian struggle for peoplehood through the voices and stories of Palestinians living in exile and under Occupation.

In many respects, contemporary narration of the *Nakba* represent a political strategy which seeks to counter the hegemonic Zionist narrative of 1948 and to combat perpetrator-induced amnesia *vis-à-vis* Palestinian claims for justice and recognition. In the wake of the failure of the Oslo Peace Accords, the *Nakba* re-emerged in the Palestinian national consciousness as a reminder of the failure of Palestinian national aspirations, resulting in a reckoning with the "unpastness" of the past, which continues to dictate Palestinian daily existence in the form of Israel's sovereignty and occupation versus Palestinian statelessness and absenteeism (Sa'di, 2008). The ensuing proliferation of testimonies, memorial books and commemorative events in relation to the *Nakba* has been a collective effort to create a socially recognized narrative of the past which serves to inform the politics of the present. In many respects, the re-emergence of the narrative of the *Nakba* as "a point of historical and political orientation towards the future" (Allan, 2007: 253) represents an attempt to narrate the past in order to articulate the injustice, powerlessness and social exclusion experienced in the present.

The lack of officially-sanctioned narratives and icons of commemoration due to the stateless status of the Palestinian collectivity has constituted the *Nakba* as a "portable" site of memory and a temporal point of departure for the Palestinian people:

> Palestine as a birthplace, homeland, source of identity, a geographical location, a history, a place of emotional attachment and fascination, a field of imagination, and place wherein Palestinians want to end their days has dominated the lives of Palestinians on an individual and collective level. (Sa'di, 2008: 387)

This longing for rootedness and return is deftly narrated by Lila Abu-Lughod in her chapter in *Nakba: Palestine, 1948 and the Claims of Memory* (Abu-Lughod and Sa'di, 2007) in which she chronicles her late father's decision to return to Palestine in the wake of the Oslo Accords. She relates how from his residence in Ramallah in the Occupied West Bank he conducted regular historical "tours" to his childhood home in Jaffa, from where his family was forced to flee in 1948 (ibid.: 77–104). Abu-Lughod writes that upon her father's first return visit to Jaffa, after over forty years of exile, he reported feelings of profound disorientation and unfamiliarity in the alien environment of the now Israeli suburb of Jaffa. He was nevertheless able to find his bearings and relocate himself in the city of his youth by asking local Palestinian children about the location of King Faysal Street, and to his relief they took him there immediately, even though there was no longer a sign bearing the name of that street (ibid.: 84). The children's intimate knowledge

of a long expunged history and supplanted geography and Ibrahim
Abu-Lughod's ability to relocate physical remnants of pre-*Nakba*
sites, such as Hasan Bek Mosque, his now re-named and Israeli-
occupied school, and the now-neglected cemetery where his father's
and grandfather's remains rest (ibid.: 83–91), testify to the living
memory of the pre-*Nakba* years that are passed on from generation
to generation through family stories.

For the Palestinian generations born after the *Nakba*,
who derive their identities from the experience of Palestinian
dispossession and statelessness, the stories and maps of the lost
Palestinian villages and cities are not lived but inherited memories.
These second and third generation Palestinian refugees were not
born and raised in the villages their parents and grandparents had
to leave, nor have they had the opportunity to visit them, and even
if they were permitted to return they would discover that their
ancestral homes no longer exist, as they have either been reduced
to ruins, or are now covered by Israeli cities and settlements.
Marianne Hirsch defines the above mode of formative recollection
as *postmemory*:

> distinguished from memory by generational distance and
> from history by deep personal connection.... Postmemory
> characterises the experiences of those who grew up
> dominated by narratives that precede their birth, whose own
> belated stories are evacuated by the stories of the previous
> generation shaped by traumatic events.... Postmemory—
> often obsessive and relentless—need not be absent or
> evacuated: it is as full and as empty, certainly as constructed,
> as memory itself. (1997: 22)

Mapping the erased and suppressed geography of former Palestinian
inhabited localities is an integral part of the Palestinian endeavor
to retrieve and retain the material significance of their loss: their
homes, mosques, villages and lands. Rochelle Davies's (2007)
account of the memorial books compiled by Palestinian refugees in
the camps of Lebanon, Syria, The West Bank and Gaza illustrates
precisely the integral role played by the refugees' preoccupation
with preserving the memories of the physical localities from which
these communities were expelled or forced to flee in 1948 and

have since been prevented from returning to. The compulsion and intricate detail with which these maps are drawn and communally preserved, detailing not only significant landmarks and geological habitat but also the ownership of homes and lands, is intimately tied to the Palestinian longing for and desire to return to the familiarity and ownership of their former homes. The village, with its connotation of intimate connection to the land, remains a key site of identification and a source of belonging for the refugees who continue to organize camp life and dwelling on the basis of their localities of origin in pre-1948 Palestine.

Nevertheless, the *Nakba* is not simply an act of recall; the experience of being uprooted from one's habitat is a tragic reality even for the subsequent generations of those Palestinians who remained within the borders of the state of Israel and for whom dispossession continues in the present. These Palestinians who Israel refers to as the "Arab minority," who managed to remain and received Israeli citizenship in the aftermath of 1948, although they are no longer subject to the military rule imposed on them until 1966 they continue to reside in a legal and existential limbo. They are citizens of a country which treats them as "present absentees"[8]: second-rate citizens whose lands continue to be confiscated by the state, and who are denied the right of return to their former homes and localities which, unlike the refugees beyond Israel's 1948 borders, they can visit, touch and smell, but they cannot reclaim (Abu-Lughod and Sa'di, 2007; Pappé, 2006).

Yet, like the children who took Ibrahim Abu-Lughod to King Faysal Street, despite nearly fifty years of absence from Jaffa's landscape, these Palestinians keep the memory of pre-*Nakba* Palestine alive. Palestinian Israelis organize annual processions to the localities of former Palestinian villages to commemorate the *Nakba*; these Marches of Return often coincide with Israel's Independence Day[9] celebrations and constitute an act of resistance in the face of denial, and more recently, attempts at outright legalized repression.

The latter development has been characterized by the actions of the ultranationalist right-wing party of the Israeli Foreign Minister, Avigdor Lieberman's *Yisrael Beiteinu* (Israel is Our Home), which has proposed extensive legislation to "ban" the *Nakba* (*Ha'aretz*,

May 14, 2009). The first legal proposal submitted in May 2009 was only narrowly defeated in the Israeli Knesset (Parliament) amidst international outrage and condemnation from Palestinian-Israeli minority rights groups and their progressive Jewish supporters who opposed the divisive and discriminatory nature of the law (*Ha'aretz*, May 31, 2009). The proposal involved a ban of any public display of "mourning" on Israel's Day of Independence and the imprisonment for up to three years of anyone who would refuse to obey the law (*Ha'aretz*, January 1, 2009). A revised proposal which banned references to the *Nakba* from Israeli school textbooks and ordered the removal of existing references succeeded in becoming law in July 2009 (*Ha'aretz*, July 22, 2009). The most recent onslaught on *Nakba* commemoration became law on March 23, 2011; the "*Nakba* Law" makes it illegal for institutions which "undermine the foundations of the state and contradict its values" to receive any public funding (Khoury and Lis, March 24, 2011).

Peled-Elhanan (2010) illustrates the textbook anti-*Nakba* law in action. She writes in relation to the Israeli government's reaction to a school textbook by Domka et al. (2009) which was recalled immediately after publication because it rendered

> the Palestinian version regarding the ethnic cleaning in 1948 alongside the Israeli one, as a "version" and not "propaganda", using both Israeli and Palestinian sources (such as Walid Khalidi's books). The change requested by the ministry of education was first of all to remove the Palestinian sources from the Palestinian version and to substitute it with Palestinian texts that are "more faithful to reality" or with Israeli sources.... In order to have the book republished, the publishers replaced the Palestinian sources with Israeli ones in the part called "The Palestinian Version" and gave it a lesser weight, without changing the structure. (Peled-Elhanan, 2010: 398)

Despite the fierce attempts by the right-wing Israeli establishment to silence the voices of the Palestinian people, the unrelenting force of the narrative of the *Nakba* is increasingly penetrating the consciousness of growing numbers of progressive Jewish Israelis who are confronting the Zionist myths[10] of their upbringing. Among these individuals are the founders and members of the Israeli NGO

Zochrot (Remembering) who work to raise awareness about the *Nakba* within Israeli society:

> The Nakba is an unspoken taboo in Israeli discourse, its memory expunged from the official history of the country and from its physical landscape. Yet the Nakba is also the central trauma of the Israeli-Palestinian conflict, and its legacy continues to unfold today—in the institutionalization of inequality and violence, in the erasure of the past, and in the deteriorating plight of the Palestinian refugees. We hope that by talking about the Nakba in Hebrew, the language spoken by the Jewish majority in Israel, we can engage the public in learning about and taking responsibility for the Nakba and its enduring consequences. (*Zochrot* Annual Report 2008)

Zochrot's commemorative and educational work in relation to the *Nakba* exemplify what Karen E. Till (2008) theorizes as socially engaged and ethically responsible "place-based practice," a mode of operation based on the conceptualization of social memory as embodied experience, "places are embodied contexts of experience, but also porous and mobile, connected to other places, times and peoples" (ibid.: 109). This notion is embodied in *Zochrot*'s commemorative activities which include public tours to the locations of the Palestinian villages destroyed during 1947–1949. These tours are accompanied by the publication of booklets dedicated to these erased localities. The booklets contain history about and maps of the village, as well as testimonies from the village's refugees, and on occasion include written reflections by the Israeli Jews who live or have lived in the towns and settlements erected on the lands of the former Palestinian villages.

Zochrot's commemorative activities echo the village memorial books compiled by Palestinian refugees in the camps as the organization routinely engages in the re-mapping of Palestine onto the amnesiac Israeli landscape. The NGO's tours often culminate with the erection of street signs bearing the pre-1948 names of the destroyed Palestinian villages in Arabic and Hebrew: "These signs are usually removed shortly after…Removal of the signs testifies to their importance; the act of their removal relates both to the *Nakba* and to its significance in space and history" (*Zochrot* Annual Report 2008).

The organization also engages in advocacy activities which seek to democratize the public landscape of Israel. These activities include actively opposing building plans which will erase the remains, without marking the existence, of depopulated Palestinian villages, such as *Zochrot*'s successful Supreme Court lawsuit against the JNF which calls for the erection of public signs identifying the Palestinian villages on which JNF sites are now located.[11] At the time of the original request, *Zochrot*'s demand was widely publicized in the liberal media with numerous articles appearing in the Israeli daily *Ha'aretz* (June 12, 2005; July 26, 2005; June 13, 2007, February 3, 2008).[12]

Attempts to preserve the physical traces of the former Palestinian presence are often met with evasion and vandalism, a case in point being JNF's refusal and delay in repairing and replacing the damaged signs in Canada Park which testify to the destroyed Palestinian villages (*Zochrot* Annual Report 2009). Nevertheless, the battle for and against *Nakba* remembrance continues to be waged publicly, legally and politically, making it increasingly more difficult for the opponents of the narrative to refute its potency and moral entitlement. The sentiment of resignation and "damage limitation" in relation to *Nakba* commemoration is illuminated in a comment made by a JNF administrator in a newspaper interview following *Zochrot*'s successful High Court petition concerning Canada Park:

> The signs don't say that we expelled them, nor that they're in refugee camps.... I suggest not raising this issue in the media, because it's very sensitive. And it would be better not to raise the issue at all. So far there is only one park where it's mentioned. In fact, many of the JNF parks are on land where Arab villages were once located, and the forests were planted as camouflage. But we're afraid it will spread throughout the country; it's apparently something that can't be stopped. (Michal Kortoza interview in *Eretz Israel Shelanu*; translated quote in *Zochrot* Annual Report 2008)

Commemorative practices such as the public display of signs bearing witness to the former presence and current absence of the Palestinian people, two unspeakable facts, are deeply unsettling to the Jewish Israeli collectivity which refuses to acknowledge the past so as to avoid confronting responsibility in the present. Such commemorative acts are deeply disturbing because they "prompt us to think about forms of descendancy, genealogies of proprietorship and histories of citizenship, and remind us that we need to reconceptualize received ideas of identity, belonging and the civic" (Jonker in Till, 2008: 109). Thus, in spite of the hostile and unreceptive environment and the concerted efforts to silence the remembrance, and even utterance, of the *Nakba*, *Zochrot's* work is opening up a valuable space for Jewish Israelis to be able to begin to confront the founding myths of Zionism, and perhaps be able to begin, at a later stage, to take ethical responsibility without the unbearable and potentially disabling burden of guilt and the fear of persecution.

Nakba remembrance carves out a space which enables the painful past of Palestine-Israel to be confronted with a view to acknowledging and assimilating the *Nakba* as a shared historical experience, an act which has the potential to enable the possibility of the two collectivities to begin to envisage a future based on coexistence and reconciliation. The public commemorative events in which *Zochrot* engages act as a bridge between the two conflicting narratives and are opportunities for active inter-cultural dialogue between Israeli Jews and Palestinians. These acts serve to democratize and reconstitute social memory not only through education and commemoration but also by posing important and challenging political questions in the form of *Zochrot's* 2008 public conference on the Israeli recognition of the Palestinian refugees' right of return. The conference was ironically held at the Zionists of America House in Tel Aviv, and the location of this historically unprecedented event can be read as a sign of the *Nakba* narrative's power of subversion and disruption of the Zionist account and simultaneously as a testament to the flexibility and strength of the Zionist hegemony.

Such inherent contradictions in the geo-political space within which *Zochrot* functions serve to illustrate the validity of some of the criticisms levelled at the organization by Lentin (2008) who argues that much of *Zochrot's* work remains at the level of the symbolic, and further, activities such as mapping the land as it existed before 1948 epitomize a re-colonization of Palestine (ibid.: 217). For her this constitutes an appropriation of Palestinian memory which perpetuates Palestinian victimhood and Israeli authority (ibid.: 215). While there is validity in her criticisms, Lentin leaves little room for self-reflexivity and improvement among *Zochrot* activists. Two of her challenges to the organization have been met or attempted at the time of writing. One of the challenges represented by her is the need for Jewish Israelis to develop political strategies for advocating the Palestinian return—a question which was first put at the organization's 2008 conference mentioned above and which forms part of a larger ongoing project on the practicalities of return in conjunction with *BADIL*.[13]

The second challenge, which Lentin admits is much more difficult, is to document the testimonies of Jewish perpetrators of the *Nakba*. Given the current climate of denial, this task is much more problematic and any progress is likely to be painstakingly slow. Nevertheless, since 2010 there are a number of testimonies on *Zochrot's* website from former Jewish Israeli combatants who fought in 1948 who have reluctantly come forward to speak about carrying out and/or witnessing expulsions of the Palestinians. These include the testimony of Amnon Noiman (*Zochrot*, June 17, 2010) which is featured in a documentary about contemporary Israeli responses to 1948 (Lia Tarachansky, *Seven Deadly Myths*, 2011).

Therefore, despite their limitations, Israeli proponents of *Nakba* acknowledgement are carving out a vital space for dialogue within Israeli society which is increasingly enfolding in denial. This denial is most explicitly evident in the concerted political efforts to silence the *Nakba* narrative and intimidate its advocates. To commemorate the *Nakba* in 2010, an event corresponding with Israel's Independence Day celebrations was held by *Zochrot* activists. On the day they put up protest posters across Tel Aviv which read: *"The* Nakba, *since 1948, Made in Israel."* and at the bottom: *"The* Nakba *law aims to scare those who commemorate the* Nakba *on Israel's Independence Day. Israel's Independence Day is The* Nakba *day too. You try to shut my mouth but I won't forget that today is also* Nakba *day."*[14]

Such activities constitute not only commemorative acts but further articulate a political solidarity against those who wish to silence those who have chosen to bear witness to the *Nakba*. Such acts are politically as well as symbolically significant given that *Nakba* commemorative activities in Israel will be criminalized by the 2011 anti-*Nakba* law. The significance of the activities of organizations such as *Zochrot* (Remembering) lies precisely in the act of bearing witness and the refusal to forget about the *Nakba* in a time of perpetrator-induced denial. *Zochrot's* Independence/*Nakba* Day activities are a reminder that denial and repression are not the same as forgetting, and moreover, there is positive potential in the stand-off between those who seek to reconcile with the tragedy of the past and embrace a future of coexistence and those who choose denial and conflict. As a result a conversation is beginning to take place in Israeli society and this conversation is being held in a common language, and even those who refuse to listen cannot deny that they are hearing.

Conclusion

Since the 1990s, the history of 1948 has been simultaneously read and re-read as a historical account from the events of the past to the present, and in reverse, illuminating a silenced history and memory from the perspective of the now. Despite its catastrophic nature, the *Nakba* is also a narrative of hope, its narration having been made possible by the long awaited recognition in the Oslo Accords of 1993 that the Palestinian people are a national collectivity with rights to self-determination. The explosion of *Nakba* testimonies and commemorations since the 1990s has been the direct result of the space, to re-narrate the Palestinian nation, opened up by the Oslo Accords with their promise of statehood. Narrating the Nakba became even more urgent when this promise, coupled with the refusal to address the refugee's right of return, began to appear as a distant and untenable prospect.

In response to these failures, the Palestinian collectivity and Diaspora intellectuals, alongside a number of critical Israeli academics and civil society groups such as *Zochrot*, amongst others, have undertaken a project which seeks to challenge and re-articulate the polarizing positions in the Israeli-Palestinian conflict. Differential access to power has meant that who gets to tell the story of the *Nakba* with the biggest impact has not always been related to direct experience and its lived consequences, but the privilege of being able to speak and be received with authority, which at present tends to lie with Israelis. Nevertheless, the conversation that is taking place between progressive Israeli Jews and Palestinians is vitally important as it is producing new narratives for coexistence which are vital for "constructing a sense of the self in the face of traditions that have crumbled and human hopes that risk being forgotten...only through the variety of relationships constructed by many people seeing from different perspectives can truth be known and community be created" (Minow, 2008: 258).

Notes

1. Teodora Todorova is a doctoral candidate at the Department of Culture, Film and Media in the University of Nottingham, UK. Her thesis is concerned with theorizing non-governmental peace politics in Israel-Palestine, with a specific focus on the contemporary civil society struggle for a just peace.
2. UNRWA Statistics (1950–2008) "Number of Registered Refugees," http://www.unrwa.org/userfiles/rr_countryandarea.pdf/. Accessed on March 4/2010.
3. UN GAR 181.
4. UNRWA Statistics (2010), http://www.unrwa.org/etemplate.php?id=253.
5. Central Bureau of Statistics (2009/10) "Population by Population Group [in Israel]," http://www.cbs.gov.il/www/yarhon/b1_e.htm.
6. *The Washington Post, Herald Times,* June 16, 1969 (ProQuest Historical Newspapers).
7. "Catastrophe" in Hebrew, the concept relates to the systematic murder of 6 million European Jews by the Nazi regime during the 1940s.
8. "Land & Housing Rights: The Absentee Property Law declares that anyone who left the country in 1948 is an absentee, and that his/her property comes under the control of the State. This Law was used only against Arabs [Palestinians], and even in reference to people who remained in the country but who were compelled to leave their land. These individuals are called 'present absentees.' The Defence (Emergency) Regulation 125 authorizes the military commander to declare land to be a 'closed area.' Once the commander so declares, no person is allowed to enter or to leave the area. By this regulation, the population of tens of Arab villages became uprooted. There is no uprooted Jewish population in the State. The National Planning and Building Law prohibits the provision of basic services such as water and electricity to tens of unrecognized Arab villages in the State. Although these villages existed before the State's establishment, the main purpose of the law is to force the people to leave their villages and move to government-planned areas. There are no unrecognized Jewish villages in Israel (Adalah, Legal Centre for Arab Minority Rights in Israel, Report to UN CERD 1998: 2, http://www.adalah.org/eng/intladvocacy/cerd-major-finding-march98.pdf)

9. *Al Nakba* is annually commemorated on May 14 according to the Gregorian calendar, while Israel's Independence Day celebrations are annually held on 5th Lyar according to the Hebrew calendar. The two dates do not always coincide, as was the case in 2010 when 5th Lyar corresponded to April 19.

10. Similarly to Smith I use the concept "myth" not to connote a "false" or "fabricated" account of history but rather "a widely held view of the past which has helped to shape and explain the present" (Smith, 2000: 2).

11. *Zochrot* (2006) "High Court Petition [Canada Park]; Military Commander's Response to Canada Park Petition;" and "JNF's Response to Canada Park Petition".

12. Translations from the Hebrew are available on *Zochrot's* website: see References.

13. Resource Center for Palestinian Residency & Refugee Rights.

14. Translations from the Hebrew supplied in personal correspondence by Eitan Bronstein, May 2010.

References

Abu-Lughod, Lila, and Ahmad H. Sa'di eds, (2007). *Nakba: Palestine, 1948, and the Claims of Memory* (New York: Columbia University Press).

—— (2007). "Return to Half-Ruins: Memory, Postmemory, and Living History in Palestine" in Ahmad H. Sa'di and Lila Abu-Lughod (eds), *Nakba: Palestine, 1948, and the Claims of Memory* (New York: Columbia University Press).

Agamben, Georgio (1999). *Remnants of Auschwitz: The Witness and the Archive* (New York: Zone Books).

Allan, Diana K. (2007). "The Politics of Witnessing: Remembering and Forgetting 1948 in Shatila Camp" in Ahmad H. Sa'di and Lila Abu-Lughod (eds), *Nakba: Palestine, 1948, and the Claims of Memory* (New York: Columbia University Press).

Alon, Gideon, and Aluf Benn (2003). "Netanyahu: Israel's Arabs are the Real Demographic Threat," *Ha'aretz*, http://www.haaretz.com/print-edition/news/netanyahu-israel-s-arabs-are-the-real-demographic-threat-1.109045 (December 18, 2003).

BADIL Resource Center for Palestinian Residency & Refuge (2010). www.badil.org.

Barakat, Amiram (2005). "The JNF will post signs commemorating the Palestinian villages that were destroyed" in *Ha'aretz*; translated article: http://www.nakbainhebrew.org/index.php?id=518 (July 26, 2005).

Baram, Daphna (2010). "A Shared Story Offers Hope to Israel: A Row Over a Textbook That Tells Both Sides of Israeli-Palestinian History Shows

A Shift In Some Israelis' Thinking – But Not Others" in *The Guardian*, http://www.guardian.co.uk/commentisfree/2010/oct/29/israel-palestine-textbook-history (October 29, 2010).

Central Bureau of Statistics (Israel) (2009/10). "Population by Population Group," http://www.cbs.gov.il/www/yarhon/b1_e.htm.

Cohen, Stanley (2001). *States of Denial: Knowing about Atrocities and Suffering* (Cambridge: Polity).

Davies, Rochelle (2007). "Mapping the Past, Re-creating the Homeland: Memories of Village Places in pre-1948 Palestine" in Ahmad H. Sa'di and Lila Abu-Lughod (eds), *Nakba: Palestine, 1948, and the Claims of Memory* (New York: Columbia University Press).

Dooley, Mark, and Richard Kearney (eds), (1999). "Imagination, Testimony and Trust: A Dialogue with Paul Ricoeur" in *Questioning Ethics: Contemporary Debates in Philosophy* (London: Routledge).

Ha'aretz (2008). "JNF Will Mention Destroyed Palestinian Villages on Signs," by Yoav Stern, translated article: http://www.nakbainhebrew.org/index.php?id=661 (February 3, 2008).

——— (2009). "Israel Moves Closer to Banning Mourning of Its Independence," http://www.haaretz.com/hasen/spages/1087792.html (January 1, 2009).

——— (2009). "Lieberman's Party Proposes Ban on Arab *Nakba*," http://www.haaretz.com/hasen/spages/1085588.html (May 14, 2009).

——— Editorial (2009). "Netanyahu Must Rein In Lieberman's Racist Proposals," http://www.haaretz.com/hasen/spages/1089216.html (May 31, 2009).

——— (2009). "Revised Bill Would Ban Funding *Nakba* Events," http://www.haaretz.com/hasen/spages/1101403.html (July 20, 2009).

——— (2009). "Israel Bans Use of Palestinian Term '*Nakba*'in Textbooks," http://www.haaretz.com/hasen/spages/1102099.html (July 22, 2009).

Hirsch, Marianne (1997). *Family Frames: Photography, Narrative and Post-Memory* (Cambridge: Harvard University Press).

JNews (2010), "Israel Set to Forbid Mourning Its Independence Day: *Nakba* Law Passes First Legislation Stage"; http://www.jnews.org.uk/news/israel-set-to-forbid-mourning-its-independence-day (March 18, 2010).

Kearney, Richard (2002). *On Stories* (London: Routledge).

Khalidi, Walid ([1959] 2005). "Why Did the Palestinians Leave Revisited," 2005, *Journal of Palestine Studies*, 34(2): 42–54.

——— (1992). *All That Remains: The Palestinian Villages Occupied and Depopulated by Israel in 1948* (Washington: Institute for Palestine Studies).

Khoury, Jack, and Jonathan Lis (2011). "Knesset Passes Two Bills Slammed as Discriminatory by Rights Groups" in *Ha'aretz*, http://www.haaretz. com/print-edition/news/knesset-passes-two-bills-slammed-as-discriminatory-by-rights-groups-1.351462. (March 24, 2011.)

Lentin, Ronit (2008). "The Contested Memory of Dispossession: Commemorizing the Palestinian Nakba in Israel" in R. Lentin (ed), *Thinking Palestine* (London: Zed Books).

Ma'an News Agency (2010). "Rights Group: Israel Penalizing *Nakba* Commemoration," http://www.maannews.net/eng/ViewDetails.aspx?ID=265702. (March 4, 2010.)

Matar, Dina (2011). *What It Means to be Palestinian: Stories of Palestinian Peoplehood.* (London:I.B.Tauris).

Mills, Catherine (2003). "An Ethics of Bare Life: Agamben on Witnessing" in *Borderlands*, 2(1), http://www.borderlands.net.au/vol2no1_2003/mills_agamben.html.

Minow, Martha (2008). "Stories in Law" in Rickie Solinger et al. (eds), *Telling Stories to Change the World: Global Voices on the Power of Narrative to Build Community and Make Social Justice Claims* (London: Routledge).

Morris, Benny ([1987] 2004). *The Birth of the Palestinian Refugee Problem, 1947–49 Revisited* (Cambridge: Cambridge University Press).

Pappé, Ilan (2006). *The Ethnic Cleansing of Palestine* (Oxford: Oneworld).

Peled-Elhanan, Nurit (2010). "Legitimation of Massacres in Israeli School History Books" in *Discourse Society*, 21(4): 377–404.

Ricoeur, Paul (1999). "Memory and Forgetting" in M. Dooley and R. Kearney (eds), *Questioning Ethics: Contemporary Debates in Philosophy* (London: Routledge).

————— (2004). *Memory, History, Forgetting* (Chicago: The University of Chicago Press).

Rinat, Zifrir (2007). "Out of Sight Maybe but Not Out of Mind" in *Ha'aretz*, http://www.haaretz.com/print-edition/features/out-of-sight-maybe-but-not-out-of-mind-1.222986 (June 13, 2007).

Rothberg, Michael (2009). *Multidirectional Memory: Remembering the Holocaust in the Age of Decolonisation* (Stanford: Stanford University Press).

Sa'di, Ahmad H. (2008). "Remembering *Al-Nakba* in a Time of Amnesia: On Silence, Dislocation and Time." *International Journal of Postcolonial Studies*, 10(3): 381–99.

Said, Edward (1984). "Permission to Narrative." *Journal of Palestine Studies*, 13(3): 27–48.

Shavit, Ari (2004). "Survival of the Fittest: An Interview with Benny Morris" in *Ha'aretz* Magazine (January 9, 2004).

Smith, Malcolm (2000). *Britain and 1940: History, Myth, and Popular Memory* (London: Routledge).

Tarachansky, Lia (2011). *Seven Deadly Myths*, http://sevendeadlymyths. webs.com/.

Till, Karen, E. (2008). "Artistic and Activist Memory-Work: Approaching Place-Based Practice" in *Memory Studies*, 1(1): 99–113.

UNRWA (2008). "Total Registered Refugees per Country and Area", Retrieved on July 30, 2009, http://www.un.org/unrwa/publications/ pdf/rr_countryandarea.pdf.

The Washington Post, Times Herald (1969). "Golda Meir Scorns Soviets," acquired from ProQuest Historical Newspapers, *The Washington Post* (1877–1994) (June 16, 1969).

Wiesel, Elie (1985). *Against Silence*, Holocaust Library.

Yoaz, Yuval (2005). "The Palestinian Past of Canada Park is Forgotten in JNF Signs" in *Ha'aretz*, translated article: http://www.nakbainhebrew. org/index.php?id=210.

Zochrot (2006). "High Court Petition [Canada Park]" http://www. nakbainhebrew.org/index.php?id=433.

—— (2006). "Military Commander's Response to Canada Park Petition" http://www.nakbainhebrew.org/index.php?id=222.

—— (2006). "JNF's Response to Canada Park Petition" http://www. nakbainhebrew.org/index.php?id=368.

—— (2008). "Annual Report" http://www.zochrot.org/images/Zoc_ AnRe08eng_web.pdf.[15]

—— (2009). "Annual Report" http://nakbainhebrew.org/images/Zoc_ AnRe09eng_web.pdf.

—— (2010). "Testimony by Amnon Noiman," http://www.zochrot.org/ index.php?id=844 (June 17, 2010).

INDEX